Schools with Heart

Schools with Heart

Voluntarism and Public Education

Daniel J. Brown

Westview Press
A Member of Perseus Books, L.L.C.

This monograph was supported in part by a grant from the Social Sciences and Humanities Research Council of Canada. The author thanks the many respondents who gave their time generously with little to gain.

Published in 1998 in the United States of America by Westview Press, 5500 Central Avenue, Boulder, Colorado 80301-2877, and in the United Kingdom by Westview Press, 12 Hid's Copse Road, Cumnor Hill, Oxford OX2 9JJ

Library of Congress Cataloging-in-Publication Data
Brown, Daniel J., 1941–
    Schools with heart : voluntarism and public education / Daniel J. Brown.
        p.   cm.
    Includes bibliographical references (p.   ) and index.
    ISBN 0-8133-9084-2 (hardcover)
    1. Voluntarism—United States.   2. Volunteer workers in education—Canada.   3. Voluntarism—Canada.   4. Public schools—Canada.   5. Volunteer workers in education—United States.   6. Voluntarism—United States.   7. Public schools—United States.   I. Title.
LB2844.1.V6B76   1998
371.14' 124—dc21   98–18416
                                                                                        CIP

The paper used in this publication meets the requirements of the American National Standard for Permanence of Paper for Printed Library Materials Z39.48-1984.

10   9   8   7   6   5   4   3   2   1

Contents

Specific Policies for School Voluntarism, 157
The Vision of Voluntarism, 161
Notes, 165

Tables

Preface

During the mid-1980s, I became acquainted with a number of public elementary schools rich in volunteers. While I saw that the donation of volunteers' time constituted an important resource for the schools, the existence of so many volunteers presented a paradox for me. My impressions of public education had led me to believe that its raison d'être was to create schools that did not depend much on their communities for support. Ostensibly, they could be independent of their settings and largely free of community constraints. Yet my exposure to these schools showed that volunteer parents contributed actively to programs in public schools and administrators appeared to welcome them. Was this activity evidence of subversive action designed to undermine the tenets of public education? Or was something else at work? Were these school volunteers actually important or were they simply doing "nice things," i.e., making insignificant contributions? Were they, in a quiet way, adding something special to the lives of "their" schools? As shown by Thornton Wilder's play *Our Town*, the ordinary may be extraordinary.

To answer these questions, I began by thinking about the people actually involved in this phenomenon—the volunteers and the school personnel who welcomed them. This inception led to an examination of the literature on parental involvement and volunteers in general. I was intrigued particularly with discussions of "voluntarism," or "benevolence" (author's note: I will use these terms interchangeably throughout the book to refer to the donation of both goods and, more importantly, services in the form of personal time). Interestingly, the literature revealed a paucity of explanation for the phenomenon I kept encountering in schools. With the help of a grant from the Social Sciences and Humanities Research Council of Canada, which established the Marketing and Attraction of Resources for Schools (MARS) Project, I undertook an investigation of the role of voluntarism in education, the results of which form the primary data source for this monograph.

I hope that this book will add to the discussion about community involvement in education. It is intended for all persons who wish to reflect on the meaning of giving to public schools. Among them are professionals and lay people who are concerned about the welfare of upcoming generations. They are individuals who want to learn why and how public schools may be altered to increase the financial resources and social capital available to them. In light of this diverse readership, this volume sets out to meet four purposes. The first is to extend the current literature on parental participation, which generally advocates involvement as a "good idea." Although a main component of parental participation is the use of volunteers, the literature does not tend to consider the presence of volunteers as a manifestation of giving behaviour, which is odd since volunteering is almost always a benevolent act. If, however, voluntarism is understood (as mentioned above) as the donation of goods and services, it becomes an aspect of altruism and may be understood as such.

The second purpose is to demonstrate some public schools' responses to voluntarism in terms of how they organize and administer the volunteers from their respective communities. The analysis of their reactions requires that the questions surrounding the usual models of school organization be revisited, which can help to increase our understanding of what we know about educational organizations and the resources needed to maintain them. I show that schools with heart, which I call "voluntary public schools," develop a bridge between the world of families (and communities) and the world of public schools and thus contribute to a societal process in which the "private" and the "public" become blurred.

A third purpose of this book is to place the discussion of school volunteers on a firmer intellectual foundation than that currently available. While much good research has been done on volunteers and parental involvement generally, it tends to be primarily descriptive or exhortative. Since the presence of volunteers constitutes a substantial phenomenon in public education, it deserves a serious search for explanations of voluntary giving and its organizational response. To that end, in its later chapters, this book examines some of the extensive writings on organizations, the debates about the foundations of human behaviour, and the explanatory power of rational choice to produce a more satisfying understanding of voluntarism than the literature now reveals.

The final purpose is to contribute to discussions on educational policy. This study of voluntarism and the responses to it has some powerful and often neglected implications for the way public schools are organized and how resources flow to them. Simply stated, the thesis of this book is that voluntarism is most probably very good for schools and all who participate in it. Make no mistake—this volume is not part of the current attacks on public education. It concludes that the use of volunteers can make a substantial contribution to the lives of children and thus public schools may be enhanced. Perhaps all public schools can become "schools with heart."

As implied by the order of its four purposes, this book is designed "outwards from the heart." That is, it moves inductively from consideration of the individual volunteers to actions taken at the school level and then to contemplation of the meaning of voluntarism in abstract terms. Each chapter is constructed in a similar fashion—data or ideas of limited applicability are introduced first and from them, generalizations are induced. This pattern also applies to the sequence of data presented. Initially, primary data (gathered specifically for this volume) are described and summarized; they are foundational. Subsequently, secondary data from the extant literature are considered as they permit generalizations to be based on a much wider set of circumstances. Furthermore, the "outwards from the heart" design is also an honest reflection of how the book came to be. It sprang not with clear explanations in mind beforehand, but rather from a spirit of discovery that guided the study. Here is the chapter-by-chapter presentation, which unfolds somewhat in narrative fashion, as it develops largely from the concrete to the analytic and finally to policy issues.

Chapter 1 presents, briefly, some general aspects of the context of public schools, a case to show the impact of voluntarism, some comments about how this research was conducted, its theoretical directions, and what they may imply. By contrast, Chapter 2, the beginning of Part I, is largely descriptive. It takes us inside selected schools and introduces a number of the participants in their own voices. The question of why people give to schools is explored initially here in volunteers' own responses. Some partial explanations are offered; perhaps this chapter is the "soul" of the book. Chapter 3 moves outward from the individuals and considers the effects of giving on schools. These include not only substantial material and learning benefits but also social capital (i.e., the linkages among students, volunteers, and others). The accounts show that "schools with heart" are rather special places. Chapter 4 looks beyond the school to consider the student equity issues via the neighbourhood factors that influence voluntarism. A basic disagreement arises from the literature about what schools are able to do. Are they captives of their environments? Or are they able to thrive within their contexts? In acknowledgement of the contextual influences, Chapter 5 moves back inside the schools and discusses the purposeful actions on the part of school personnel to encourage benevolence. Chapter 6 completes this consideration by revealing other developments in schools that benefit from community giving. It juxtaposes the general relationships that are currently typical between most public schools and their environments against those of a model of a "voluntary public school."

Chapter 7 starts Part II and marks a shift in the treatment of the discussion; it pulls together Chapters 2 through 6 and contemplates the deeper meaning of individual giving and community. I claim that school voluntarism and schools' responses build a bridge between two galaxies within our social universe, which are the public and the private domains. Chapter 8 continues the theoretical emphasis by reexamining the fundamental explanations of benevolence. Is it genetically based? How does it link egoism and altruism? One particular theory, rational choice, emerges as having considerable power to understand the phenomenon. A sketch of the dynamics of benevolence and its responses is offered at the levels of individuals, organizations, and society. Chapter 9 puts these forays into the theories to use by linking them to policy issues. It explores questions about the optimal balance between resources from benevolence and resources from governments in support of schools. Specific policies are advanced and the general "vision" of voluntarism is asserted. An appendix is also provided. It contains details about the primary data sample and rationale for the research methods used for this monograph.

The sequence of chapters is deliberately designed to be flexible for the diversity of readers. Chapter 1, as mentioned above, offers a general overview. However, if you are interested primarily in educational inquiry, then the conceptualizations in Chapters 7 and 8 and the commentary on research methods in the appendix may be your most useful starting points. If you are mostly captivated by educational policy, then Chapter 9 on policy and to a lesser extent Chapters 5 and 6 on administration and organization may be considered introductory. If you enjoy immersing yourself in the data to generate an initial understanding of voluntarism in schools before you tackle the conceptual bases or the social issues, then start at Chapter 2 and proceed through to Chapter 6. You will have covered the essential evidence in the narrative. If you take the cricket approach, as I do, then head for the table of contents or author/subject index and hop around. It is my intention, as author, that this book will not only inform; it will also be enjoyed.

Daniel J. Brown

Acknowledgements

A number of persons provided assistance in bringing this work to fruition. The most recent were individuals I asked to be critics of chapters. They were Adrienne Burk, Jean Hills, Geof Isherwood, Dante Lupini, Carol Merz, and Carolyn Shields, and they did their jobs well. Other contributors were less direct but very important. There was Dan Lortie who tolerated the intellectual immaturity of his advisee at the University of Chicago and who never shied from an earnest debate. R. Oliver Gibson offered both academic impetus and personal support during the early years of my career at SUNY–Buffalo. Peter Atherton, now deceased, gave his assistance in securing the grant. More recently, a number of helpful commentators and supporters intervened, each making a difference in some way: William Boyd, Steve Jacobson, Robert O'Reilly, Austin Swanson, and Richard Townsend. I also thank Cathy Pusateri of Westview Press for her guidance and assistance. Two persons offered important assurance that the journey was worth taking: Tony Bryk and K. Forbis Jordan. Their critical interventions stayed the course. Another, Bruce Cooper, effected an able review of the complete manuscript and made many useful suggestions. One person, however, stands out. That was James Coleman, who served as a career-long inspiration. A scholar's scholar, his encouragement weighed greatly in my willingness to pursue the tasks of compilation and writing, to tell the story. My intellectual debt to him is evident in the following pages.

Many graduate students, affectionately called "martians," also contributed directly to the volume by exploring variations of benevolence, gathering data, and challenging my assumptions. Their names appear in the Martian Honour Roll in the appendix. Support from the University of British Columbia in the form of an eight-month sabbatical is acknowledged gratefully. Most importantly, my thanks go to the many school administrators, teachers, and volunteers who gave their time to answer questions about voluntarism in their schools. These heroes and heroines provided the primary knowledge base for this study and their benevolence speaks well of them.

At this point, the usual insertion states that if the author's spouse and children had not suffered the deprivation of the writer's company for substantial periods, "this book would never have been written." Not so in my case. I set aside this work many times to respond to the usual demands of life with others. I was there. From high chairs to dentists' chairs, I was there. From nightmares to camping, I was there. From preschool to basketball, from midnight rambles to visits to Grandma's, from bedtime songs to emergency wards, from birthday parties to principals' offices, from setbacks to breakthroughs, I was there. And I shall continue to be there. This book, therefore, has its genesis in the realization of the importance of acts of giving in my own life. My parents, Doug and Rita Brown, taught me throughout my childhood about the daily import of benevolence. Consequently, this book is dedicated to their memory.

D.J.B.

1

Is Voluntarism Important?

Many difficulties beset public schools in North America, an assertion so commonplace that it warrants substantial investigation. Among the prominent concerns, however, are three: "the problem of resources," "the problem of autonomy," and "the problem of integration." Simply stated, the problem of resources refers to the paucity of dollars available to public schools to educate children. The problem of autonomy is the restriction on the ability to make school-level decisions in order to address local priorities. And the problem of integration refers to the insufficient care or social support provided to the students. Note that these problems are organizational; they pertain to the way schools are structured and administered. The research for this book suggests that voluntarism provides a special opportunity to lessen the first and second problems and make important progress in addressing the third one, though not without some pitfalls. Sounds reassuring, doesn't it? Advocates for the use of school volunteers certainly think so. To investigate how voluntarism can address the three problems, it is important to appreciate, first, the severity of the three challenges for public schools.

Three Problems of Public Education

Public school educators often point out they have insufficient resources to "do the job." Teachers and others usually want to provide more services to their students than they can currently deliver. For example, to meet their ideals, schools generally say they require more assistance in classrooms, more clerical help, more aid in the supervision of students, as well as additional equipment and more teaching supplies. Instead, resources are dwindling precisely at the time when growing numbers of students speak native languages that are not English, more special needs students are entering regular classrooms, and the requirements for curricular change are frequent.[1] Although schools have always faced a "scarcity of resources," to use the economists' term, the funds available to them have been curtailed in many jurisdictions in the recent past. Two reasons are offered for this reduction in real dollars. The first is the financial retrenchment imposed by many states and provinces on all governmental services. In an effort to diminish their deficits, they say that "there is just no more money available." The second reason is that public schools are facing greater competition for the available tax revenues because of the demands made for other governmental services, particularly health and welfare.[2,3] As a consequence of the cutbacks, the cry of educational administrators for adequate resources has grown even more shrill than it was in the past. The era of substantial budget increases and public willingness to provide more tax dollars is over.

A second problem closely related to the amount of resources that public schools receive is the constraint on the resources they have. Public schools are very rule-bound. Principals complain that they are not authorized to engage in flexible decision-making with regard to school resources (particularly personnel, maintenance, equipment, utilities and central office services).[4] It seems that tax dollars become lost in "the system" and do not necessarily "follow the child." Those who have prime responsibility for the education of children say they do not have control over significant quantities of educational resources, despite the large amounts of funding that come from states, provinces, and districts—a substantial annual cost to educate each pupil. Thus, a "problem of school autonomy" persists.[5,6] According to one American study, many frustrations accompany the lack of control that school personnel feel:

> Generally speaking, the 183 professional educators who work in the nine urban schools in our study are forced—by circumstances and by law—to deal with factors over which they have almost no control. They feel directed—by events and by mandates—to engage in activities that will not help their students perform well in school. Only a few of the 183 teachers feel in charge of who they are and of what they do. (Frymier, p. 12)

The probable impact of these constraints on learning has been argued by John Chubb and Terry Moe (1990), who rather audaciously link less-than-desirable student achievement levels with the extent to which schools are restricted in their ability to allocate resources internally.[7] They insist the lack of autonomy is attributable to governmental control.

Beyond these two complaints, public schools also face the myriad social problems which are shared with the wider society. These constitute the "problem of integration." Children endure and bring to school problems such as violence, family breakdown, substance abuse, crime, and unwanted pregnancies.[8] Elementary teachers often remark that their roles are increasingly like those of social workers as dislocation enters their classrooms. At few times previously have school-age children been required to cope with the lack of sustaining social structures to the extent that they do today. Clearly, children's needs for care have seldom been greater; the task to provide that level of support is monumental. Unfortunately, many of today's public schools may be currently viewed as "colonial outposts"—isolated from the public they serve.[9] No longer one of the main centres of the lives of persons who live nearby, schools have become places which some parents fear to enter. Many communities have grown to neglect their local schools, institutions which once enjoyed strong neighbourhood support.[10] Clearly, if schools are to address these problems of social integration and reconstruction, they must be strengthened, rather than weakened. It appears that voluntarism offers hope for this healing since it can enhance schools' resources, freedom to act, and build strong community connections.[11]

Many proposals for the reform of public education have been presented and several of them are designed to address parts of the three problems of resources, autonomy, and integration outlined above. States and districts are trying various strategies.[12, 13] There are many initiatives promoting parental school choice, school-based management, and teacher empowerment. Saturn schools are being established. Charter schools are being approved and their initial evaluation has begun.[14] Private schools are cited as models for change.[15] These reforms are international[16] and breed a sense of euphoria among activists during this time of experimentation. The desire to improve public education is accompanied by fierce commitments and intense debates. Will the putative reforms correct the problems of resources, autonomy, or integration? Maybe not. There are substantive questions about the likely failure of most reforms and the paucity of "real" educational change. One reason for circumspection is that reforms are cyclic in the long term, as Larry Cuban has pointed out. Waves of centralization and decentralization have washed across schools during the last century and they will continue.[17] Another reason for pause is that no matter how brilliant a reform idea, it is quite likely that its implementation will founder, leading to the abandonment of the change.[18] The outlook for reforms is, therefore, both optimistic and pessimistic. What, then, can really be done? The following case illustrates some possibilities.

The Story of the Little School

This is the true story of a small elementary school in British Columbia which sits in a pastoral setting on the fringes of a suburb. The school's enrollment at the time of the story in 1990 was 116; it had 4 1/2 classrooms serving grades K–7. A fair proportion of students spoke a mother tongue which was not English and many of the 30 extended families it served were poor. One little girl wrote on her wish list, "I wish we didn't have a house full of rats." When school was dismissed at noon, a boy said, "I don't want to go home; I want to stay for the day." Most of the students were neither well dressed nor well groomed.

The extent of parental participation in school activities was sparse. Perhaps six parents would show up at parent group meetings. The school's fund raiser, a chicken sale, had brought in a paltry $69 and only because the teachers had bought the chicken. Parents were not available for field trips. Some did not have cars; some did not drive; others did not want to pick up their children after school basketball games. They appeared to feel that it was the school's responsibility to see their children home. Several families were recent immigrants and had been peasants in their native countries. They were farmers and defined success as the ownership of land. Schooling seemed not to be valuable to them.

When the year's events were being planned, a mother suggested a fashion show at $5 per ticket. This idea was received very skeptically by the principal and teachers. In their view, no school in the district was less suited to a fashion show. But the mother persisted and persuaded the principal to schedule the event. The same mother volunteered to coordinate the show. She approached four children's clothing stores and asked them to be sponsors by lending clothes. Ten other businesses were requested to donate prizes. They offered awards such as a car lubrication, a hair styling, a hair electrolysis, and a ring. The coordinating mother wrote the commentary for the show and asked the grade seven students to make the decorations. Parents took their children to the stores to try on the clothes for the fashion show, but most could not afford to purchase them, even on sale. Two days before the event, only 20 tickets had been sold to parents. The decision was made to change the price to $10 per family or $2 per child. A booth was set up so that visitors could pay at the door.

It was 7:00 and time for the show to start. Almost no parents were on hand; the principal panicked. She should never had allowed this disaster to happen. At 7:10, the small faculty and staff parking lot had a few cars, at least someone was coming. By 7:20, the gymnasium was full; more chairs were needed.

A variety of clothes was featured: neon coloured sports wear, matched couples wear, and dressed suits. Some dads were on hand with their video cameras to record the moves of their progeny. Toddlers ran amok. Ample numbers of relatives and friends attended. The results were rather startling. Students with limited skills in English were the stars as they had no need to speak. Some wore clothes they could never afford. "Weak" pupils had their moments of success in school. Two teachers commented, "Some are so well dressed, I can hardly recognize my own students," and "Who says that clothes don't make the person?" Coffee was served and prizes awarded.

During the next few days, the school checked its accounts and found that it had realized $565 for the evening. By contrast, the complaints seemed minor. One parent said that her child's name had been left off the program. The vice principal requested the name be added and the revised program be sent home as a souvenir. Some of the businesses griped that a few of the parents who had borrowed the clothes were ill-mannered and so they would not participate in such an event again. But overall, the school agreed the show was a success.

This narrative was related by a teacher in the Little School. While the financial payoff in particular was celebrated, the event evokes a number of issues about benevolence in the form of personal time given to a school. One is, can it be successful at carrying out an important task? The principal and faculty were certain the show would be a failure because they believed they knew the parents to be either unable or unwilling to participate. Yet, the initiative of one mother demonstrated that there was a way to hold a successful fashion show (giving behaviour can be remarkably insistent). But can voluntarism contribute a significant amount of resources to a school? Although the time and dollar values of the event were not large, their contributions to the life of this school were important. Resources were donated to serve a desired objective—participation in an event which was chiefly social but also had student learning associated with it and resulted in some funds. The school received time and money it never would have gained otherwise. Further, the dollars acquired were both marginal (in the positive, economic sense) and discretionary. Now the school had several hundred additional dollars to allocate with few constraints. There is nothing like an extra dollar in one's pocket—it makes the subjective difference between affluence and poverty, even for a school. Thus, problems of resources, autonomy, and integration were addressed in a small way through the actions of a few individuals.[19]

It would seem that voluntarism could prove vitally important to public schools. To understand how and why, the journey leaves the example of the Little School to engage in a fuller consideration of both the primary and secondary data sets which inform this book. To begin this exploration, the next sections refer briefly to how the initial research was done as well as how it was conceptualized relative to previous works in the literature. The chapter concludes with some general thoughts about what implications this work holds for educational policy.[20]

Notes on This Monograph

The initial data which led to this book were gathered from interviews of a total of 185 principals, teachers, and volunteers. Interviews were conducted in 72 schools situated in a variety of contexts in British Columbia, a Canadian province in which public revenues for education had been curtailed severely during the 1980's and 1990's. One of the ways schools reacted to the lean years was to rely on benevolence. Since Canadians are less known for voluntarism than Americans (according to Seymour Martin Lipset), the British Columbia setting provided a conservative context in which to investigate giving.[21] How were the schools chosen? They were sampled in a manner which was unabashedly purposeful—no random sampling here. Rather, 54 were selected from ones known by reputation within their respective 17 districts for their active volunteer programs. Focus was on the exceptional, rather than the status quo, which was represented by 18 "unselected" schools that provided contrast. The unselected schools were regarded as typical elementary schools within the same districts. The overall emphasis on the uncommon schools was diminished by the secondary data which was assembled from the extant literature.

Secondary data were often provided by surveys of current levels of voluntarism in public schools and districts. The secondary data sources, of which there are many embedded in this volume, came from around the world but mainly from the United States. Some of the data were provided by works that have lighted the way for the study of community involvement in education.

While this volume has few clear predecessors, works of special note that have covered some common ground include Litwak and Meyer, Lightfoot, Comer, Coleman and Hoffer, Epstein, Chubb and Moe, Michael, and Bryk, Lee, and Holland. However, this book differs in a number of ways from most of them.

First, this monograph concentrates on benevolence in schools, not just on specific schools or on all forms of community participation. It attempts to tell the story of voluntarism in education more completely than it has been told before. Information comes from grassroots efforts in individual schools rather than from substantial interventions directed by teams of researchers. Further, it is based on an investigation that was conducted not with the certainty of the committed but with the wonder of the explorer.

Second, this volume places a strong emphasis not only on the acts of giving but on the administrative and organizational responses to them. Voluntarism is considered in this binary fashion because the managerial reaction and the structures that support or impede it are seen as central to understanding the entire phenomenon. A focus on the individual participant would be incomplete; people are social beings.[22]

Third, there is a need to come to grips with the fundamental explanations behind benevolence and the organizational reactions it engenders. Too often, benevolence is explained merely in terms of personal traits and its organizational response is not even acknowledged. But this volume searches for linkages between these social phenomena and some established models of individual and organizational behaviour. The culminating point of this search for explanation is Coleman's (1990) rational choice theory which casts a wide net and is used to interpret much of the primary and secondary data. The sense of purpose expressed by the volunteers, the growth of social capital constructed, and the deliberate planning on the part of schools to foster benevolence are just some of the behaviours that become clearly interpretable as rational actions. While other theories compete by offering useful perspectives, each falls somewhat short and Coleman's "wins," thus providing a useful framework for this volume. Of course, all this contemplation points to some directions for educational policies that require a sound footing.

Voluntarism and Educational Policies

As suggested, benevolence may address not only the problems of resources and autonomy, but also of social integration. Perhaps the Little School could become a "voluntary public school," a school that depends on giving as well as public support. Yet, for some, the idea of benevolence is a dangerous one. It raises the possibility that schools could succumb to the limitations of their neighbourhoods.

The dominant principle that now guides the direction of resources to most public schools in North America is equality, either for students or for taxpayers.[23] Equality of access for students and the ability-to-pay for taxpayers are paramount values in the design of support for public education. The equality effort, seeking to standardize the provision of schooling, implies that the contributions of parents, families, or neighbours are not wanted (or are unimportant) and that the state provides the child's education and has sufficient resources to do so. The axiom is simple: schools are context-bound and need to be freed from community influences. But what has happened? State provision of education appears to have resulted in schools which are underfunded, rule-bound, and disassociated from their immediate publics. Emancipation has produced schools which sometimes resemble citadels. The three problems of resources, autonomy, and integration require us to question the vision of fully public schools, embraced from the early part of the twentieth century onward, and to consider a reconception of support for public education.[24]

This book presents evidence and ideas to help the reader imagine support for public education which is a mix—partly public and partly private. It offers a simple choice to policy makers: we can hope for funding on a fully equitable basis and do without needed services, or we can ask for private voluntary help and accept the effects, both economic and social. I submit that the vision of voluntarism is a straightforward one. Neither nostalgic nor utopian, it offers assistance to public schools and the persons who support them. Such an approach has its precedents. Benevolence towards schools has been apparent for over 400 years in Great Britain and North America. This long tradition may be rediscovered and contribute much to today's schools, perhaps bringing them closer to a conception of "good" ones.[25] So is voluntarism important? Absolutely. To see how it works, Chapter 2 provides some answers.

Notes

1. Murphy and Beck make this gloomy statement: "Most critics see little hope that the ever-widening goals of education can be reached in the current system of schooling." (p. 78)

2. See Fowler, Boyd, and Plank on the problem of public support for public education internationally.

3. In some jurisdictions, support for private schools also reduces the dollars available for public schools.

4. See Brown (1990), pp. 1–8.

5. See Goodlad on the need to permit decisions to be made at the school level, pp. 264–274.

6. It seems that bureaucracy as an organizational structure is a favourite target of criticism. Complaints about its ineffectiveness abound. See Clark and Meloy who address overall bureaucratic failure, Lawton who says that bureaucracy cannot address technical and structural problems, Tyack who refers to "bureaucratic arteriosclerosis," (p. 3), and Wagstaff and Reyes who say the central office is too removed from schools.

7. See Chubb and Moe on the difficulties of inflexible decision making that public schools face (p. 2). Also see Wise on bureaucracy as an idea alien to schools and Conway and Jacobson who call for more teacher control.

8. Problems in the greater society have formed part of the impetus for the reform of schools. See Murphy (1993), Guthrie, and Hodgkinson on family dislocation; Kirst, McLaughlin and Massell who note that about half of America's children will live with a single parent at some time (p. 4); and Wagstaff and Gallagher who report the recent growth in female-headed families (p. 103) and student experimentation with drugs (p. 107).

9. This rather apt metaphor was suggested to me by Alfred Hess, Jr. of the Chicago Panel.

10. Schools and communities were once closely connected. See Crowson for a detailed account of the relationships between schools and the communities they serve. Hawley calls for a reconciliation between families and schools (p. 428) and Murphy (1991) notes the shift from bureaucratic to more communal views of what schools should be. The disassociation between the public in general and its schools in general is observable in the annual Phi Delta Kappan poll. See Elam (1996), who shows that 57% of public school parents gave public schools in their community an "A" or "B," while 87% of nonpublic school parents gave nonpublic schools the same grades (p. 46 and 47). Thirty-eight percent of nonparents

(persons without children in school) gave the public schools in their community an "A" or "B" while 67% of them gave the nonpublic schools the same grades. The disenchantment is nicely captured by Jennings who attributes the problem to negative media reports, the disengagement of educators, attacks from the far right, and a general lack of change.

11. I could have added the obvious problems of economic decline and the need for industries to be competitive in a world economy but the extent to which schools should assume this goal is a matter of some disagreement.

12. For a series of cases of reform efforts, see Murphy and Hallinger. One is the general call for parental participation, most noteworthy in the work of Joyce Epstein (1990). Her typology of involvement covers communications between home and school, parental involvement at school, and home-based efforts of parents to help their own children in school. Only the second is of main concern in this volume but it tries to tell the story of voluntarism more completely. See also Swap. A response to the autonomy problem consists of several proposals for the provision of school choice by parents (Chubb and Moe). Their advocacy for choice is a manifestation of the rise of the economic paradigm as a basis for educational policies world-wide (Boyd). Although choice of school is voluntary and may result in gifts, choice plans are not the focus of this book. Another current idea for reform focuses on the flexibility problem. It is school-based management (Brown, 1990). There is evidence to show that school-based management can solve many problems of inflexibility of decision-making in schools and the lack of accountability to boards, though we do not know much about its effects on learning. While both choice and school-based management may involve parent volunteers on advisory councils, the concern in this volume is largely restricted to private resources and the control over them. One final exclusion is needed: voluntarism is not the same as school enterprise, defined as exchanges with school environments. Enterprise also produces private resources and may result in social capital, but it is not based on giving. Rather, its practice is founded on short-term exchanges as evident in contracting, tuition fees, the sale of goods and the provision of services by schools. Enterprise is the subject of another work which will investigate entrepreneurship among educational administrators.

13. For an international review of restructuring in education, see Beare and Boyd.

14. See Education Commission of the States for a survey of charter school legislation, numbers, enrollments, and potential impacts on students, parents, and teachers. Nathan puts forward a cogent defense and many positive claims on behalf of charter schools. He says, "The charter school movement brings together four powerful concepts: freedom and choice for families, entrepreneurial opportunities for educators, explicit accountability for schools, and thoughtful fair competition for public school districts." (p. 18)

15. For an overview of the salient demographics of nonpublic schools in the United States, see Cooper (1988).

16. The English and Welsh experience with economic decentralization is probably the most noteworthy example.

17. See Cuban.

18. Effective change requires ample time and resources. See Fullan on educational change.

19. The story illustrates another point—the linkage between giving and exchange behaviours. The organizer, helpers, and children who performed gave their time and energy to the event. However, the teachers, shopkeepers, and purchasers of tickets all contributed in light of the expected return they would receive. The teachers, of course, expected their usual paychecks, the shopkeepers, an increase in business, and the purchasers, an evening's entertainment. Conceptually, the distinction between giving and exchange is considerable but they are often associated empirically in schools.

20. See also Chapter 9. For an elaboration on all aspects of the research methods and data set, see the appendix.

21. See Lipset.

22. The study of individual giving is a relatively neglected area of inquiry. According to Weisbrod, the contributions of individuals exceed that of foundations and corporations by many times. Inquiry on the social determinants is also underrepresented, according to Jencks, p. 326.

23. See Swanson and King on public school finance.

24. See Ellwood Cubberly on developments between 1900 and 1930. Such a reorientation is reflected in Nathan Glazer's remarks which are directed toward most public services: "I am increasingly convinced that some important part of the solution to our social problems lies in traditional practices and traditional restraints. Since the past is not recoverable, what guidance can this possibly give? It gives two forms of guidance: first, it counsels hesitation in the development of social policies that sanction the abandonment of traditional practices, and second, and perhaps more helpful, it suggests that the creation and building of new traditions, or new versions of old traditions, must be taken more seriously as a requirement of social policy itself." (Glazer, pp. 7–8).

25. See Bryk.

PART I

Experiences with School Voluntarism

2

School Gifts,
Givers, and Giving

This discussion begins by addressing the things the sampled volunteers did when they gave to schools. What good deeds did they perform? A description of these tasks allows us to form a rudimentary understanding of school gifts. Next, it makes sense to ask who the benefactors were. What did they look like? What were their backgrounds? More precisely, why did these benefactors give? Volunteers and those who worked closely with them responded to this question. The answers are then compared to what is known about reasons given for all social behaviour, of which giving one's personal time is one example. Finally, I pause to seek a formal definition of giving in order to separate it from what it is not.

The Good Deeds

One day, 25 fathers, mothers, and teachers gathered together at "their" school. They had worked for months to raise $25,000 from fun fairs, casino nights, and donations. In addition, they had been offered cement from a cement company, logs from a logging company, the services of a truck that could dig post holes, and lunches from local stores. Most of these dollars had been spent on carefully-selected equipment. After lots of hard work, their adventure playground was in place. Though this story may seem exceptional, it is not. Such benevolence is common.[1]

Playground construction was only one task among many that the sample of volunteers undertook in schools. Some of their jobs aided the central purpose of academic learning. Often, they served the function of tutors[2] and classroom aides by listening to children read, helping in arithmetic, or assisting in spelling drills. These roles, which required instructional skills, were perceived to be helpful to teachers. As one volunteer said, "The teacher has the latitude to work with the entire class while

I take the child and work with him or her on an individual basis" (ad33).*
Teachers agreed:

> The volunteers provide more adult bodies in the classroom to meet the indi-
> vidual needs of the children. The children receive a better program because I
> am able to offer more varied, exciting, and interesting activities. I could not
> carry out some of my programs without the use of volunteers. (ad33)

> The classroom is much better because control and management are much
> more positive. I am not trying to rush around madly attending to all of the
> students at once. (ad46)

> It's like having an extra set of ears and eyes. It's great! (ad34)

Such tutorial help on a one-on-one basis was mentioned frequently as a job
that volunteers undertook. Often, benefactors associated their tutorial work
with the aim of providing individualized instruction to a particular pupil.
They played a direct and active role in the learning process of a child.[3]

Not all direct instruction on the part of volunteers was, however, confined to the tutorial mode or even the to classroom. One volunteer invited classes to her orchard for lessons on plant cultivation. As a principal mentioned,

> We had one of our mothers, who is a constable with the police force, give
> talks to 80 percent of the classes on her role and the types of things she deals
> with. I had a lady who gave a demonstration on face painting. We had First
> Nations people come in. A father, active in the dance troops, performed for
> the school. A grandfather did a demonstration of carving. (sp67)

Other examples of group instruction included assistance with an acid
rain project, banking, parent literacy, letter writing, and a introduction to
"big books."

A large number of other assignments were also undertaken by volunteers in the sample. For schools which needed transportation and supervision for field trips, most of the benefactors' work involved unglam-
ourous chores of maintaining order or waiting for buses in the rain. But
the assistance was sometimes than more that:

> My son was in an early primary class and the teacher was new to our area.
> She was not aware of the field trip opportunities which were available in
> our community. As she was planning a theme, I would put her in touch with
> the resource people which were associated with that area. (volunteer ad35)

---

*The letters and numbers in parentheses throughout the text indicate the identity of the
interviewers and the page in their reports.

Donors also offered adult supervision as requested for playgrounds, after-school games, and particularly, sports days. These voluntary contributions prompted one principal to comment: "The tone on our playground at lunch time is really positive because of the commitment that volunteers have made to organizing and supervising games for the children to play" (ad31).

Some volunteer support work was almost unrelated to instruction. It included safe arrival checks, noon hour supervision, health inspections, and school lunch programs. One benefactor became known as "the hot dog lady" (he33). Also, volunteers helped with jobs such as photocopying and library card cataloguing. As one volunteer remarked, "There is no need for the teacher to waste her time doing that. Now she has more time to help the kids" (rt50). Many of these tasks were quite removed from student academic learning and distant from the prescriptions of the curriculum, but they were regarded as critical nonetheless.

Teachers tended to see donations of time as an assortment of small but interlocking pieces of classroom life. One primary teacher described the contributions in this way:

> All parents are invited to come in from 9:00 to 9:15 every day to read with children. Parents read with a group or one child. Volunteers assist on Wednesday mornings with cooking. One parent does computer work once a week for 40 minutes, writing and publishing stories. A parent takes students, one at a time, to have them read into a tape recorder to show growth in reading. Another parent comes in once a week to help with clerical tasks such as filing, filling in portfolio information, and organizing scrapbook portfolios. In the morning, this volunteer will also bring in supplies, tidy up, and organize the recycling. Two parents come in on special occasions such as Friendship Day and eight are called upon for driving. (sp67)

Her mention of special occasions constituted yet another area of giving of time to schools. Some events in which volunteers helped were mainly social, such as Christmas or Easter parties. Others had a financial goal. Examples were bake sales, hot dog sales, or campaigns to raise money for library books, computer hardware and software, or instructional supplies.[4] Although efforts usually benefited the school, some schools were most generous to external causes.[5] The principal of an inner city middle-to-low income school reported proudly,

> To show you the generosity of this community, we have just raised over $4,000 for the . . . Terry Fox Cancer Fund. That amount is the highest in the city or close to it . . . a reflection of how the parents feel about the school. (rt38)

Another principal summed up her views on fund raising in this way:

Because the parents are so heavily involved in fund-raising, we have things we would not have due to our size. We have lots of computers. The computerization of the library was paid for by the volunteers. Every grade seven is given a T-shirt when they leave and everyone at Sport's Day gets a ribbon. It allows us to 'make' the school. (he33)

Fund raising was often undertaken with considerable planning and organization on the part of the volunteers.[6] It was a major activity of the parent advisory council, a group whose officers invariably contributed a large number of hours of volunteer time to the school.[7]

Educators in the sample, particularly those in the selected schools,[8] considered the overall duties accomplished by volunteers to be highly necessary to the education of children in their charge. They made remarks such as "We do things (with volunteers) we would not be able to do (otherwise)" (ob48). "Without the volunteers nothing would happen" (ob57). One head teacher summed up this assessment very clearly: "We couldn't run the school the way we want without volunteers. If we had to do everything ourselves, lots would be left undone" (ps54). For them, the volunteers were a *sine qua non* of many services provided to their students.

So volunteers assume a great deal of work in schools. But what kinds of jobs are the most common? The primary data did not reveal the relative frequencies of occurrence of instruction, support, or special events and there are only a few studies that tell the frequency of tasks observed across schools.[9] Two studies indicate that contributions to direct instruction may be most common, followed by support (such as transportation), while special events (such as fund raisers) may be observed less often. How many volunteers are involved in the different kinds of tasks? Again, the data are sparse. It is likely that most volunteers donate time to support service, followed by instruction, and then special events.[10] Note the inversion: voluntary instruction is probably encountered often in schools but more volunteers participate in activities that support learning indirectly.

The depiction of sample schools is that they are ones in which volunteers are plentiful. That observation is an artifact of purposeful sampling. Contrarily, typical schools may not receive much volunteer help—there are often only a few volunteers in the average elementary school.[11] The picture brightens when selected schools in Hancock's study are considered—they showed a mean of 182.5 hours of volunteer time per week with a peak of 500.[12] Unfortunately, the number of donated hours per student is seldom calculated; one solitary estimate is 0.64 hours per student per month for a typical school.[13, 14] How much time can each school expect from a volunteer?[15] Estimates of averages vary from 1.7 to 2.2 hours per week with ranges from 15 minutes to 154 hours per month.[16] Some people give a lot of time.[17] Others give little. Many give none. According to one study, over 70% of parents have never been involved in assisting a teacher or staff member of a school.[18] How many volunteers work on what kinds of jobs once they arrive at school? One estimate is that 45 percent offer direct aid to instruction.[19] Clearly, a good deal more research is needed to produce reliable estimates of voluntary contributions to schools.[20] Having said that, it is easy to call for more research under circumstances of lack of knowledge. However, there is a sense in which the value of hours donated cannot be measured in any valid way, even if they are counted accurately. We may never have any idea how important or unimportant these contributions may be since only the intimate knowledge of each act of giving time and its effects on the recipient(s) can begin to explain its significance or insignificance.

Although one survey revealed that 25% of elementary schools did not use volunteers at all,[21] the national effort of persons who donate time to schools in the United States appears to be substantial.[22] It is likely that 1.1 million volunteers contributed their time to American elementary and secondary schools in 1984–85.[23] The sense that voluntarism for schools involves substantial numbers of persons is augmented by captivating descriptions of programs in large school districts. Chicago, Tulsa, Boston, Montgomery County, Washington, D.C., Dallas, Los Angeles, and San Francisco are among the sites wherein significant efforts have been made to engage volunteers. If the enrollments and hours or numbers of volunteers are added for these districts alone, then 1.083M children potentially benefited from 636,000 hours combined with the time given by 70,594 volunteers for elementary and secondary schools.[24]

It is important to note that the picture for volunteers in elementary schools should not be assumed to apply to secondary schools. There, volunteers perform different kinds of jobs than they do at the elementary level. Although some make instructional contributions (e.g., speakers), most are involved in extracurricular activities, such as assistance with athletics. Their roles appear more specialized than in elementary schools. Secondary schools may also have far fewer volunteers. According to a national survey, 75% of elementary schools have them but only 32% of high schools do.[25] Some secondary schools may prefer to charge fees rather than to rely on fund raising which requires volunteer hours. Contrarily, the level of volunteer activity may be higher in nonpublic secondary schools that hold more special events, particularly for fund raising.

The jobs that volunteers do in elementary schools may not be greatly different from the work they perform when donating their time to other institutions such as those who serve health, welfare, and the arts. There, benefactors teach, perform clerical duties, and fund raise,[26] but unlike their school counterparts, their most frequent activity may be fund raising, particularly for those institutions not supported by public money.[27]

Nonprofit organizations appear to benefit considerably from volunteer time, which may be worth 50% more than all the money they receive.[28] Actually, the propensity to give time may be rising.[29] How much do people give? Canadians, who match Californians in population, gave one billion hours of volunteer time in one year, the equivalent of one half million full-time jobs. They were willing to donate 3.7 hours per week on average.[30] Giving time is popular.

Who Volunteers in Schools?

It is fairly easy to form a picture of the usual person who donated time in the sample elementary schools. When respondents were asked to offer a profile of the "common volunteer," they said that she was a mother aged from 30 to her early 40's with children in primary school (kindergarten to grade three). Further, she was a Caucasian who either worked part time or was a home maker. This profile was affirmed widely by the respondents. Fathers were encountered much less frequently than mothers.[31] There were far fewer volunteers among parents whose children were in the intermediate grades (four to seven). Most volunteers were white[32] and most of the benefactors did not have full-time employment.

Some interviewees augmented this demographic profile by adding that their school's usual volunteer often belonged to a two-parent family and spoke English well. A small number said that she came from a high socioeconomic background but others noted that her circumstances matched the majority of parents who sent their children to that particular school.[33] A few interviewees insisted that part of their volunteer profile included the personal characteristic of not feeling threatened by the school.[34]

Does this simple portrait of the common volunteer who is female, between young adulthood and middle age, a parent, Caucasian, and not employed full time fit with the descriptions that others have found? It seems to. Studies support this general depiction for elementary schools.[35] The profile of the common volunteer also resembles that of benefactors outside education, though not completely. For instance, volunteers in other institutions are often employed full-time.[36]

A few of the respondents were asked if they could make up a profile of a non-volunteer. A bit of a challenge! This question was a rather negative one, posed as, "Who does not come through the school gate?" After some thought, they said that this person had a demanding family life, was unaware of the parental role at school, was an immigrant, and did not drive a car. Note that they did not answer in demographic terms exclusively, but chose to mention the constraints on the lives of persons who elected not to donate time to their schools. This kind of response did not permit an adequate contrast between the makeup of the common volunteer and the non-volunteer. Perhaps the question of who does not come through the school gate may be more helpfully answered by observing those people who are less well represented than the person in the profile but who do contribute nonetheless. Who is the "uncommon volunteer?"

It is possible to piece together a depiction of uncommon volunteers (found mostly in selected schools), though only a tentative picture may be constructed of them. Some were dads. As one principal said,

> The fathers are a big deal at this school. The male volunteers do things with the children that other volunteers do not do. They have lots of fun with the children and the children respond differently. (ad37)

Some donors were nonparents with special skills and talents (I shall use the term "nonparent" to refer to all persons except those who have children in elementary school). Here is an example of one volunteer who recalled the work of another:

> My son decided he wanted to be a decoy carver. The program organizers could not find a senior to work with him, so in our case, he worked with a twenty-nine year old fellow. We thought at the time, "Oh, what are we going to have to put out in costs?" We were told by this young man that our son could make use of his beautiful set of carving tools. He would supply everything our son needed if we picked up the costs of two sheets of sandpaper. (volunteer dd42)

Many donors were not Caucasian. At one selected school, most of the volunteers were Indo-Canadian.[37] Some in other schools were seniors. One was 94 years old and helped four mornings each week, reading to students individually giving instructions on how to knit bookmarks. She started volunteering when she was 79 and the school held a birthday party for her each year (sm38). Some were teenagers. A teacher remarked that 70% of her volunteers were teenagers (mostly students). The remainder of her benefactors consisted of a few parents and a rabbi (sm37).[38] While the primary data did not offer a great deal of information on the uncommon volunteer, accounts from other studies demonstrate a spectrum of participants.

There are many isolated examples of volunteers who do not fit the profile of everyday benefactors in schools. They include groups of older volunteers (such as LA DOVES, the Dedicated Older Volunteers in Los Angeles),[39] seniors in Ann Arbor who formed TLC (Teaching-Learning Communities aimed at high risk children),[40] and older persons who offered expert help on subjects such as volcanoes, coats of arms, and ballroom dancing.[41] There seems to be an association between vocational or avocational interests and the contributions people make. Senior benefactors were frequently retired teachers or other professionals.[42]

Some uncommon volunteers are much younger than seniors and have an occupational connection to schools. For instance, there were students from teachers' colleges who explored future roles.[43] Other nonparents were sometimes sent by their companies to contribute a small number of hours a week.[44, 45] Some of the common volunteers in the primary data were teachers who had taken time out to raise their children and wanted to maintain contact with a school before returning to the classroom formally.

Volunteers come in many forms. The rather jumbled picture of the uncommon volunteer leads to the suggestion that if a profile could be constructed, it would be of a person who is male, a senior, nonwhite, and not a parent. No proper generalization can be made (particularly about employment status), but for certain, these volunteers are rather distant from the "lady bountiful" stereotype.[46] Does the "quasi profile" of the uncommon volunteer fit with persons who donate time elsewhere? There may be some overlap with benefactors found in secondary schools.[47] Importantly, nonparents (and particularly seniors) may be a considerable latent source of support for schools.[48] A Gallup survey revealed that a full 51 percent of persons without children in schools indicated they were willing to work as an unpaid school volunteer.[49] Remarkable!

Why Do They Give?

The volunteers and those who worked closely with them were asked why people contributed time to schools. Initial reasons offered, such as "to help others," did not produce much insight since volunteering and helping others are highly overlapping actions. But when reasons were probed, many kinds of explanations were offered. Some of the volunteers contributed to schools mostly in order to serve themselves. They admitted unabashedly that they volunteer for their own good alone. For instance, one of the purposes of volunteering was to escape from a home life often dominated by small children. "It gets me out of the house" was a frequent response. More positively, volunteers said that they were searching for fulfillment and stimulation. According to two,

> Volunteering is a growing experience. . . . If you stay at home and only occupy yourself with your own family, you don't grow too much. . . . If you take on different things you learn your strength . . . which you may decide to pursue later on. (ps47)

> Volunteering helps you learn a lot about yourself and about dealing with other people. . . . Volunteering is a source of personal satisfaction and it helps develop self-confidence. It broadens your horizons and enriches your viewpoint. Certain jobs you take on can be very challenging. (st46)

Others found their work at school to be a substitute for paid employment. One principal described an important contributor:

> Our treasurer who volunteers and organizes all the money and so on—she's very, very, very good at that. She's got a real accounting sense and accounting background. She doesn't have a job; she's got too many kids so I think this gives her a real sense of fulfillment. She can do all this math and all this tallying and all those spreadsheets so she gets a charge and still manages to be with her children a lot. There's no doubt about it; a lot of them do it for themselves. (ob44)

For some, there was great satisfaction derived from serving in a teacher's role. They enjoyed instructing children and may have been denied the opportunity to pursue teaching as an occupation at an earlier time. These people were expressing or observing immediate satisfaction with what they had done.[50] What about the long term? Some were following their hope for political recognition, as articulated by this principal:

> I've known of parents who worked through the local school PAC's (parent advisory councils), they got into the district PAC's, and then they became a trustee.[51] That's happened. So there's the will to volunteer but there's the political perspective—ambition. (ob45)

Others sought an economic payoff. While most did not mention the possible connection between their volunteer work and future employment, a few were benefactors for that reason.

> Some of my volunteers are substitute teachers that are new to the school district and are seeking employment. They want some experience in the district and volunteering gives them the opportunity to meet other staff members. I usually call upon these people when I am sick and they come in for me. I like it because they already know the students and they are familiar with my routine. (teacher ad54)[52]

A great many other volunteers offered a rather obvious but different set of reasons as to why they and others donated their time to the neighbourhood school. Most spoke an interest in gaining a knowledge of the school. Others wanted to improve the school attended by their children. One demonstrated the kind of information she was seeking:

> If you don't get involved with volunteer work at school, you do not know what's going on. I think it's quite important if you want to know the quality of education the kids can receive. You're more aware that some teachers are better than others. I would like to be able to pick the teacher next year for my kid. . . . it would help her in her education because she has the better teacher. (ob46)

First-hand information was very important to them. Others simply wanted to lend a direct hand in the education of their children.[53]

> I believe in the enrichment of a child's education and this is just not possible without the help of parent volunteers. I want teachers to do the creative, wonderful things with the class and I will do the joe-job stuff. (volunteer gc43)

> They have a duty to their kids. They want to help in whatever ways they can, whether it's coming in helping in the library or going to the classroom and helping teachers to copy materials . . . for them. (vice-principal ob44)

When some were asked how long they would continue to volunteer, they often said that they would persevere as long as their children remained in that particular school. Many said they had an obligation to their own children.[54] Family ties may be stronger reasons to contribute time than others.[55]

Yet, it is almost impossible to serve one's own child at school without assisting the others at the same time. For some mentors who were invited to volunteer because of their expert ability, their sense of duty was enhanced:

> I am a firm believer that the school system on its own rarely turns out really bright people. I think it needs help from the outside. If you want something to prosper, you have to contribute to it." (dn73)

Other benefactors simply stated that they needed to show the children that they cared. For a few, volunteering was a matter of family tradition. For others, there was a sense of repayment over the long term.

> Someone helped me through a difficult period of time when I was ill as a teenager. He volunteered his time, hours and hours, when I needed help. . . . In reflection, the real reason that I volunteer is because of the influence of this other person and the impact he had on my life. (gc40)

Although repayment may be given because a person perceives a debt to a group or person,[56] the desire to help without sense of repayment also appeared to be strong among the respondents in the sample.[57] Support for a cause is also most evident in Richard Titmuss' study of giving blood, in which the desire to help (with no attendant personal benefit) was the main reason for donation.[58]

A few donors articulated a distinctive set of reasons for volunteering. Although mixed with the prior ones of personal advancement and duty, they hoped to achieve another purpose.

> I love being with the children. My dream was to be a kindergarten teacher and I am fulfilling part of my dream by volunteering in the school. (ad 55)

to establish a more personal relationship with the people who have such an influence on my child. (gc44)

I am attracted to the kids and I can see something happening, some response, and that's what keeps me coming back. I can identify with them. I had that problem (English); some can't speak very well. I remember, I used to sit in the back of the library. Also, there is the feeling of being caught between two cultures—trying to retain your own culture while desperately trying to fit into a new culture at the same time. (rt64)

I was new to the community and I didn't have any friends. Our family had recently undergone a number of serious illnesses and I wasn't able to work. I missed the interactions with other adults. (ad 36)

These reasons speak of bonding either with children or adults. Voluntarism was seen as an avenue whereby givers could develop ties with others. Bonding was a less-frequently mentioned aim for donating volunteer time to schools than personal advancement or sense of duty to one's own child or other children.[59] However, it may be a byproduct of the act of giving rather than an initial aim.

Were the benefactors successful in their purposes of achieving their own personal goals, fulfilling their duty, or bonding with others? Chapter 3, on the effects of voluntarism, provides some tentative answers. But these people did not always remain constant in their aims. The reasons for offering to volunteer were not always the same as the reasons for continuing to give. For some, there was a transformation. Why they started was not why they stayed.[60] Persons who persisted in their roles as benefactors frequently offered an account of how their concerns changed:

My original motivation was to be a part of my child's day. As I experienced the school I found that I had time to do more. The better I felt, the more I did, and the more involved with the program I became. It is cyclical, if a person will just get involved. (gc50)

There seems to be a hierarchy of levels of involvement. A parent may initially become involved for her own child. As time passes, these parents take on issues. Volunteers have something important at stake in the school and want to be involved and have some control over what is happening. (ps 61)

The pattern was clear. Initially, the focus of interest was on one's own child. Later, involvement was generalized to the welfare of the children in the classroom and then the school. Long-term volunteers mentioned their responsibility to help the entire school, their influence on policy, work with other adults and their sense of accomplishment. Some continued well after their children were gone. One principal mentioned that a former mother had spent one half day per week working in the school library—for 21 years.[61] These continuing benefactors became part of their schools.

At this point, I ask the reader to accept the participants' explanations for why they donated time to their schools. After considering some predispositions for individual giving in the next section, we shall return to this topic again in Chapter 8 where more fundamental explanations such as self-interest and altruism will be probed.

Predispositions for Individual Giving

There is a useful trichotomy of "predispositions to give" that aids in the understanding of the reasons donors of time offer for their giving behaviour. Its parts are labeled *rational choice, normative conformity,* and *affective bonding.*[62] The three-way division is based upon the assumption that humans are purposive agents who will act toward the attainment of their goals.[63]

Some respondents in this study said that they, indeed, volunteered "for themselves," suggesting that they were acting explicitly in their self-interests.[64] Their explanation corresponds well with "rational choice" for which the key axiom is utility maximization (to chose the alternative with the highest payoff).[65] Although, simply stated, the predisposition of rational choice focuses on the calculation of costs and benefits and the selection of the alternative with highest expected value, this study has revealed no evidence that volunteers have done that exactly. Rather, they expressed hope that their personal aims of escape, fulfillment, or employment would be achieved through acts of giving time. Utility maximization was thus extended to outcomes which are not certain but are deemed probable. In this way, benevolence goes beyond the self-interest of the volunteer.[66] This outcome does not conflict with the predisposition of rational choice as its rationality does not require purely personal gain; it may include someone else's welfare as long as that welfare was valued. Rather, voluntarism links self-interest and other-interest in an unusually intimate way.[67] Thus, the volunteer can value the welfare of her own children and still offer an explanation for her behaviour which is seen as a predisposition for rational choice.[68] This extension of rationality to parental care for children crowds the next predisposition in the trichotomy, which is duty or "normative conformity."

A considerable number of the volunteers said that they felt an obligation to serve children, either their own or others. They characterized the obligation as a repayment, a tradition, or simply a duty. This norm of voluntary service may be internalized by persons who espouse it,[69] reflecting fundamental values concerning what is important in an individual volunteer's world, as shown by some of the comments. Religious teachings support giving to others, particularly in the Story of the Good Samaritan.[70] Note that the norm prescribes behaviour; a rational assessment of consequences is not required for a person to obey—it is seen as "a matter of principle." Although some respondents appeared to be assessing the consequences for their own children, others were simply acting on their sense of duty to serve.

Association was the third kind of reason given or predisposition for giving provided by volunteers. They donated their time because of their wish to develop relationships with children or adults. Labeled "affective bonding," this purpose is linked closely to a process of identification with the members of groups or a group as a whole.[71] It is not offered as frequently as the other reasons for giving one's time initially (at that point in the pattern of giving, the donor is probably not considered to be a group member). However, affective bonding may grow in importance if a person's identification with those served increases over time. This topic is discussed further in Chapter 3.

There appear to be two intriguing areas of overlap among rational choice, normative conformity and affective bonding as predispositions for individual giving since they are not as mutually exclusive as simple logic would suggest. The first occurs when the volunteer cares for near-strangers (as would be the case of the volunteer who helps with classroom duties but not individual students). When that happens, sense of duty and bonding may appear to be absent, at least initially. Reasons such as personal fulfillment may be offered as a substitute motivation.[72] Robert Wuthnow cautions us that explanations based upon personal interests may be considered more legitimate than those claiming a personal sense of duty under such conditions.[73] This possibility suggests that rational explanations, when encountered in empirical studies, may be reported more numerously than their actual presence warrants. A second overlap pertains to the donation of time on behalf of one's own children. Although volunteering was interpreted as a duty by many respondents, it can be stated that the interests of the donor and her child are the same and so caring for her own children is similar to caring for herself. The donation of time to a person's own children also emerges from the affective bond children are likely have with their parents, though very few interviewees expressed their predispositions in those terms.

Why do volunteers volunteer? The trichotomy provides some simplified, interim answers. While a single explanation may be adequate for an individual, as an aggregate the benefactors often chose rationally to pursue their interests, secondly they acted on principles based on their values, and thirdly they wished to bond with others perhaps because of their identifications.[74] Although there is a certain satisfaction in breaking down the reasons for giving time and assembling them into a moderately coherent trichotomy, one special issue remains unaddressed. Wuthnow poses it this way: "The real question may not be whether we try to help others, but whether the giving we do is still mainly a way of giving to ourselves."[75] This problem is contemplated in Chapter 8.

What Is Benevolence?

Definitions are always difficult to construct. Prior authors have struggled to build a definition of philanthropy, a term closely related to benevolence and voluntarism. Here are two attempts:

> voluntary giving and receiving of time and money, aimed (however imperfectly) toward the needs of charity and the interest of all in a better quality of life. (original in italics, Van Til, p. 34)

> the expression of benevolence, generally associated with the giving of money or goods to charitable causes. (Ellis and Noyes, p. 7)

Although the writers each preceded their definitions with considerable analysis, they failed to capture much of a sense of the gifts, givers, or reasons for giving that are evident from the accounts offered in the primary data in this study. For instance, both include charity as integral. While charity implies the need to alleviate suffering, it cannot be said that all children in schools are receivers of compassion.[76] Neither definition mentions the benefactor or recipient as an important component in the relationship and both include terms very similar to philanthropy, thus rendering their meanings rather indistinct.

A core element of voluntarism or benevolence (the two terms are used synonymously throughout this volume) is a resource in the form of service (time or labour), money, or a good. The resource is transferred from one person to another, thus affirming that giving is a social action. A special feature of the transfer is that it carries no certain return to the benefactor. Thus donation has no guarantee of payoff; any benefits to the giver are tentative. Consequently, the difference between one-way transfers and two-way social exchange is substantial. With exchange, repayment is either immediate or strongly implied (often by contract) in the future. With one-way transfers, some positive intention is required on the part of the giver toward the welfare of another or others. This intention may not always be the primary reason for giving but it rules out accidental gifts such as lost money and malicious gifts such as Trojan horses. Transfers that are compulsory, such as taxes, are also excluded. Gifts are given freely.

Here is a definition that draws from those considerations above to focus more closely on giving as generally understood: *Voluntarism or benevolence is the transfer of a resource from one actor to another with no certain return and positive interest on the part of the giver for the welfare of the recipient.*[77] This definition deserves some comment. Quite importantly, it does not exclude the donor's own interest as a primary predisposition for the transfer of a resource—just that some positive intentions toward the recipient are required. The definition is specifically silent on the donor's interest in any benefit that may accrue. No implications for self-interest or altruism are asserted.[78] Further, the definition does not refer explicitly to control, although control plays an important part because voluntarism is seen as within an individual's choice to participate. The definition does not include any reference to collective action on the part of the donors, and as such, they may be individuals or organizations. Also, the reference to resources in the definition identifies voluntarism and benevolence as conceptually separate from political participation, which refers to activities aimed at influencing decisions in governmental organizations.[79] The important connection between resources and control is revisited in Chapters 6, 7, and 8.

The definition of benevolence as a one-way resource transfer with no certain return but a positive interest includes many contexts of giving, from education, health, and welfare to everyday life. This inclusiveness helps us to recognize the ubiquity of voluntarism. However, the general nature of the definition misses salient elements of benevolence as found in school organizations. It may be useful to try and incorporate some of the particularities of giving that take place in schools. Drawing from the descriptions of gifts, givers, and reasons for giving to schools discussed thus far, I shall offer a more precise account of what school voluntarism appears to be. The resource in question is usually time although I admit the account of playground construction near the beginning of this chapter involved donations of money and materials.[80] Note that donated labour differs from money or goods because time cannot be exchanged for anything else; it can't be disassociated from the donor. Other aspects of the definition remain parallel to the specification of benevolence: its apparent benefit remains with the recipient; the condition of uncertain payoff stays; nothing is said about the hope for future reward; the positive interest condition does not vary.

Thus, a pertinent definition of benevolence as it pertains to schools and which is reflected in this book is the following: *School voluntarism or benevolence is the donation of time, from a person external to a school, to a school itself. It implies no certain return but it requires a positive interest on the part of the donor for the welfare of the student(s).* A delimitation of this definition is that it focuses on giving time as a small-scale activity and not on large-scale resource exchanges among organizations, frequently called philanthropy in education.[81] It excludes giving on the part of personnel employed by a school, although their benevolence is included in definition of voluntarism per se. Lack of certain return implies that school volunteers are unpaid.[82] This specification also focuses on giving by family members as individuals rather than as representatives of the family or a place of work. Note that the recipient may be an individual child, a group, or the entire school. One difficulty with this definition is that it requires the benefactor to be outside the school when donors often become "part of" their schools. See Chapter 3 for the empirical analyses of how the separation of giver and school is overcome to produce powerful alliances and Chapters 5 and 6 for some of the organizational influences on school voluntarism. The exploration continues.

Notes

1. Nanaimo Free Press, Vol. 116, No. 154, p. 3, Oct. 16, 1989.

2. Note that I have considered the job of helping one's own child with homework to be less of an act of giving than contributing to the welfare of several children in the school which one's child attends. Consequently, the enormous effort that millions of parents make in this way is not within the scope of this volume.

3. Individualization is revisited as an effect in Chapter 3 and as part of the teacher's role in Chapter 5. Use of tutorial assistance from volunteers has been noted in Hancock (p. 68) and in Robinson, (pp. 10–11). It is exemplified in the case reported by Epstein and Dauber. They describe a remarkable social studies and art program in which parents and others made twenty-minute presentations and monthly visits to classrooms. The experience was rated positively by teachers and students alike. More generally, Brudner associates direct contact with the attempt to "humanize" governmental services (p. 67).

4. As an illustration, one school's drive to raise funds for library books resulted when parents transferred their children to a school and then observed that the library required updating. Their view was that just because the school was small was no reason why their children should not have an ample selection of books. However, the vice principal noted that the school's funding per student for library resources was higher than the allocation to others in the district. Their school's relative advantage did not dampen the determination of the volunteers (pm63). Another school raised $133 per student in a fund raiser.

5. One adopted a nearby community park (ew73).

6. Some volunteers found fund raising attractive because it was a clear-cut role. See Chapter 4 for the story of a successful drive.

7. See the section in Chapter 6 on the active roles of school councils.

8. See the appendix for the constitution of the primary data, which included 72 schools.

9. For instance, see Robinson who surveyed 39 schools, and Hancock, who chose a sample of 37 schools in northwestern Florida that permitted her to contrast those with many and those with few volunteers.

10. In England, Cyster and Clift used 1,401 questionnaire responses to elementary school parents in England and Wales; they also conducted some interviews. The Social Planning and Review Council of British Columbia study within a single district interviewed 112 school volunteers and found the same pattern

11. One estimate for the average number of volunteers per elementary school is eight. See Robinson (p. 11).

12. When her schools that are low in volunteers are included, the average drops to 116 hours per week. The low schools had a mean of 46.1 hours per week and the lowest logged 10. See Hancock (p. 62). An obvious factor not taken into account in these figures is school size.

13. See Goldberg (p. 8). The Social Planning and Review Council of British Columbia undertook a study in a school district not included in the primary data. Its sample contained all community schools in the district and a random selection of 13 elementary schools. Persons interviewed included 65 administrators, teachers, or support personnel and 112 volunteers. The reason for the study appears to have been the support staff union's concern about the tasks performed by volunteers.

14. Although there are other figures of hours given that can be compared with enrollments, they aggregate elementary and secondary data in districts with volunteer programs. See Michael (pp. 46–90).

15. There appears to be almost no quantitative investigations giving a sense of the contributions of volunteers within schools. If school enrollments, the number of volunteers and donated hours are known, it is not difficult to compute the number of hours of benefit per year received per student or the number of hours donated per volunteer. For instance, one selected school in the primary data enrolling 350 students (of whom 140 lived in subsidized housing) received 5140 hours per year from 115 volunteers; its hours per student was 14.7 while its hours per volunteer was 47.

16. See Goldberg (p. 8) and Robinson (p. 11).

17. One example was a library volunteer who typed, prepared new books for circulation, and helped with correspondence for three mornings per week, two hours per day for ten years (vk58).

18. See Epstein (1987, p. 125). Her investigation was based on interviews with 82 first, third, and fifth-grade teachers

19. Twenty-four percent help with extracurricular activities. See the NCES 1984–85 survey, noted in Michael (p. 14).

20. The number of volunteers per child, hours donated per student per year, and the hours donated per volunteer across elementary and secondary schools would seem to be grist for many dissertations that could make comparisons with other kinds of contact with the community, public resources from tax revenues, and giving to other institutions.

21. See National Center for Educational Statistics (1987–88).

22. See Michael for an extensive investigation into volunteer activity in public and private schools in the U.S. Since their monograph is mainly a descriptive report, the authors do not offer much explanation or criticism of the information they compile, apart from methodological assessments of previous studies.

23. See NCES (1987–88).

24. See Michael (pp. 47–86). The descriptions were generated by 13 site visits lasting two days each that included interviews with volunteer coordinators, superintendents, principals, and volunteers, among others. Since the data on both volunteers and time given are not available for all districts, one or the other was included in the totals reported here. See also the NCES Survey, (1987–88).

25. See Michael (p. 109). Although this pattern is strong, teenagers can benefit from parental contributions to their education during the precarious period of early adolescence, according to Eccles and Harold. See Salloum (p. 139 for an account of the tradeoff between time spent and money raised.

26. Inter alia. See Weisbrod (Appendix E) for data from the United States.

27. See Duschesne (pp. 9 and 44) for Canadian data.

28. Weisbrod also reports that 79% of voluntary labour is donated to nonprofit corporations while 18 % is donated to governmental organizations. He adds that volunteer time constitutes 6% of the total labour force and that the total value of the volunteer time is 50% more than the total contributions of money (p. 131)

29. See Jencks (p. 332).

30. These figures come from a Canadian national survey of voluntary activity of the period covering November, 1986 to October 1987. Twenty-seven percent of the sample over the age of 15 donated time during that year. See Duschesne (p. 61).

31. I have no idea what percentage of the mothers were married; my estimation is that most were.

32. While volunteers of other races were evident, the majority of students served by the schools in the sample were Caucasian.

33. See Chapter 4 on neighbourhood factors that influence voluntarism.

34. See Chapter 5 for how administrators try to reduce the unease of prospective benefactors.

35. A survey of over 1,000 volunteers in non-selected schools in a district in British Columbia showed that the volunteers were almost exclusively parents, mostly women with children in the elementary grades, and persons who were usually homemakers or employed part-time. See Goldberg. Other studies that support elements of the profile are Epstein (1987, p. 129), Lareau (p. 95), Michael (pp. 20–21).

36. The Canadian profile shows a person who is female, between 35–44 years of age, married, has a high school education, and is employed full-time (See Duschesne). The American profile, provided by Michael (pp. 20–21), shows a female who is married, has a high school education, and is employed full-time. Sorokin, in a survey of "good neighbours" now over four decades old, concluded "Thus, *the American 'good neighbor' is an optimistic, friendly environmentalist with average school intelligence.*" (p. 206) By "environmentalist," Sorokin probably meant that such persons believe that a person's environment was responsible for their good behaviour, rather than heredity. Most were women. (See Sorokin, 1950.) A study by McPherson and Smith-Lovin of 815 voluntary associations in Nebraska revealed that fully one half were exclusively female groups.

37. See Chapter 4 on ethnicity and school neighbourhood contexts

38. A focus on the uncommon volunteers suggests that their contributions are sometimes more specialized than those of the common volunteer. Specialists tended to be preselected and invited into the schools on the basis of their expertise; mentors were archetypical examples. They undertook single predetermined

tasks within a particular period. Generalists encompassed a category that includes the majority of volunteers and were harnessed by the schools in the aforementioned variety of activities (instructional, noninstructional, and special events work).

39. See Hill (pp. 86–89) on grandpeople programs. See also Wilson and Corcoran (p. 112) and Conyers (pp. 14–16).

40. Michael (pp. 46–47).

41. See Reynolds (pp. 80–88). He offers what are perceived to be the advantages (such as special skills and time to serve) and disadvantages (transportation, availability, and health) of having retired volunteers. See pp. 61–64. Cherlin and Furstenberg found that today's grandparents are much more numerous than in past generations and they desire to have more companionship with their grandchildren than their predecessors.

42. Often, these volunteers asserted that they wish to maintain an interest in life, make a contribution to society, and share their information. See Robinson (p. 6 and 89). For an account of older volunteers that accentuates their availability because of their increasing numbers, see Fischer and Schaffer.

43. According to a survey by Hodgkinson and Weitzman, 29% of all voluntary assignments for teenagers were performed as extra-curricular activities at schools. Time contributed to schools may also be a part of service learning in which students gain credit via community service, according to Kraft. See also Robinson (p. 6).

44. See Michael (p. 61).

45. Some "volunteers" were persons who were currently teachers themselves. They "adopted" students in their own schools or just gave a lot of time to student clubs and activities when their role specifications did not require them to do so. Brian Knight noted that teachers who undertake voluntary extensions to their regular roles should not be considered volunteers in the same sense as others. The exclusion of parents who help their own children with homework supports his argument (private correspondence). See also Michael (p. 59).

46. See Daniels (p. 10) on the invalidity of the stereotype. For instance, in Canada, the people from the poorest province (Newfoundland) have the highest ratio of dollar donations to income, according to Frank and Mihorean.

47. Secondary schools volunteers are parents, businesspeople, seniors, and college students. There is some question if students make their parents welcome; parents appear not to dominate the numbers of secondary benefactors. Students themselves are volunteers, though often not in their own schools. They donate time to nursing homes, give the proceeds of walkathons to charity, and offer musical performances to their communities. See Tierce (p. 141) and Wilson and Corcoran (p. 115).

48. For a review of the contributions of older volunteers in all fields, see Fischer and Schaffer.

49. This figure is subject to a sampling error of + or –4%. See Elam (1992, p. 52). Of the public school parents who participated in the survey, 72% (with a 7% sampling error) indicated their willingness to participate.

50. Among Canadian volunteers in general, using one's skills and experience, and attaining a feeling of accomplishment were rated highly as reasons for volunteering. See Duschesne (p. 33).

51. School board member.

52. Sixty-five percent of Canadian volunteers said that learning new skills was an important reason for volunteering, though only 39 percent said that they hoped to improve their job opportunities. See Duschesne (p. 33).

53. An extensive review of the literature on why parents become involved in their children's education boils down to three reasons: they want to participate, they think they can help educate their children, and they are given the opportunity. See Hover-Dempsey and Sandley.

54. Sixty-nine percent of Canadian volunteers said they participated to benefit their own children or themselves. See Duschesne (p. 33). Daniels found that her respondents placed their family interests above their own careers. See Daniels (p. 28).

55. According to Sorokin (1950), ". . . an overwhelming majority of neighbors *consider the ties of kinship to be the most important and valuable ties, over and above other social ties and relationships."* (p. 207) (original italics).

56. Sixty-one percent of volunteer Canadians said that they owed something to the community. See Duschesne (p. 33).

57. Desire to help may be enhanced by a cause to make the world a "better place" since 88 percent of Canadian volunteers gave it as a reason for contributing their time. See Duschesne (p. 33). Pitirim Sorokin audaciously compares the actions of such people to saints when he says, " . . . *the 'good neighbors' and saints are deviants who rise above the level of moral conduct demanded by official law. Their actions are 'superlegal'."* (p. 208) (original italics).

58. See Titmuss (p. 221). As he observed for blood donations, the recipient is not known to the donor and there is no permanent loss to the giver (p. 74). These characteristics make the donation of blood quite different from the donation of time in schools, since recipients are almost always known and the loss of time cannot be regained.

59. The desire to meet people and achieve companionship was registered by 74 percent of Duschesne's sample (p. 33).

60. It is also important to note that many did not stay. They melted away as their children progressed from kindergarten upwards through the grades. They seemed to achieved their purposes of helping themselves or their children and then they moved on.

61. Others move to positions of greater accountability. A picture is painted by Daniels, who studied 70 women active in civic life in Seattle and Portland. She says, "Volunteer careers initially develop in the interstices of family life. Women put in time, as family responsibilities permit, during their years of child rearing. The development of a focused working life may have to wait until these responsibilities are substantially over. However, from their first tasks in the PTA, church, or political party, women begin acquiring experience and achievements. One successful performance led to another; one indication of special interests or ability leads to more assignments calling upon the same skill or working in the same area." (p. 69).

62. See Knoke and Wright-Isak (pp. 210–228). The trichotomy was developed in the context of giving resources to voluntary organizations. They pose the simple question, "Why do people contribute varying amounts of personally-controlled resources to organizations?" (p. 211).

63. Knoke and Wright-Isak (p. 212).

64. Wuthnow's corresponding models are called therapy (p. 100) and growth, which also reflect self-interest (p. 112).

65. Knoke and Wright-Isak (p. 213).

66. See Knoke and Wright-Isak (p. 215).

67. This relationship was suggested by Kenneth Boulding (1989): "If A is benevolent toward B and A gives something to B, up to the point where A's perception of B's increased welfare increases A's own welfare by at least as much as the gift in itself diminishes it, then we have what an economist might want to call "rational benevolence." (p. 110).

68. Knoke and Wright-Isak p. 215) offer four examples of groups that may be the recipients of gifts and whose welfare is deemed important: kinsman, cause, group, or nation.

69. Knoke and Wright-Isak (p. 216).

70. The story ends with "Go and do thou likewise." (Luke 10:37). It is quite likely that many persons are influenced by these teachings even if they are not practicing Christians. There are similar norms in other religious teachings.

71. See Knoke and Wright-Isak (p. 219). Boulding concurs (1981, p. 15).

72. Wuthnow (p. 96).

73. Wuthnow (p. 96).

74. Note that these explanations are considered to be incompatible and incomplete without each other. See Knoke and Wright-Isak (p. 228). One reason why the explanation of fulfillment (part of the rational choice predisposition) is seen as incomplete is that fulfillment can occur in many ways besides giving. See Wuthnow (p. 96).

75. Wuthnow (p. 89).

76. Bremner makes the point that philanthropy is broader than charity which is confined to circumstances of compassion. For Bremner, "The aim of philanthropy in its broadest sense is improvement in the quality of human life." (p. 3).

77. This definition is compatible with the roots of voluntarism, derived from the Latin words voluntas (will) and volo (I wish). "Voluntary" means an action performed of one's free will, action left to choice (not required or imposed), and unpaid work freely undertaken (see the *New Shorter Oxford English Dictionary*, p. 3,600). "Voluntarism" is associated with the principle that churches and schools should be supported by voluntary contributions, the doctrine that sees will as the dominant factor in human behaviour, and the principle that action regarding social welfare should be of one's own accord rather than compulsory (*New Shorter Oxford English Dictionary*, p. 3,600). The definition is also coincident with the traditional meanings of benevolence which are derived from the Latin bene (well) and again, volo (I wish). Benevolence is associated with the act of giving and is seen as a disposition or desire to do good, to be generous to all persons. It is also connected closely with the gift itself, being an act of kindness (*New Shorter Oxford English Dictionary*, p. 214).

78. Altruism, which is associated with a lack of self-interest, is addressed in Chapter 8.

79. Verba, Nie, and Petrocik make a clear distinction between ceremonial or support participation and the political participation designed to effect influence or even control of public institutions (p. 2).

80. This restriction permits the distinction sometimes made between voluntarism and volunteerism, in which voluntarism pertains to acts of free will while volunteerism is associated with the turnout of volunteers. I do not need to use the differences between the two in this investigation. See Ellis and Noyes (pp. 5–6).

81. See Lagemann in a special issue of the Teachers' College Record on large-scale philanthropy in education

82. Payment is excluded from consideration but compensation for costs incurred is not. See Ellis and Noyes on monetary profit (p. 4).

3

Some Effects of Benevolence

The Little Lake City School District was considering the closing of schools because of declining enrollment. A study indicated Lakeland School would be one of those recommended for closure, one of the reasons being the cost to bring the school 'up to standard' by needed painting. A parent group indicated to the Board of Education that if the school were to remain open, parents would paint the school. The school was not closed and parents honored the commitment to paint. Finances for paint and necessary equipment to do the job were raised through various fund-raising activities, including a kick-off pancake breakfast. Volunteer parents, teachers, and the principal have worked numerous Saturdays in scraping, sanding, priming, and applying paint to the outside of the buildings. Mothers as well as fathers have been on rooftops, scaffolding, and the tops of ladders. Windows previously painted have been scraped to give the school a consistency in appearance. The project continued during the heat of the summer and fall months. Child care was provided for children to allow the parents to paint. Grandparents of children previously attending the school volunteered time. A great pride in accomplishment has been achieved. This document was selected by the Association of California School Administrators (ACSA) Task Force on Public Confidence as descriptive of a promising practice or exemplary project worthy of highlighting for the California educational community.[1]

There is a maxim in the lives of educators that goes something like this: in order for a change in schools to be justifiable, it should benefit the students' academic learning. That stance has some merit. Innovations that do not fit this criterion may be interpreted as superficial—change for change's sake. If schools see learning as their organizational purpose, then they should expect improvements to result in demonstrable academic progress. Such reasoning becomes more compelling when the results of innovations are measurable in terms of increased national test scores in reading and arithmetic. Unfortunately, the scores are not illustrative of the whole story. When the test results do not change or go the wrong way, teachers say that such measures are too narrow to capture the other chief aim of schooling, namely, children's social development.

Educators often express the desire for schools to contribute to the development of the student as a person who will later take a place in society.[2] The social goals of schooling are usually difficult to assess although some may be measured by changes in absences, vandalism, or dropout rates. While such indicators are useful, they are confining not just because they are narrowly conceived but because social aims transcend effects on students alone. Though many persons agree that schools exist mainly to serve the students, the example of painting the school in Little Lake City reminds us that schools promote several additional functions. They support the persons employed inside them, they benefit persons who give their time to them, and very importantly, they ideally sustain the community of which they are a part. Benevolence is an innovation adopted to some extent by almost all public schools. It produces some remarkable effects—some highly visible, some quite intangible. Let's take a look at what the respondents and others perceived to be its consequences for students, volunteers, and the community.[3]

Effects on Students

A number of impacts on students were evident from the primary data. As shown in Chapter 2, many volunteers in the selected elementary schools contributed their time as tutors, aides, and guests. Although academic learning was not measured, it seems plausible that the children would have shown a higher performance on their reading and mathematics tests because their learning was assisted.[4] Beyond the present study, two research reviews suggest that the relationship between overall parental participation in schools and resulting student achievement is a strong one.[5] An example is an inquiry conducted by Reginald Clark in Chicago. He compared ten low-income black families, five that had students who were high achievers of literacy and five that had low. The parents of the high achieving students frequently initiated contact with the school while parents of the low achieving students did so relatively rarely. The former expected to play a major role in their child's schooling while the latter did not. Unfortunately, Clark's study did not discriminate between achievement resulting from help with homework and that achievement that resulted from parental participation in activities on the school site. The two contributions are quite hard to disentangle when they occur simultaneously.[6] Some studies that try to measure the relative impact of various factors on achievement virtually ignore parental participation and just consider the family background effect.[7] Yet, if strengthened academic achievement was the principle effect of voluntarism, then the story would be positive but short. There are many more effects.

The students, particularly in the selected schools,[8] appeared to have their links to their families increased when parents helped out. An example commonly mentioned was the cooking demonstration:

The kids are learning different meals and how to cook different things. When a mom comes in to cook for the class that child sort of beams, "That's my mom doing it." (volunteer ob48)

More generally, a principal observed,

the children who have parents involved in volunteering feel good about the fact that their mom or dad is helping out and not just being the recipient of service. They're actually participating in the process of improving on the education for their kids . . . being part of the team. (ob55)

This sense of connection was not confined to students' own parents. Respondents perceived that pupils came to appreciate that parents generally were associated with their school and that the parents' roles transcended their own familial responsibilities. One volunteer commented,

It makes me feel good that I know all the kids and all the kids know me. . . . If the kids have problems, they come to me. . . . If I see kids in trouble in the streets, too, I'll help. I can go to the kids and say, "Tell your mom to phone me" or do this. I guess they feel that "She's part of us." I do feel like I'm part of the kids and I can talk to the kids. (ob48)

Another affirmed the support given students:

So many children . . . feel that the store owners are against them. They feel that the adults are always finding fault with them. By having business people, seniors, and other members of the community come into the schools, we can bridge that gap. The children realize that they have friends out there that respect them and vice versa. (volunteer, dd44)

A sense of linkage or "connectedness" generally characterized the relationships that were a part of student life in the selected schools.[9] But what constituted those linkages? Two volunteers offered their views:

My volunteer work has an impact on the way in which my children perceive school. They see me involved and they see that I value their education. I hope this makes them more apt to like school and have a more positive attitude toward it. (ad45)

I am a volunteer because I feel that education is really important and I want my children to receive the same message. (ad47)

Teachers and principals who were interviewed concurred with these two volunteers. They perceived that the children began to see the importance of school because their parents and others volunteered time and worked with school personnel as a team. In essence, the message from the volunteer to the child was this: "I'm here to support your efforts to learn because your achievement in school is important to me and to you." Embedded in that statement is what I shall call the "learning norm,"[10] which, if accepted by students, may explain why they develop positive attitude changes toward school work as a result of volunteer contributions in schools.[11] But there was another lesson for them.

The learning norm (students should learn what they are asked to learn) was accompanied by a further prescription that pertained to the way learning was undertaken. Respondents, again mostly from selected schools, believed that it was

> good for kids to have other adults around; good for them to see that adults are interested and involved in their education; for them to understand they are a part of society with its responsibilities and privileges. (principal, wv45)

Principals, teachers, and volunteers commented at length on the children's contact with adults and the models of service to the school and community that the benefactors provided. For example, the construction of the adventure playground showed the children what parents and others were willing to do. Another was provided by one teacher who remarked about her volunteer seniors in this way: "They referred to the student they were working with as 'my child.' They had taken possession of their 'little buddies'" (dd84). In essence, the message transmitted to the student from the volunteer appeared to be, "I could be at the office; I could be having tea; I could be in Sun City but I'm not. I'm here to lend a hand to you and your school. I'm a community member and I care about you." This is what I call the "caring norm" (students should care for others through social action). It was a vehicle for the learning norm and showed that pupils' welfare could be augmented with the help of others' donated time.[12, 13]

When combined, the learning norm and the caring norm sound potent enough, but are they effective? It is difficult to say that they have a marked influence on student learning behaviour. Evidence on academic learning suggests that it increases with the presence of volunteers, but the learning norm may not account for the change. The real impact of the caring norm may come from ten to thirty years after the donation—a long time to wait. However, respondents in selected schools were sometimes able to offer evidence that the "climate" of their schools had changed when volunteers became more prominent. A principal in a selected, poor, urban school said that as a result of the greatly increased parental involvement from 1986 to 1988, graffiti and vandalism had almost vanished. He also asserted that there had been a reduction in discipline problems. As evidence, he noted that in September and October of 1986, his log showed 64 entries regarding discipline; eight parents were confronted and some severe measures were taken. During September and October of 1988, there were 14 entries and one meeting with a parent (db05).

If the caring norm actually works, then adults could make a claim on the future resources of the child. Although there is some probability that the volunteer may never be repaid by gifts of time because of the absence of sanctions on the child for non-repayment, the relation may be symmetric for two persons, such as a tutor and tutee, since direct repayment may be returned later. It becomes asymmetric if repayment occurs not to the original benefactor but to others who may be deemed deserving by those who benefited earlier. Adults who once gained from donations of time as children later return the favours and repay their social debts, perhaps to a younger generation. They "put something back," as shown in Chapter 2.

There were two less frequently observed effects on students that were evident in remarks from principals, teachers, and volunteers. The first of these was the development of trust. Resources were transferred unilaterally to the child, who became the trustee.[14] I do not know what precise obligations and expectations evolved between volunteers such as tutors and their students; they were not uncovered from the data. I surmise that they consisted of guidance and approval from the tutor and effort at learning and appreciation from the tutee.[15] The second effect noted in the primary data was one of acceptance. Many respondents asserted that tolerance and appreciation of others was established by the presence of volunteers in schools. For instance, cooking demonstrations by persons of differing ethnicities or with disabilities were seen to increase levels of understanding and acceptance by students who learned about other families. The construction of trusting relationships and children's tolerance of others, while minor themes in this inquiry, likely merit their own investigations.

Effects on Volunteers and Others

As might be supposed by the responses noted in Chapter 2, many benefactors in the sample of elementary schools expressed personal satisfaction with their volunteering experiences. They reported feeling needed, happy, and a sense of accomplishment. One donor expressed her satisfaction in this way:

> I get the satisfaction from people (after we had the Casino Night) saying, "Oh, good job." That was the most money we've ever raised, about $8,000. I felt so great about it; I was kind of on my high horse. (ob44)[16]

This kind of response is characterized by a sense of fulfillment from an exchange with persons cared for.[17] Volunteers considered their work to be meaningful and something to "fill up their lives."[18] But not all benefits were strictly personal ones.

Several volunteers found that their labour with tutoring, fund raising, organizing, and generally working with adults provided practice for their entry or re-entry into paid employment. One principal spoke about his volunteers this way:

> They find the work worthwhile and satisfying. The motivation of volunteers can change over time. They don't come in with the intent of using the school as a training ground but as they become more capable and involved, they sometimes go on to clerical jobs in the district. (ps47)

Another said,

> For some who have been at home, when they become active in school, they end up working shortly after. The school experience is in this sense very empowering. (do38)

Some had no prior experience in the job market; others, such as university students, used volunteering as a way to find out about work in schools. Their hope was to pursue teaching careers. Whether initially intentional or not, the acquisition of skills for employment appears to be a noteworthy achievement.[19]

Donation of time to a school requires unavoidable contact with students and school personnel. An "awakening process" took place, as illustrated by this remark by a volunteer:

> When I was in elementary school I thought the teachers were cheap—not taking us on field trips, etc. Now I know the schools are underfunded. I hope this will change. Some teachers put their money in for trips. I see teachers more positively now. (rt53)

Teachers in the sample schools who had volunteers concurred. One remarked rather glowingly about a mentorial program:

> Those adults who came into the school went away raving about their experience here. Many write thank you letters and request that they be asked back again and again. They have become wonderful spokespeople for what they saw happening in the school. (teacher, dd73)

A principal of a non-selected school said of his volunteers, "We do some things they think we don't; we don't do some things they think we do" (wv49). A teacher said that "it gets them on your side" (rt53). A principal of a selected school mentioned that volunteers "know the day-to-day operation. They actually see what is happening, how teachers deal with kids, and how kids behave. As a result, there is a better understanding of the school and what school life is like" (ob48). The growth in what the principal called "understanding" was widely supported by the remaining respondents. Misperceptions of schooling were exploded. Teachers were perceived as "human beings" (teacher, he33). One volunteer summed up her view of the transition in this way:

> It is easy (for community members) to dream up what schools are like and develop uninformed theories of what is happening in the classroom in 1993. When you invite people into the school it breaks down a lot of barriers. They see the "humanness" of education. They see what teachers are trying to do. They see the kind of work that is involved in running a classroom. (volunteer, dd74)

Other studies have shown that parent volunteers in particular learn much about the teachers' roles, the efforts made by schools on behalf of students, and the difficulties faced by educators.[20]

A further way in which linkages were built between the school and its community was described in another volunteer's reflections. She said that voluntarism

> makes the school more open. It makes new parents feel more comfortable. Having parent volunteers in the school gives the parents who can not come to help a sense of security because they know that there are familiar parents present to help with their children. By including members from the local community hall (who no longer have children attending the school) in special school events, there is a bridging between the school and the community. (volunteer, sp91)

The schoolhouse became known to the people outside it as a consequence of benevolence. We shall return to the bridge metaphor in Chapter 7.

Many volunteers, particularly mothers of students, observed that a closeness developed among those who "turned out" for activities.[21] Here are two comments:

> It seems to be the same moms. . . . You see them at the ball park with their kids, at the soccer fields with their kids. . . . You bump into them all the time. . . . It's a little group we all move in (like a gaggle of geese); we go from one school to another. (volunteer, vk46)

> I'll pop over to any of these people's houses or they'll drop off at my house just to organize things. We'll get together, we'll go out to dinner if we

want to talk about something. We'll phone each other ten times a day. We become friends. (volunteer, ob48)[22]

References to "family" were common as a metaphor for the volunteer group. Some even extended the concept of family to the school, particularly when it was small.[23] This growth of ties among parents and others may explain why volunteers were willing to share information about the school with other members of their community.

Principals felt that volunteers promoted and even defended their schools when necessary. As one principal from an unselected school said, volunteers can provide a "cushion between the principal and the community . . . they can defuse situations in the 'coffee circuit'" (wv57). A selected school's principal spoke of her benefactors, "they want to be part of the best school anywhere" (db59). Another suggested volunteers were willing to defend "their" school.[24] Volunteers were described as

> backyard ambassadors, goodwill agents who can spread meaningful first-hand observation. They get an understanding of the difficult and the positive. They have more credibility in expressing themselves in the community than we have ourselves. (rt53)

How does a volunteer who simply decides to help out on behalf of her child become a "backyard ambassador" or advocate for the neighbourhood school?[25] Coleman suggests that processes such as this one may be called "identification" in which persons perceive that they share a common interest with another person or group. For the benefactor, the group is the school and its contingent of volunteers. The common interest may start with the welfare of a benefactor's own child but this can generalize to all the children and even the school as a whole. Coleman asserts that identification is a reasonable action on the part of individual donor, whom he calls an "affine agent," and the recipient, who both benefit from the relationship. They "act as one."[26] The presence of volunteers and their interaction with other members of surrounding neighbourhoods also suggested to many respondents that their schools were much more closely connected to their respective communities than they might have been otherwise.

The Generation of Capital

A remarkable feature about the receipt of gifts by elementary schools is that the benevolence was perceived to be almost entirely positive.[27] All participants were seen to be better off than if the gifts were not given. The good news is welcome news for schools![28] These mostly glad tidings came in three packages. First, quantities of material resources in the form of supplies and equipment that arrived at schools thanks to the efforts of donors are examples of physical capital.[29] Second, students and volunteers benefited from enhanced curricular learning, development of skills (some directly related to employment), and growth of positive attitudes toward their work, comprising the development of human capital, a major goal of schools. But there was a third set of effects that was even more profound. It was comprised of the linkages among students, volunteers, and others; it constitutes social capital. Coleman states the three kinds of capital that persons have at their disposal:

> genetic endowments, that, when developed, constitute their human capital; material endowments in the form of land, money or other goods, which constitute their physical capital; and the social context surrounding and supporting them, which constitutes their social capital. (Coleman, 1990, p. 652)

Although social capital is necessarily shared and physical or human capital may be strictly owned by, or resident in, a person, it is possible for someone to benefit from varying amounts of the three. People, particularly children, may be rich in wealth but poor in the social relations needed to sustain their lives.[30] Quite likely, many of the students whose parents volunteered in their schools benefited from an aspect of social capital that Coleman calls "sustained attention," the continual contact with a few adults.[31] Can the relative importance of the three kinds of capital be compared? Somewhat. A few of the principals in selected schools were asked if they would stop fund raising if their budgets were increased said that they would continue, mainly because of the school spirit and community goodwill produced.[32] For some of them, the social capital generated from fund raising was more important than the physical capital. One principal interviewed in another study on volunteers seemed to endorse the production of social capital by saying, "These are services we cannot buy."[33] The sense that the services were "priceless" is also supported by the examples of the little school, the adventure playground, and the painted school in which social capital was generated for their participants.

Linkages among students, parents, and other community members have not received prominent attention among educational researchers. For instance, the effect of such connections is virtually ignored in the most substantial study to date of volunteers in public schools.[34,35] However, when social cohesiveness is valued in a school, it becomes a prominent feature of school life. Alan Peshkin's description of the town of Mansfield showed a community with integrity and identity derived from a shared outlook. People felt attached to Mansfield's school and

there was extensive participation in many school extra-curricular activities.[36] The same effect appears in private and parochial schools in which
caring may be valued even more highly than intellectual skills.[37] Such
connectedness or social closure can be analyzed. On the one hand, the
network of relations surrounding both children and adults may be quite
open, as is typical. That is, there can be relatively few linkages between
children and persons outside their families, or between parents whose
children attend the same public school, or between parents and other
community members. This openness is likely to be the case when parents
and others have minimal contact with the schools that the neighbourhood children attend. On the other hand, the network may be comparatively closed, in which case there are many relationships with considerable amounts of communication (particularly among adults who pool
their voluntary labours at the neighbourhood school as shown by the primary data) and also between volunteers and other community members.[38] The effect of network closure on the child is quite strong, as shown
by Coleman.[39] For him, the relative social closure with its information exchanges permits the growth of social capital from which the child benefits considerably. This is because social capital has the capacity to generate rewards and institute norms and sanctions that are much more
powerful than the child's parents can provide on their own.[40] The data
presented in this study support his assertion that social closure has some
notable effects. Let's review them.

When volunteers donate their time to schools, children affirm connections within their families (thus increasing the sustained attention given
to them). Students also gain contact with the parents of other children.
Two norms evolve: first, that the child should value learning, second that
the child should care for others.[41] Children's behaviour may change from
less to more positively social. As mentioned, the relationship between
children and their benefactors may be characterized as a trust relation.
Acts of giving also have social effects on the volunteers themselves. They
gain considerably in their understanding of how their schools function.
Some observe a closeness among their group of volunteers and some are
willing to be advocates for their school in the community, becoming am-
bassadors of goodwill. They appear to undergo a process of identification with the school so that they become "affine agents," which suggests
that their interests and those of the school are shared. Such linkages, built
as a result of people working together in pursuit of their common interests, lay the foundations for construction of social capital.

According to Coleman, social capital is a very useful resource for
groups and individuals. In this study, its utility is demonstrated through
the provision of the two other kinds of resources to children and volunteers. Social capital offers access to both physical and human capital

when they are needed.[42] It also may play an important part of the construction of human capital possessed by students. In fact, social capital may be a necessary component.[43] It certainly seems to have high contributory potential if one compares the ability of a group of volunteers who have many connections among themselves within their community to a group of parents who have few contacts with the school. The former's capacity to generate resources for students is much greater than the latter's.

Social capital may be conceived as a byproduct of persons working together toward common objectives.[44] This is an important insight. This study shows that many of the volunteers did not anticipate that their modest contributions to their children's schools would grow into a network of friends and relationships. Contrarily, some of the volunteers were aware that by working together, such relationships would develop and they volunteered their time partly for that reason.[45] Rather than being incidental, social capital was constructed intentionally. This reversal presents an interesting theoretical paradox. Just what are the antecedents and what are the consequences in this discussion? For some respondents, giving preceded the construction of social capital. For others, the already-existing relations expedited the benevolence observed. Exactly what is the order of things? We shall return to this problem in Chapters 7 and 8.

It is time to pause and contemplate more precisely certain aspects of social capital. The reader will have gained an empirical sense of it as conveyed by the comments and examples. Words such as "linkages," "network," and "relations," have been used to suggest a general meaning. More particularly, social capital may be a set of obligations among persons, as would be found in a trusting relationship. The bonds between tutor and tutee may be the best illustration in this study. Social capital may also consist of information channels; this point is accentuated by specific volunteers who came to school to find out how it functioned. Most importantly, social capital may be understood as conceived norms that which direct behaviour. The prescriptions most evident in this study are the learning norm and the caring norm that were seen to be shared by students, volunteers, and others.[46] The concept of social capital will be useful when some of the impacts of voluntarism on schools as organizations are contemplated later in the volume.

This chapter highlights three noteworthy effects of benevolence, namely the provision or construction of physical, human, and social capital. As demonstrated in Chapter 2, children benefited from the increase in physical capital available to them. Students and some volunteers derived increases in human capital as a consequence of giving. Perhaps most importantly, respondents in this study perceived an increase in linkages among students, volunteers, and the surrounding community which laid the groundwork for the construction of social capital. Naturally, this account is incomplete thus far. It is as if the reader has been invited to walk around an elementary schoolyard, listen to the music of the children's voices and observe the supervisory volunteers, but not yet visit inside the school. Before the visit to listen to persons who work there, we shall look outward into the neighbourhood and ask about some other implications of gifts conferred on schools. Specifically, does the acceptance of gifts mean that some students are treated less equitably by public schools?

Notes

1. This anecdote is the complete text of a document entitled "Painting the Outside of the Entire School." See the Little Lake City Elementary School District.

2. See Bryk, Lee, and Holland.

3. I have entitled this chapter "Some Effects" because other outcomes of voluntarism are reported in Chapters 5 and 6.

4. Mentors in the selected schools believed strongly that their students' knowledge was extended beyond the standard curricula.

5. Henderson indicates that all the studies she surveyed supported similar findings which included low-income and minority students. She concludes that the effects are substantial and long-lived. See Henderson, pp. 149–151. Epstein concurs, although her definition of achievement is broader than Henderson's and includes persistence in school and positive attitudes. See Epstein, (1990, p. 110). Also see Ho (p. 45), who reviews the evidence on academic effects.

6. A study that recorded 171 teachers' perceptions determined that volunteering and learning at home were strongly associated, showing a correlation measure of 0.561. See Epstein and Dauber (p. 294).

7. Wagstaff and Gallagher place school-community relations at the epicentre of teaching and learning (p. 114). Also see Chubb and Moe, p. 105.

8. There were 54 schools in the primary data that were identified as having active volunteer programs. See the Appendix.

9. For similar results, see Johnson (p. 101).

10. "Norm," as used here, as a prescriptive statement that endorses certain behaviours or as a proscriptive declaration that prohibits them.

11. See Streit (p. 86) and Henderson (p. 150).

12. The caring norm emerges in other settings and is illustrated in the study by Daniels on women volunteers. She found that her respondents defended ". . . common values that all should uphold. By creating situations in which citizens become mindful of their responsibilities to others, and are then moved to donate money or to offer service, volunteer women can create commitment, even fervor, as well as channel interests and energies in the participants. An important aspect of hidden work, then, is the embodiment of social values through the activities involved in the work." (p. 278).

13. For some reflections on the centrality of caring in education, see Noddings.

14. Coleman calls this relation "conjoint" because the interests of the trustor and trustee are seen to be the same. See Coleman, (1990, p. 246). The interests are

primarily learning on the child's part but also include the general welfare of the child.

15. See Coleman (1990, pp. 91–116). It is also possible that the children learned that it was safe to put their faith in adults beyond their own families. See Streit (pp. 86 and 98).

16. Note that although her "high horse" expression was used inappropriately, I included the quotation because it conveys her spirit and delight.

17. See Wuthnow (p. 95).

18. Tutoring in particular may be a great source of satisfaction. See Daniels (p. 181) for a special account. According to a survey of volunteers in unselected schools, work in the classroom was the most enjoyable among the tasks. See Goldberg (p. 18). See also Streit (p. 98).

19. According to Duschesne's general survey of Canadian volunteers, interpersonal skills, communication skills, and organizational/managerial skills feature prominently among the benefits of volunteering (p. 74).

20. See Henderson (p. 151), Hancock (p. 69), Robinson (p. 10–11), and Streit (p. 125). This effect may be found for many public sector benefactors. See Brudner (p. 70).

21. This effect was probably augmented for those volunteers who had attended the same school as children.

22. For a statement on how social conditions affect friendship, see Allan.

23. For ways in which the companionship of friends offers a sense of belonging, see Allan (pp. 154–155).

24. This kind of advocacy was valued by the principals whose communities were seen as being critical of students' behaviour. As one stated, it was important to "get out the message that the majority of students are good kids." ew74)

25. Ilsey notes that persons who volunteer have their values aligned with the organization to which donations are given. However, there is no evidence in this study that values have changed. See Ilsey (p. 22).

26. See Coleman (1990, pp. 145–161). Boulding supports the idea that the more persons identify with a group the more they will give for little in return (1989, p. 173).

27. See Michael for a similar conclusion.

28. Some problems emerge in Chapter 4 with regards to who participates and in Chapter 5, where potential child abuse is considered among the organizational effects of voluntarism.

29. See Chapter 2.

30. See Coleman (1990, pp. 653–655).

31. Actually, Coleman defines sustained attention to include the support received by all persons during times of dependency in their lives (1990, p. 653).

32. Note that "community" is used in two senses in this volume. The first is simply the geographic neighbourhood or collectivity surrounding a school. The second is a set of relationships or network among people in a large or small group. Since both senses are used widely, the reader is asked to infer the specific meaning from the context.

33. On the one hand, I am never quite sure to believe that assertion, though I hear it often. Would principals still encourage fund raising if few material re-

sources were gained? The social and human capital produced by themselves may not be deemed worthy of the effort. On the other hand, Hancock suggests that the services can't be acquired in any other way (p. 70).

34. See Michael.

35. The attainment of community within schools has been advanced by Tom Sergiovanni as an important goal for educators. He emphasizes the ways in which a sense of community can contribute to school curricula, classrooms, teaching, leadership and the students themselves. However, he does not feature giving as a way to build community in schools.

36. See Peshkin, 1978.

37. For insights into Amish schools, see Hostetler and Huntington (p. 111).

38. School personnel may also be included in this network, but discussion of them is mainly confined to Chapters 5 and 6.

39. See Coleman (1990, 590–609).

40. The closure of relations among adults can also provide a balance for the strong ties that develop among children. See Coleman (1990, pp. 593–594).

41. Note that the learning norm and caring norm are shared by many and not just by students.

42. See Bryk, Lee, and Holland for an excellent study that offers evidence regarding the connection between social capital (mostly in the form of norms) and educational achievement in Catholic high schools.

43. Coleman's (1990) view of schooling is that the production of human capital is a multiplicative function of the available amounts of physical capital and human capital. Succinctly, the relationship is $h = p \times s$. I would like to muck about with this equation in light of the data encountered in this study. The function may be modified in this way: $L = p \times h \times s$, where L is the learning gained. It tells us that unless the physical resources (p, such as learning aids and material environment), human skills (h, such as instructional abilities on the part of the teachers and volunteers), and social support (s, such as norms) are all present, the development of human capital in the children is likely to be small.

44. See Coleman (1990, p. 317).

45. See Chapter 2.

46. Norms may be internalized or reinforced by external sanctions. See Coleman (1988, pp. S98 to S105) for an exposition of social capital.

4

Issues of Student Equity

The only gift is a portion of thyself. . . . Therefore the poet brings his poem; the shepherd, his lamb; the farmer, corn; the miner, a gem; the sailor, coral and shells; the painter, his picture; the girl, a handkerchief of her own sewing. This is right and pleasing, for it restores society in so far to its primary basis, when a man's biography is conveyed in a gift.

—Ralph Waldo Emerson

Persons from all "walks of life" offer gifts—not just of articles as Emerson observed, but of personal time. This chapter is concerned with the social and demographic factors that may influence the benevolence of different kinds of people who are geographically proximate to public elementary schools. The reasons for their willingness to give were addressed in Chapter 2; now it is time to consider their ability to give and the opportunities for voluntarism. These factors offer immediate explanations of why voluntarism functions as it does. The most important factor is the socioeconomic makeup of the community surrounding the school, since the raison d'etre for the existence of public schools is that the society would be much better served if financial support for education was independent of community wealth. We will investigate this factor with reference to benevolence for the neighbourhood school. But we will also consider a factor that is much newer historically—the possibility that ethnic variations in the school's context make a difference in the extent of voluntarism. The reason why ethnicity may be important is similar to the one for socioeconomic background. Reliance on voluntarism could introduce greater differences in the levels of support than exist currently for children, especially minority children. Two other neighbourhood factors are considered. They are family/work life, and location (urban, suburban, or rural). Note that all of these factors are beyond the control of schools; they are fully contextual and cannot be influenced by schools or districts. They are inherited in a sense—what schools "have to work with." Fate determines them. Let's see what schools observe as they look outward onto their respective landscapes.

Neighbourhood Socioeconomic Setting

The following description is of a public school that is sometimes referred to as a "private school" by the parents who send their children to it. The school's most distinguishing characteristic is that its programs are French immersion, which means that instruction is almost entirely in French from kindergarten to grade seven. During 1988–89, there were 467 pupils and a faculty of 20 teachers. The location is urban and the school drew from a wide area of a large city. Parents typically drove their children to school, an act that required time and effort each morning and afternoon. The profile of a volunteer at this school was as follows: she was a female in her thirties. She wore trendy clothes and was called a "lady" by her friends. She had some university education and may have held a graduate or professional degree. She worked part time or not at all outside her home. She was Caucasian and her family had been in the country for several generations.[1] What did she contribute to her school? She may have been active in fund raising, helped in the library, aided in traffic control and safety, or prepared classroom materials. She may also have attend school consultative committee meetings with 20 to 30 other parents. The five officers of the committee donated much more time than the typical volunteer—up to 20 hours per week; the committee's chair volunteered almost full-time. Such efforts were backed up by a nonprofit society established as a registered charity so that parents who donated money could receive a receipt for income tax purposes. As a consequence of fund raising, the school was able to send its students on exchange trips that were not supported financially by the school board.

A rather different picture of certain nonselected schools was offered by respondents from them. One teacher said,

> Children are constantly moving in and out of this school and many of the "new" children have already attended a number of schools prior to their enrollment here. Their parents don't become involved in either the school or the community. A number of these children spend about four months in a school, then move again. (ps41)

Another observed,

> Many of the parents are single parents who are either working at low-paying jobs or have returned to school to upgrade themselves. The economic situation of these parents, coupled with responsibilities of parenthood, doesn't allow them to volunteer. (ps48)

A principal from a selected school mentioned,

The lower the (socioeconomic level), the less likely that they will come in and do volunteer work. I think they probably feel threatened as I have noticed at our parent meetings that the parents who are not well educated tend to be very quiet. (ad39)

These insights from three educators who spend their daily work lives in schools suggest that certain problems may reduce the probability that some schools will receive gifts of time. Their observations were backed up by those of many others in the study.[2] A number of researchers agree that the global characteristic of neighbourhood socioeconomic status has a large impact on voluntarism.

Phil Hallinger and Joe Murphy conducted a study of eight "effective" elementary schools. They contrasted the parental involvement in schools in high socioeconomic status (SES) neighbourhoods with those in low socioeconomic status:

Parents in the high-SES communities were heavily involved in many aspects of the educational program and provided various types of support to the schools. They contributed their time as classroom aides, their money to support expansion of the school's programs, their expertise to raise additional funds for the school program, and their energy to assist in organizing school wide festivals. The school was a well-integrated, highly prized, and central part of the community.

In the low-SES communities, parents were minimally involved in the life of the school. Parent-initiated involvement was rare, and there was little overall involvement of parents in the educational program. School staff expected little from the community in terms of substantive support for the school. . . . Thus, in the low-SES communities the school was more isolated and self-sustaining.[3]

Other studies confirm this depiction.[4, 5, 6, 7] But just why does socioeconomic status affect benevolence? The excerpts from Hallinger and Murphy give a clue: participation may differ because of the centrality or isolation of the school in the lives of the parents. Annette Lareau offers evidence from two schools studied in depth. The upper income parents she investigated were often both involved in the child's "school career" while the lower income parents were less so.[8] She describes school as an alien world to lower income parents, who lacked understanding of how schools worked, could not validate teachers' actions, and were sometimes intimidated by teachers.[9] For those lower income families, work life (including school) was separated from home life.[10] They tended not to mix with more educated people and lacked informal ties with teachers. In contrast, her higher income parents had the advantage of both occupa-

tional prestige and networks linked to the school.[11] Separation characterized relations between lower income families and their school while "in-
terconnectedness" described the relations between upper middle income
families and their school.[12] Clearly, neighbourhood socioeconomic status
appears to have a strong effect on the extent of voluntarism observed in
elementary schools. But it is not the income, education, or occupational
level of parents that makes the difference directly; it appears to be the
view of "school" as separate or connected to home life and the ability to
work effectively with teachers and other school personnel. As a volunteer from one of the selected schools mentioned, the typical volunteer's
most important characteristic was not her social standing but simply that
she was comfortable in the school and knew how to "do well for her children" (db22). There is a puzzle in this comment. Let's look at a large,
quantitative study and see what its data say.

Charles Benson reported the results of an investigation of parental involvement undertaken in Oakland in 1976.[13, 14] Parental socioeconomic
status was measured by income and educational level. Let's look the relationship as shown in Table 4.1. Although his results contained three income groups and five levels of involvement, they are compressed here to
contrast lower income parents compared with all higher income parents,
and those that he calls low involvement compared to all higher levels.

No statistic or microscope is needed; the pattern in Table 4.1 is clear to
the unaided eye. Parents with lower income and education had only a
50/50 chance of being involved if selected at random. Parents who had
medium or higher income and education displayed a 70% likelihood of
participation in their school or community. But look again. About 30% of
persons whose incomes and education were middle or higher donated little or no time. And most importantly, almost 50% of those with only high
school education and modest incomes participated in school or community affairs at a medium level or higher. These data suggest that lower income parents have a considerable propensity to offer their resources in
support of schools which their children attend. Perhaps the relationship
between income and parental involvement is not as strong as believed.

The primary data for this study included 17 selected schools that were
categorized as lower income by their principals. Note that "selected"
refers to schools that were known for their high levels of voluntarism.
Some of these schools were in lower income neighbourhoods; others
were in settings that were characterized by high crime levels, high tran-
siency, and many families on welfare. The principal of a small, urban
school described his school's context in this way:

I call this school a "shopping plaza school." Families who want to be middle
class don't stay. There are lots of renters here. Many parents are recent immi-

TABLE 4.1   Relationship Between Parental Income/Educational Level and Extent of Parental Involvement

| | Income/Educational Level | | |
Extent of Involvement	Lower	Middle or Higher	Total
Low	141 (50.7%)	126 (29.6%)	267
Medium or High	137 (49.3%)	300 (70.4%)	437
Total	278 (100%)	426 (100%)	704

SOURCE: Adapted from Benson, p. 62.

grants; 40% are single parents; some are blended families; some are on welfare. There are problems with alcohol. You watch the marriage breakups as children progress through the school. (db88)

When the principal of this school assumed his position, he noticed that the school had few volunteers. His response was to "open the school up." At the time of his interview (1988) there were five to six full-time volunteers and 65 benefactors for this school of 280 students, 16 teachers and 10 other staff members. The parent advisory group of 32 persons met regularly, had a telephone network, and contributed to events such as the Christmas party, Easter party, annual school-community dance, and fund raising efforts. Nonparents were welcomed into the school. Persons in a nearby senior citizens' home were encouraged to visit, use the gymnasium, and given children's art work. Community members were offered "passports" to use the school library.

There were other instances in which schools in poor neighbourhoods were observed to have few volunteers but then "turned around." One teacher in a selected school commented,

> Our school is an inner city school with a large proportion of low income families. The school is the focus for some of these people for socialization and contact with the outside world. A few years ago, morale was at an all-time low and things only started to change once the parents became involved in the school. We began by selling bicycle helmets and then we had the students design school T-shirts and we sold them. The school is now a lively place to be . . . and everyone seems much happier. (ad55)

There was something of a sense that "it can be done" in the schools that managed to attract volunteers even though they are located in neighbourhoods with far fewer resources than their uptown counterparts.[15] The volunteers themselves often had different profiles in schools in poor neighbourhoods, as illustrated when two selected schools were compared. One was lower income and the other middle income; both had immigrant populations. The lower income school had four regular weekly volunteers—three oriental and one Caucasian, all university students. They had come to Canada as child immigrants and their aim was to gain work experience. In contrast, the middle income school had a Vietnamese father who donated his time at night. He was the only immigrant volunteer in that school. Most donors were mothers who were "reasonably well off," well educated, and in their mid-30's. What did the benefactors do in their respective schools? A teacher in the lower income school said,

> Because of the high ESL population, many of the things the volunteers do involve oral language groups, interaction before doing seat work, retelling the story and oral marking—these are child-directed activities—not paper work. (rt54)

The vice-principal at the middle income school noted a broader range of contributions:

> Some work in the classrooms with individuals or groups of kids; some work outside the classrooms, but for specific teachers doing "make and take" or photocopying. . . . Others work in the library helping maintain inventory. One father who spoke very little English became quite adept at washing books. (rt55)

Clearly, the lower income school had attracted benefactors from outside the pool of parents, while the middle income school relied mostly on parents for help. Although the activities in the lower income school was constrained, volunteers undertook tasks that accommodated their backgrounds and skills, particularly with reference to languages spoken. Principals, teachers, and volunteers in the selected lower income schools frequently mentioned the noteworthy benevolence of persons on welfare, immigrants, and college students. They certainly did not fit the profile of the common volunteer developed in Chapter 2.

The willingness and ability of some parents whose children attend lower income schools to donate their time is acknowledged in other studies.[16, 17] Despite the established pattern between benevolence and socioeconomic status, studies on public schools, while not numerous, all lend credence to the idea that lower income parents can and will participate in their children's schools when they are "made welcome."[18] Certain lower income schools have considerable amounts of physical, human, and social capital. They are *rich schools in poor neighbourhoods* and they deserve special attention as sites of future research to determine more fully how the usual impediment of low socioeconomic status is overcome.[19] In general, it appears that high levels of voluntarism tend to occur under two conditions—when neighbourhoods are upper middle income and/or when schools are administered to welcome and support volunteers.[20]

Neighbourhood Cultural Context

A suburban principal in a nonselected school divided ethnic groups into two categories—Asian and European. Those from Asia included East Indian, Vietnamese, and Chinese. Europeans included Portuguese, Italians, and others.[21] She observed that many persons with either of these backgrounds do not expect to influence the school, a tendency she said was most marked among the Asians. When she considered first-generation immigrants of both backgrounds, she noted, "It is almost impossible to get them involved" (db45). This principal raised two characteristics of persons whose ethnicity was associated with a paucity of voluntarism: lack of expectation to participate, and recent arrival in the country. For many immigrants whose native language was not English, recent arrival meant that they did not have the time or opportunity to develop much skill in oral English, whether they were adults or children. Some schools served a great many immigrants. The principal of one school that had sixty percent English as a Second Language students said that there were about 50 languages from 20 countries represented in the student population. She remarked that the school coped with the language diversity in this way:

> The grandmothers are the care-givers and they speak no English. We have to have translators—either multicultural workers or our staff members, many of whom are bilingual. I can only think of one (teacher-parent) conference where a translator wasn't needed. We just assume one is needed unless we are told otherwise. (rt47)

The inability to communicate in English can pose a considerable hurdle for voluntarism, according to many respondents. One unselected school contained 30 to 40 percent of its students from Asian backgrounds but had no Asian donors. An East Indian volunteer complained,

> I try to get them involved but some of them come to meetings and they don't know what's going on. They can't speak English. They just sort of sit there and they don't speak out. (ob54)

Language difference is not the only difficulty that schools face. Some old-world cultures have no tradition of benevolence in schools, as noted in the comments of two volunteers. The first was a recent Swiss immigrant; the second was from Hong Kong:

Where I came from, voluntarism, basically, was nonexistent. The school was not interested and actually discouraged parents from participating. Teachers looked at students as their domain and didn't want parents to interfere. The only thing that was tolerated was once a year students went on a field trip and they needed a couple of parents to come along to supervise. (vk41)

You don't question the decisions made by the school. We have a saying in Chinese, "If the student is not disciplined at the school, that's the teacher's fault. But if they don't do their homework, it's the parent's fault." So the mom and dad will nag and nag and nag and bribe and do all sorts of things trying to get the kids to do their share of the work, work hard and be the right person. But education is all the teacher's. That's a very distinct rule and they don't cross. I don't think you're ever welcome to even voice an opinion. They run the school. (ob54)

Another mentioned that in Hong Kong, if parents receive a telephone call from the school, they know the child is in trouble. For these respondents, the separation of school and home is very strong. It is similar to that observed in lower income families.[22] There is even a hint of distrust of North American education:

In this community, people are oriented to keeping their own culture. We have 80-year old grandmothers who don't speak English. Many of our students were born in this area—some families are third generation, and the children come to school not speaking English. . . . After school, many children go to Chinese school. The feeling in the community is that we are not strict enough as far as discipline is concerned. At Chinese school, the students sit in desks, in rows, in rooms with bare walls. The discipline is very strict. The people are striving to maintain their culture and language. (principal, rt45)

These examples were reinforced by the voices of other volunteers, teachers, and principals who were interviewed. Certain ethnic backgrounds are strongly associated with the lack of propensity to volunteer. This pattern is also observed in the United States. The national study reported by Michael showed that the number of volunteers per school decreased as minority enrollment increased.[23] While language and tradition may not explain the relationship between minority ethnicity and voluntarism completely, they were factors association by the persons interviewed. Their views are supported by a study of parent involvement in Austria, Taiwan, and the United States.[24] Help with class trips, in the school office, or in the library was much more likely to occur in the U.S. schools. However, when parents were asked for their main reason for *not* participating, for Taiwaneese it was the conflict with their work schedules and for Austrians it was that no one asked for assistance.[25] Explanations for lack of voluntarism varied.[26]

The primary data included six selected schools having high proportions of children of Asian descent. Did they overcome the daunting difficulties posed by language and tradition? All six schools had a substantial number of Asian volunteers although very a few of them were recent immigrants—donors were almost all persons who were born in Canada. Here are two accounts of how they became volunteers:

> when I was in high school I volunteered in Hong Kong. I am a Catholic, and we went to a senior's home for two hours each weekend. I felt happy then. They would hold your hand and say, "Please come back." . . . My friend was deaf and she taught me sign language. I . . . was asked to be an interpreter for Citizenship Court two times. I was needed and I knew my friend appreciated it. I think that when I've been helping somebody, I feel happy. . . . I was brought up and told to help by my Dad, to always help when you can. That is part of the Chinese culture. . . . When the school, in Portland, first asked me to volunteer, I thought [that] it was not my job and also that English is not my first language. I talked to a neighbour. She said "Go and help only one half hour a week; go and try it." . . . I went to orientation and they told me I should feel comfortable. "If you don't want to do something, you don't need to." I got used to it and when I was asked to help here, I said "yes." (Chinese volunteer rt46)

> The first meeting I came to they were looking for somebody. I didn't know what I was getting into. Slowly, I started enjoying it, organizing things, and it became fun. Something different . . . meeting people; being boss. Before I started this I was just a housewife. Now I can get to meet different people, get to organize fund raisers or little things. They're probably not important to anybody else but it's nice to have a challenge. (East Indian volunteer ob44)

Another recalled how her involvement had increased gradually:

> Most of us volunteers were born here. That's important because we can communicate. The difference is that we have a lot of Indo-Canadian parents in the schools that don't speak English. And because I can speak both languages I can get them involved. I can phone them up and tell them what's happening. I act as an interpreter. (East Indian volunteer ob54)

The Asian benefactors found ways in which others of their own backgrounds would be willing to help, for instance, by making telephone calls in their own language to support "yes" votes for a school tax referendum. Their accounts demonstrated how some people were able to find ways to overcome the language impediment that stopped others from donating time to the schools attended by their children. While a few anecdotes do not make a persuasive case for the ability of all recent immigrants to make a contribution to schools, they showed how common interests and the desire to give sometimes paid off.

The problem of the old-world tradition of separation of home and school may be treated similarly to the language barrier. One principal viewed mothers' gradual acceptance of benevolence toward schools in this way:

> Some of these moms that I feel are the ones that are the movers and shakers, actually, I believe were born here in Canada. There are some born in the old country but they're not necessarily the leaders. The reason I think that—they've been encouraged by some of the more Canadianized moms who would say, "The only way that you can help out and make a difference in your kids' lives is to get involved. So come and be a part of it." (ob49)

Many respondents agreed that a period of one generation was usually needed in order for people to learn English and accept the tradition of voluntarism found in the local school their children attended in Canada. But not all volunteers required that time span. A volunteer from Taiwan saw voluntarism as a "quick way into the society" (rt55). One said pointedly,

> Before we came to Canada we knew there would be a big difference—culture shock. We want to help ourselves and our children. We knew the first year would be difficult. Other Chinese parents do not allow their children to join in things so quickly (like soccer and swimming), but we feel, if you don't want to join in—if you are to isolate yourselves—why come here? (Chinese volunteer rt69)

The benefactors from among the six selected schools revealed an immersion in volunteer work and a determination to encourage others to participate. Most of the active volunteers were born in Canada. For some of them, the barriers of language and tradition were challenges, unquestionably. But they were not so great as to be overwhelming. Donors made an effort not just to participate themselves, but to find ways in which persons of their own particular ethnicity could be persuaded to make contributions despite limited skills in English or reticence because of the old-world separation of school and home.

There are a few studies available on the involvement of parents of different ethnicities. A notable one investigated Latinos. When a bilingual preschool program and a migrant program were set up in a community with a significant proportion of Hispanic Americans, participants felt more shared responsibility than they did for conventional activities such as annual open houses, teacher-parent conferences, or work on school site councils.[27, 28] Another study that surveyed several hundred African

American, Hispanic, and "Anglo" parents found that the rates of participation to assist in school events or as audiences were all close to 90 percent.[29] A further study found that Afro-Americans had higher rates of involvement with their respective Parent Teacher Associations than other
groups.[30] When participation is studied and the effects of socioeconomic
background is controlled, David Kerbow and Anette Bernhardt determined that "schools with very high concentrations of African American
and Hispanic students show significantly higher levels of both types of
parental involvement" (original in italics, p. 126). These inquiries suggest
that ethnicity itself does not determine parental participation in schools
or voluntarism in particular. When combined with the results from the
primary data, the conclusion on the effect of neighbourhood culture is
equivocal. It may be that the more accommodating schools can be to parents of various ethnic backgrounds, the more support they can engender.

Other Neighbourhood Features

The data revealed two other kinds of contextual factors besides socioeconomic status and ethnicity that probably impinge on voluntarism for
public schools. Each may have the potential to affect the ability and opportunity of prospective donors to give their time. One of them constitutes the
main activities in which most parents engage: a combination of work and
family life. Parents who work outside their homes have lives that share
similarities regardless of their socioeconomic background. One principal
stated directly, "Non-working mothers are becoming a luxury and that has
had an impact on the number of people available" (he31).[31] Parents are often not available to volunteer during school days because of work schedules and even find difficulty donating time during evenings.[32] An intensive
study of three schools concluded that most of the parents

> seemed comfortable in collapsing their energies around the family at home.
> For these parents, evenings are just a blurry and brief respite before another
> work day; any expendable energy is spent preparing meals, organizing bath
> times, and helping with homework. (Smrekar, p.15)

The view that persons with busy lives volunteer less time is backed up by
polls in both the United States and Canada. Adults who are employed
part time are more likely to volunteer than those employed full time.[33] A
study of voluntary organizations in ten communities found that daytime
participants tended to be largely females who were not in the labour
force.[34] Although there is some contrary evidence to indicate that mothers' employment is not an important influence in their ability to volunteer,[35] the simple availability of time constitutes a plausible explanation

why those who do volunteer were often employed part-time or do not work outside the home.[36] When the putative explanation for lack of participation is lack of time, it is quite possible that the difficulty of scheduling volunteer hours is a proxy for a more profound reason, however. Persons may be saying that their personal priorities do not fit with benevolence to schools although they may give ample amounts of time to the welfare of others. Wuthnow calls this phenomenon "bounded love," in which the total amount of compassion in anyone's life is limited and may be restricted to the immediate family. He infers that most people do not want to emulate Mother Teresa; they learn to say "when."[37]

The other contextual factor that may influence voluntarism for schools is the neighbourhood's location—urban, suburban, or rural. Some respondents in selected schools indicated that their rural setting was one in which people knew one another well.[38] A few examples of benevolence were evident in rural circumstances. For instance, a secretarial volunteer donated two days per week to office duties even though her children were no longer in the school and she was required to drive 16 miles each way on country roads in all weather conditions. She used the experience as job preparation was often asked to help in her community (jr60). Two other respondents commented on the perceived effect of farm life on school voluntarism: "With the farm families, the wives take an active role in the farm and their time is flexible. They adjust their times for us as do the fathers" (principal, sp60). A volunteer in a different community concurred:

> Not a lot of working moms . . . there are some that work but not as many as in town. The mothers here can be at home because of the farm. We can be flexible with our work hours. I'll cut something out in the morning and do a little more at night so I can help. (he35)

One benefactor invoked a sense of obligation when she said, "We're all in one area and we're out here. It's all we have" (he36). Perhaps the rural isolation contributed to her willingness to help.

While the primary data on rural schools are not extensive, there is a small amount of evidence that suggests that rural schools form a centre for their communities.[39] Although survey data are conflicting on the propensity of rural people to donate time,[40] a notable case is a rural volunteer program that was well supported in the town of Kingfield, Maine.[41] On the one hand, the rural spirit may be quite imaginary; everyday experience tells us that urbanites and suburbanites often pull together.[42] On the other hand, the small number of interviewee in rural areas in this study gave the impression that their schools were special to them and that their sense of community was strong. Some insisted that because farm work permitted flexible time, mothers and fathers who worked on farms were able to participate. The implication for school voluntarism is that there may be a "rural advantage" but the paucity of data does not allow much more than tentative comment.

Summary of the Contexts

Capacity and opportunity for making donations are affected by what may be called socio-demographic factors that appear to increase or decrease the ability or occasion to give. Schools in well-off neighbourhoods tended to have ample numbers of parental volunteers. Personnel in schools in poorer neighbourhoods often complained that parents did not donate their time. Recall that the problem of variations in support of schools by parents is a prime reason for public school funding. But how does socioeconomic status affect benevolence? According to earlier studies, there is a separation between work (and therefore school) and home for lower income families, while middle income families see school as integrated into their family lives. The implication is that there is little participation in school life on the part of lower income parents. But evidence from this and other research does not bear out that hypothesis; there are just too many exceptions. Some contrary evidence is offered from the 17 selected schools included in the primary data. I call them "rich schools in poor neighbourhoods." Substantial levels of voluntarism seemed to occur either in higher socioeconomic schools or in other schools (some of which may be labeled "turnaround" schools) that specifically welcomed volunteers.

Language difficulties and old-world traditions also appear to be major barriers to benevolence in schools. Persons who spoke little English were often reluctant to come to their children's school and donate their time; those who considered schools as places where teachers' authority is supreme were less likely to help. Recent immigration may be associated with both these subfactors. Despite the impediments, some persons born in Canada with strong ties to their Asian-Canadian communities donated time to schools and encouraged others to do so. It is possible that, on the right terms (as illustrated by the story of the little school in Chapter 1) minority group members may give their time to schools in extensive numbers.

Two other factors in the school context were considered briefly. Evidence from the primary data and previous studies revealed that the press of time can be severe for parents, particularly when both work full-time. There is little left over for benevolence outside the family. Under such conditions, nonparents may be invited to assume volunteer roles in schools. While little was said about urban or suburban status, rural settings may offer a context in which persons are more willing to pull together when asked. Despite the acknowledged deficiencies of some rural schools, they may have a "rural advantage" for voluntarism.[43]

While some evidence suggests that the two main contextual factors, neighbourhood socioeconomic status and neighbourhood ethnicity, may have a substantial impact on voluntarism, other data indicate that those factors are not associated strongly with the extent of benevolence observed in schools. A less certain conclusion applies to the work and family lives of parents and geographic location. In short, the idea that the school context determines voluntarism may be challenged, as Joyce Epstein has done.[44] There is a sense of "all for vol and vol for all," if the reader will pardon an exaggeration and some flippancy. School volunteers may been viewed as a club or even an aristocracy that almost everyone is invited to join. But not everybody accepts the offer. Further explanations are needed for why some schools attract many volunteers and why others do not. Having considered descriptions of the volunteers themselves in Chapter 2 and the school context in this chapter, we shall look inside schools in Chapter 5.

Notes

1. Note that there are many similarities and some differences from the profile of the common volunteer induced in Chapter 2.

2. They noted that parents often could not afford a baby-sitter or pay for day care in order to help out at school. Some did not own cars and so they could not provide transportation for field trips.

3. See Hallinger and Murphy (pp. 343–4).

4. See Cyster and Clift (p. 160).

5. A common pattern shows that as the level of education rises, so does the percentage of persons who volunteer. See also Michael (pp. 20–21) and Duschesne (p. 23).

6. Further, as household income rises, percentages of volunteers also goes up. See Duschesne (p. 25). The socioeconomic disparity is upheld in a study on co-production. A national interview sample of 1,638 persons in the United States found that level of parental education was related to volunteer time donated. See Sundeen (p. 556).

7. Of course, the relationship between socioeconomic status and academic achievement has been well documented. For instance, see Chubb and Moe (pp. 101–140).

8. See Lareau (p. 82).

9. Lareau (p. 112).

10. Lareau (p. 115).

11. Lareau (p. 119). The main consequence of these differences was that children of higher income parents were rewarded with an education tailored for them, while children of lower income parents received an education which was generally standardized. Also see Lareau (p. 170).

12. Lareau (p. 8). The social origin of teachers is also an important part of the mix of factors. Particularly when the origins of teachers and students are not

matched (when teachers from middle income families teach children from lower income families), not only are parents less connected to schools but the effectiveness of teachers may be reduced. See Alexander, Entwisle, and Thomson (p. 681).

13. See Benson (pp. 56–74). Benson labels his perspective the "class-dominant model."

14. A parent involvement index was used to assess willingness to belong to the P.T.A., do volunteer work, or be a leader outside school. See Benson (p. 61).

15. The specific ways in which volunteers are welcomed and retained are described in Chapter 5.

16. See Lareau (pp. 56, 89). A study of parental political involvement in lower income schools says something similar: they will come if they are encouraged and schedules permit their participation. See McLaughlin and Shields (p. 157). An extensive study of 75,000 low-income children in 150 communities concludes that active parental involvement (including homework and governance) is a real possibility for low-income parents. See Olmsted (p. 135). Henderson's review of the literature on parental involvement asserts that ". . . parents do not have to be well-educated to make a difference." (p. 153). Ho and Willms confirm that lower income parents are as involved as others. Becker and Epstein's study suggests that not even eighth grade is necessary for enthusiastic parental participation (p. 107). Research by Comer and Haynes on poor, black neighbourhoods reports that in two schools, parent programs were established and evoked three levels of response: turnout for general activities, donation of time to classroom and school activities, contributions to the school parents' organization (pp. 273–277). There is no question that persons with low incomes and education volunteer a lot of time. Duschesne's Canadian data show that persons with less than $10,000 per year donated the most volunteer hours, followed by those between $10,000 and $20,000 per year. The largest group of volunteers had high school education only (46%); those with primary school donated the largest number of hours (p. 61). Perhaps it should not be surprising to find that working people give generously of their time. Using United States Internal Revenue Service data from 1983, Jencks found that the mean "charitable" deduction rises as income rises. However, the deduction as a percentage of adjusted gross income varied so that the poor and rich gave the most and persons in the $25,000-$49,999 category gave the least (p. 322).

17. The occupations of volunteers may be related to the kind of volunteer work they do. For instance, managers comprised 16% of volunteers but did 27% of the consulting; construction workers were only 4% of volunteers but undertook 12% of repairs, maintenance, and building of facilities. See Duschesne (pp. 48–49).

18. According to Moles' overview of the relations between schools and disadvantaged parents, ". . . the evidence suggests that limitations on collaboration between schools and disadvantaged parents are real and serious but that the possibilities for overcoming them are exciting and attainable." (p. 42)

19. This is Daniels' interpretation (p. 267). Interestingly, none of the previous studies questions the willingness on the part of lower income parents to donate their time to schools. They assume that, as a starting point, all parents are interested in the educational welfare of their children. Actually, there may be a commonality of interests across income groups

20. This conclusion is also reached by Johnson, who suggests that parents initiate contact in affluent schools and school personnel in other schools deliberately welcome parents, give them meaningful work, and provide support (p. 102).

21. Obviously, she did not intend to include all the ethnic groups that her school served.

22. Lareau (p. 8).

23. Michael (p. 14).

24. See Krumm.

25. See Krumm (p. 18).

26. For a detailed statement of the cultural challenges to immigrants of Asian descent, see Yao. She mentions difficulties with arranged marriages, suitable dress, changes in food, intimidation by one's own children, change in respect for teachers, presence of superstitions, and variations in the meaning of body language, among others. (p. 149) When taken together, these problems appear formidable.

27. See Delgado-Gaitan. A study of culturally diverse families by Ortner revealed that the use of welcome committee and home visits were associated with reduced student mobility rates. For a description of an exemplary volunteer program in a largely Latino school, see Rioux and Berla (p. 132).

28. Another source is the data from the Schools and Staffing Survey from 1987–88. The representation of volunteers in that study varied only slightly across percentage of minority enrollment. Schools with less than 5% enrollment had almost exactly the same percentage of volunteers per school as schools with more than 75% minority enrollment. See Michael (p. 108). No particular pattern between ethnicity and voluntarism is observable in Duschesne's data (p. 30).

29. See Chavkin and Williams (p. 73). For an examplary volunteer program in a primarily Afro-American school, see Rioux and Berla (p. 179).

30. See Muller and Kerbow (p. 30).

31. Her remark concurs with the findings of Miller and Kerbow who showed that when mothers were employed full time, their overall participation was low but when they were part time or not in the labour force, they were much more involved in school activities. (p. 35).

32. Single parents are restricted in their ability to donate time to schools if they work outside their homes but they do participate in school activities. See Epstein (1987, p. 130). When fewer parents were available, selected schools usually attracted nonparental volunteers (defined as persons without children currently in schools), such as university students, grandparents, and others from the community. See Chapter 2 on the uncommon volunteer.

33. See Michael (pp. 20–21 and) Duschesne (p. 26).

34. McPherson and Smith-Lovin (p. 68).

35. Some interviewees asserted that parental employment status did not impede their donation of time; see also Becker and Epstein (p. 106).

36. Further aspects of family structure may make a difference, too. While married people volunteer more, (See Michael, pp. 20–21 and Duschesne, p. 21), single parents, divorced, widowed, separated, or never-married persons may volunteer less time in schools (See Epstein, 1990, p. 23 and Ho, p. 143). However, even that pattern may be questioned. The principal of a selected school noted, ". . . over 50% of our families are single parents on social assistance and they still do a lot of

volunteer work." (ad45) At this point, it is important to recall that volunteering and involvement are not the same thing. Inability or unwillingness to volunteer may not preclude intense interest in one's child's schooling or assistance with homework.

37. See Wuthnow (pp. 201–205).

38. I stopped by a small town's florist to purchase some flowers. The florist asked for what purpose and for whom the flowers were intended. On hearing that the school superintendent and wife had invited me to dinner, she said, "Fuchias are her favourites."

39. See Monk and Haller for a well-crafted article on small, rural schools. Schmuck and Schmuck also suggest that rural schools enhance community identity (p. 15). Even critics of rural schools acknowledge their social closure as discussed in Chapter 3 (See Cole, p. 144).

40. Fewer people in metropolitan centres volunteer their time according to Duschesne (p. 16), but town and rural schools report that they have no volunteers at all more often than do suburban or urban (Michael, p. 110)

41. Reported in Michael (pp. 68–71).

42. For other ways to classify neighbourhoods, see Litwak and Meyer (pp. 140–154). They saw them as varying in population mobility, strength of tradition, homogeneity, inter alia.

43. A third factor, financial retrenchment, was seldom mentioned by respondents. It was expected to be suggested because it is a frequent problem facing schools, particularly the 72 in the primary data. See Chapter 1. Retrenchment may be perceived as less of a neighbourhood characteristic and more a feature of the institution because it is associated with the administration and organization of schools. See Chapters 5, 6, and the Appendix.

44. She suggests that status variables may not hold the key to understanding parental participation in general. See Epstein, 1990.

5

The Administration of
Voluntary Public Schools

One of the selected schools, Great Lake Elementary, is situated in a village on farm and ranch land in the interior of British Columbia. The village itself contains only 97 homes and 300 people. All speak English. Most have western European origins except for a few families who send six Native students to the school. Most pupils are from two-parent two-income families. During 1989, Great Lake Elementary had 2.5 full-time equivalent teachers, one of which was the head teacher. Not only is the school very small, it shares gymnasium and playground facilities with the community centre. At the time of the study, it served 32 families who sent 45 students to grades K–7.

The educators estimated that, over a year, the school received the benefits of one full-time equivalent volunteer's work per day from a core of eight to ten donors. The task volunteers performed included many of the usual ones, such as small group tutoring, clerical work, and student supervision. Less common activities were puppet construction, dance lessons, substitute teaching, and secretarial time. Fund raising events were scheduled almost weekly, in part for a foster child in Kenya supported by the school at a cost of $22 per month. They included special dress days (nerd days, cowboy days, rock days, colour days) administered by the student council, others run by the home-school association, and food days managed by family groups. The most substantial event was probably the school-community Christmas auction in which sales of students' and local artisans' crafts raised money for a toy for each child in the village. Toys were presented by Santa Claus while the teachers led a Christmas carol sing-a-long.

School personnel believed that the considerable part the benefactors played in school affairs was because of close ties between the community and its school. The head teacher made a point of buying gas at the local station and patronizing the local post office, restaurant, store, and bakery although a larger town was less than a half-hour drive away. In return, he acknowledged the daily donation of buns to the school as reciprocation by the bakery (db22). The closeness between school personnel and families required a delicate balance. For example, the head teacher lived outside of the village to attain an "element of freedom." But the closeness was seen as a factor contributing to the good relations between school and town. A teacher mentioned that when she converses with townspeople, "we talk about animals and the weather and how it affects the farms" (db29). Further, as a consequence of school size, teachers taught students for more than one year. A teacher mentioned that because of long association, pupils "call me 'dad'. They make that mistake often" (db32). Distinctions between family and school were blurred.

The level of school-community interaction was seen as neither spontaneous nor strictly a natural product of the village setting, however. Involvement of persons outside the school was small at one time. The teachers resolved to increase their contact with people in the community. They assessed school needs which they linked to potential volunteers via the chair of the home-school association. Parents, grandparents, and retired persons were approached both formally and informally. The head teacher set up a database of volunteers' backgrounds, skills and availability. Another teacher likened the process to "planting a garden" (db27). The head teacher understood that the school and community needed to provide mutual aid but that "gardening" required lots of assistance. He was inclined to delegate some of the tasks to teachers and volunteers partly to reduce the amount of his family time that had been surrendered to school-community activities.

Once inside the school, volunteers required help and direction. Teachers made sure that volunteers' schedules were accommodated and ensured gentle introductions to their roles. One offered the benefactors easy tasks at first to build their confidence. Later, each volunteer was asked about his or her experience to determine the significance and meaningfulness of the job. When the time came to offer acknowledgements, twelve certificates were presented to benefactors on awards day and the students made 63 thank-you cards. Volunteers were recognized in the newsletter, in home-school meetings, and in other public encounters.

The case of Great Lake Elementary presents several elements of the administration of voluntary public schools. Gifts do not simply appear at school gates. The encouragement of time donations is a preoccupation of administrators and teachers who work in "voluntary public schools." Care is given to maintain and augment the resource flows.[1] A high level of donations requires schools to face the challenge of how to manage the private resources previously unavailable to them. Teachers in particular accommodate and direct the willing hands. In this chapter, aspects of the administrator's special role in voluntarism, the recruitment of benefactors and the management of volunteers are addressed from accounts given by people in the selected schools.

The Administrator's Role in Voluntarism

All Visitors
Must Report To The Principal's Office
VISITOR-STATE STATUE 2917.21.1 OF
THE OHIO CODE PROHIBITS THE
TRESPASSING ON SCHOOL PROPERTY
THIS REGULATION PERTAINS TO THE
BUILDINGS AND GROUNDS[2]

As a consequences of signs such as this one, many parents consider schools to be places that are hostile to them. A principal of a selected school commented, "In general, parents are terrified of coming in the school and doing things" (ob59). It seems reasonable to conclude that fear is a possible explanation for the paucity of volunteers in schools.[3] But why would parents and others be reticent to pass through the school door? One parent gave a hint: "I think that sometimes administrators don't want volunteers. They don't want any interference at all" (vk46). There is some evidence that principals do not support voluntarism and act as gatekeepers to restrict parent involvement in schools.[4] Principals may perceive volunteers as intruders into their domains,[5] despite the fact that potential benefactors making up the total pool of prospective donors appear to comprise the majority of both parents and nonparents.[6, 7] Unlike some principals who likely have discouraged benevolence, the principals in selected schools seemed alert to the potential goodwill around them. Let's take a closer look at principals' actions on behalf of voluntarism as reflected in a quotation from 1914:

The schoolmaster has a new task: he must rain not only on pupils, but the volunteer helpers; guide not only the teachers, but the zealous public. (Cabot, p. 2, quoted in Haughness, p. 78)

When respondents were asked how the levels of benevolence came about in their schools, they noted frequently that the principal was either responsible for the initiation of the program of volunteers (in cases when the school was perceived to be hostile or noncommittal to volunteers before the principal arrived), or that the initiative of the principal had increased the level of participation. Why and how would principals engage the people in their neighbourhoods as benefactors? Not many administrators provided clear answers.[8] The ones that did offered justifications such as, "The bottom line has to be the children" (gr72). One suggested that many of his contemporaries had a desire to control the personnel in their schools. In contrast, his orientation was "You need to trust people. I become the facilitator—the guy who removes the roadblocks. I liken my role to being a parent. You must give up control for influence" (db89). Another principal stated,

> Many adults have had negative experiences in school. These people are intimidated by the school and must be made to feel welcome. We have an open school and the process of welcoming parents is most important to me. (ps48)

Although the principals commitment to the merits of benevolence appeared to be firm, the data revealed few insights into the grounds for their actions. They persisted in their work toward their visions of voluntary public schools, despite complaints about lack of resources for teachers for training time and not much central office support. Some spoke of "resource pools" of talented people in their communities and believed that they would respond positively when asked to contribute (dd73).[9] Interestingly, there was a touch of entrepreneurship among some persons in the selected schools; they took calculated risks to find resources for their schools. Perhaps they may be considered to be hunters acting out their primordial instincts but most just said they were "community-oriented" rather than "entrepreneurial."

Principals committed to benevolence worked long hours in their schools and communities to achieve it.[10] Over and over, interviewees enunciated the words, "make them welcome" when they referred to their prospective volunteers. Some spoke of the "attitude of the school" and others stressed a "school climate" that favoured benevolence. An illustration of this kind of behaviour emerged from an interview with an elementary principal in southern California who was involved in a study of school volunteer programs there:

> [Creating a climate] means letting these people know what their being here does for us. When you have a neighborhood that is composed of a high majority of single parents, mostly Spanish speaking, when there are evidences of how little the people feel for most of the property and institutions nearby, and when teachers really need the help of a Spanish-speaking volunteer, then you know what a beautiful experience it is to see an 80-year-old grandmother come to work with our kids or to realize that a single mother changes her work schedule to be with us for one of her days off each week. Creating a climate is bringing the grandmother a cup of coffee, or parking

your car out on the street on the day the working mother comes because there is never a space near here at 9:30 in the morning. For some reason, nobody seems to park in the one marked 'principal', so it is always there for her. It means so many things, but most of all, [creating a climate] means making them comfortable.[11]

Making outsiders welcome was not just the job of the principals in the selected schools. Administrators also enlisted the services of others. A few made the willingness to work with parents a factor a hiring consideration for the acquisition of new teachers in their schools. Most shared their priorities with their faculties and supported teachers' efforts to create a positive school climate for volunteers.[12, 13, 14]

Were the volunteers actually made welcome? Results summarized in Chapters 3 and 4 suggest that they were.[15, 16] But at what costs was voluntarism achieved? One principal took the time to know almost all of the parents of 280 students on a first-name basis.[17] Time spent in fund raising activities in particular can be substantial for principals.[18] The expenditure of time on the part of administrators in return for time donated by volunteers may be interpreted as an investment of a small amount of public resources to help to produce a significant amount of private resources that aids public education. Just to what extent the work load on administrators increased as a result of significant numbers of volunteers in the selected schools is unknown but it can be substantial as the next sections show.[19]

Recruitment of Benefactors

Gifts of time were sought actively by the selected schools. They used obvious devices to communicate their invitations to parents, such as newsletters, brochures, notices for special events, and handbooks. The impact of these mechanisms was amplified by informal meetings of parents and teachers as well as open houses. Direct, face-to-face contact was the preferred method of asking for aid. Some principals spent "time in the hall" before and after school partly to meet parents. When specialized services were desired, school personnel asked others in their communities to suggest names. One teacher maintained a record of the school's volunteers and their contributions. Whether by "mass media," social gatherings, or personal contact, selected schools sought help with more determination than nonselected schools.[20] There was an annual recruitment cycle evident from the data. Initial efforts to attract parents were made through newsletters in September so that prospective volunteers were alerted to pending requests for events such as the Christmas party or sports day. Some schools held a spring tea for the kindergarten parents and their students who would start in the next school year.[21]

Although the principals of selected schools often contributed to the recruitment effort, they were not the ones perceived by respondents to do the "real work." Instead, principals were usually restricted to a coordinating role for recruitment.[22] One teacher showed how she laboured to acquire aid:

> I ask parents when I see them if they can come in and help; I send home a monthly newsletter requesting help and I hold monthly class meetings in the evening where both the children and parents attend and we discuss the activities for the month and the help that is required. (ad41)

Another teacher suggested that important impediments to parental participation could be overcome:

> just because they are unable to come into the school to help because of smaller children at home or because they have a job to go to is no reason to exclude them. If they want to be involved I will find something for them to do. I always have a volunteer video tape during our special days or events so that the working parents may borrow the tape and share in the experience with their child at a later date. (ad55)

Principals agreed that teachers were among their most active recruiters of benefactors.[23]

A second group, the volunteers themselves, received high praise from the respondents for their efforts at recruiting assistance for schools. The usual pattern was illustrated by two volunteers:

> I'd say, "Help." I would tell them what's happening. I'd call up people I knew and people I met at the school and send out lots of letters. . . . basically whoever I know will help me. (ob46)

> Volunteers often recruit friends whose interests may fit a particular type of activity (such as computers). People new to the neighbourhood become involved in this way—someone suggests that they come along and help out. (ps45)

Not only did the volunteers "spread the word" that more donors were needed, but they seemed to be sensitive to the concerns of the newcomers:

> I called these three persons up because somebody was needed to come in to help on Pizza Day. They said they would like to help if I personally asked them. As a matter of fact, most of them are not very good with English, so they said, "Yea, I'll come and help but you've got to be there to help me in case I don't know what they're talking about." I think in their case this is the first step. (ob59)

This volunteer helped develop a "buddy system" matching recently immigrated families with those that had been in the country longer. Linking a school to new members of different ethnic backgrounds through individual volunteers is an important component of voluntarism. Litwak and Meyer would call the above volunteer an "indigenous person" and even a "common messenger"—one whose contact with her cultural group is used to bridge the distance between the school and its community.[24]

Both teachers and volunteers in the selected schools worked hard to attract gifts of time. Determination to overcome likely obstacles to the participation of prospective benefactors was shared. The giving spirit may be infectious since even students were reported to offer their parents' expertise on occasion.[25] The substantial effort at recruitment made in the selected schools appeared to pay off. Indeed, the abundance of volunteers presented a different challenge. One principal voiced the problem, "When you ask for 50 and 80 show up, what do you do?" (db66).

In contrast to the experience of the selected schools, unselected schools in the primary data revealed a paucity of donors.[26] One might ask why aren't there more of them? Why are there so few? The answer may be the existence of a "free rider," a person whose child benefits from the work of volunteers although he does not contribute. The clearest example of a free rider is the parent who does not volunteer in his child's school.[27] If the person does not have a child in a particular school, the possibility that the person does not benefit becomes stronger. The genius of the selected school's volunteer programs lay in how they converted free riders into willing benefactors.

How is this done? Selected schools seemed to deliberately match incentives for donating time with the predispositions of potential benefactors. The incentives were utilitarian (clear payoffs or social status), normative incentives (fulfillment of civic duty, sense of sacrifice or fair share), and affective incentives (emotional attachments or support of sentiments).[28] Notice that the incentives correspond to the predispositions for giving that volunteers gave in Chapter 2—rational choice (clear benefits), normative conformity (obligation to children), and affective bonding (desire for association with others).[29] As pointed out insightfully by Knoke and Wright-Isak, if an organization dependent upon voluntary giving wants to attract resources, one way is to develop a set of incentives to match the three predispositions. The selected schools, which were successful at converting free riders into volunteers, were clearly skilled at persuading individuals to donate their time.[30, 31, 32] While this study did not permit an estimation of the quantitative balance among the three kinds of opportunities or incentives provided by the selected schools, the exploration of such a topic would be intriguing.

Clearly the recruitment of volunteers in public schools "could be the start of something big." As shown by Great Lake Elementary and others, the 54 selected schools worked hard to find and invite prospective patrons. They used methods such as written communications to student's homes, gatherings at schools, and personal contact in order to ensure that parents in particular were aware of the request to donate their time to their children's education. While principals played mainly an administrative role, the persons who made the direct requests were often committed teachers and enthusiastic volunteers. These willing workers and indigenous persons made contacts and offered encouragement to the people they thought might give their time. While selected schools were successful at recruiting donors, many unselected schools were not. The paucity of volunteers is explainable, at least in part, by the idea of a free rider, a person who looks on and profits from the work of others. The selected schools provided incentives for community members to stop being free riders and participate, if only to pass through the school gate and stay for a few hours. Let's see what reception awaited them.

Management of School Volunteer Programs

Once prospective volunteers expressed an interest in donating their time, they visited the selected schools. While many had been recruited for specific tasks, others were asked to help on an ongoing basis. Principals generally undertook an informal selection process to ensure that the volunteer was "suitable."

> I do some gentle steering if I think that someone will not work out as a volunteer. I am careful not to hurt their feelings and I try and stress the important factors of being a volunteer—usually the people who feel that they do not fit drop out of the volunteer program. (ad51)

Another said bluntly during his interview, "Unwilling parents not wanted!" (wv49). Just what criteria the principals used to judge the prospective benefactors' suitability were not made clear.[33] Principals discouraged some donors and occasionally wished they could be still more selective. A parent, who supervised volunteers, observed, "There are some people who volunteer, who we really do not want, but we take them anyway and say, 'great'" (sp78).

Some volunteers may have posed an inadvertent distraction to the children and so they were seen as unsuitable. Others were reported to have reasons for volunteering that were quite malevolent, such as a desire to abuse children. When the volunteers were completely unknown to principals, health and police checks were often deemed necessary.[34] One principal recalled a case:

> I know of a 21 year old male who was using a school to get closer to older kids. There were "red flags" but no reported incidents. Eventually, when he

drove students home after being told not to, he was told that he could no longer volunteer and was not to come on the school grounds. (sm46)

Subsequently, this principal changed her policy on screening. She explained how it worked:

These people who want to volunteer require a closer look because of the possibility of potential abuse. It's explained that a criminal check is necessary and that there is a $75 fee for the procedure. If the school really wants the volunteer, the school will pay; otherwise, it is the person who wants to volunteer who pays. (sm46)

Police checks in that school were required thereafter for persons with whom school personnel were not acquainted, but very seldom required for parents.

Many who had been accepted by a school did not have much knowledge about their future roles as volunteers. Principals and teachers in the selected schools usually held orientation meetings in which they explained guidelines of volunteer work. Explanations of rules included topics such as the authority and responsibility of teachers, expectations regarding student discipline, limitations imposed by union contracts, the need to maintain regular schedules, and the confidentiality of information about students.[35] To the extent that these norms were understood and accepted by the volunteers, they constitute growth of social capital (the network of relations between volunteers and school personnel). In contrast to the social capital developed between volunteers and students, this type of social capital did not evolve as a consequence of people working together; it was simply adopted.[36]

When the volunteers had been made aware of the general rules, they were assigned to particular jobs. Principals, teachers, and parent advisory councils tried to match the interests and skills of the volunteers with the needs of the school. They did not always succeed:

Volunteering for a job and committing oneself for a year is not as exciting as I thought it might be. Shelving books in the library is not too exciting . . . putting the cards in the pockets is not too stimulating. (volunteer, vk58)

Principals concurred, saying that unengaging work assignments were avoided whenever possible. It was important to them that the tasks served the interests of volunteers as well as the school's objectives. A few respondents reported that parents were given a choice of assignments. More often, school personnel assessed the volunteer's capabilities as well as desires and made the placements to avoid mismatches, as in cases of benefactors who were not seen as being particularly competent:

If I had a mom with weak skills, I would slot her with a strong mom and use her for out-of-class [tasks], so the teacher ends up with as little difficulty as possible. I asked the staff assistant to help in finding jobs she could do. (principal, rt56)

Some donors were seen as capable of valuable contributions in certain ways but not in others:

A Chinese lady brings in interesting things and goes on field trips with us. She helped with the painting, but said "no" to reading. A Japanese mom helped with cooking and walking field trips in the community. She also said, "No reading." Some moms without enough English perhaps don't want to help in the classroom. (teacher, rt51)

The matching process for both short-term and long-term assignments was usually carried out with the result that principals, teachers, and volunteers were satisfied with the arrangements (interests of both were served). When the congruence was not successful, sometimes volunteers showed up only once.

Volunteers worked at many jobs in schools. Examples were "read-a-long," computer assisted instruction, head lice identification, early warning, and dance committees.[37] While most tasks required only low-level skills, some training was considered by school personnel to be necessary. As might be surmised, most donors were trained and monitored almost entirely by teachers.[38] One teacher explained her orientation for benefactors:

I usually have the parents come in at lunch time and I explain the craft project for the day. I give the parents guidance, have them look for certain things and give them the words to use to explain the activity. I monitor the work that they are doing—it is on-the-job training. (teacher, ad52)

This teacher built clear expectations into her instructions for her volunteers. The expectations may be interpreted as authority relations which were part of the social capital. Such obligations were conveyed in other ways, too. For instance, a number of volunteers felt they were largely self-taught and learned as they contributed.[39] Principals and teachers sometimes rotated benefactors among positions (occasionally increasing in the level of challenge) so they would build a repertoire of knowledge and skills and thus increase their human capital. Donors used their previous volunteer experiences to contribute to their current schools:

Many of the parents who are presently volunteering here have been volunteering from the time that their children entered preschool. . . . Many of the jobs that volunteers undertake in this school are more advanced versions of the jobs they did in the preschools. (ps55)

There were no complaints about the training provided,[40, 41] but once training was under way, the supervision of volunteers offered some challenges.

Although there were not many reservations expressed, there were three recurrent problems associated with the use of volunteers. The problem of confidentiality was mentioned the most frequently. School personnel reported that a few volunteers did not respect the norm that some information about students is not public. "There is a tendency for some to be chinwaggers" (principal, do41). A few thought that some volunteers came to the school to snoop.[42] Breakage of the confidentiality norm, while not frequently mentioned, is the most evident example of lack of acceptance of one of the school obligations that benefactors were asked to honour. A few teachers observed that they could not speak freely in the presence of volunteers. Oddly, no incidence of the employment of sanctions was reported.

After confidentiality, the next most noted difficulty was the reliability of some volunteers.[43] A volunteer and then a principal from the same school reflected on the problem in these ways:

I cannot always come when I say I can. For example, this morning my youngest daughter was sick and I had to stay home with her and I couldn't drive my oldest daughter's class on their field trip. The trip had to be canceled but I just couldn't be there. (ad52)

Volunteers do not punch the clock or draw a salary and they can't be expected to have the same commitment to the task as [a teacher] does. Programs that require volunteers must be ones that can be changed, postponed, or even cancelled. It is important to have back-up plans for programs or activities that are considered important. (ad54)

This volunteer and principal acknowledged transgressions of the rule of reliability (i.e., to be on hand when promised). Yet, there was no hint of sanction. Most likely, minor infractions were not considered to be serious.[44]

The third problem was student safety, a difficulty that arose most often when volunteers were asked to drive students on field trips. One principal related, "It is embarrassing when you have to go out and check the tires because you aren't sure if the car is going to make it off the school grounds. I have had to tell parents that we won't be able to use their vehicle" (ad53).[45, 46] Aside from confidentiality, reliability, and safety, few other concerns were expressed. Additional sporadic problems included donors disciplining their own children harshly, criticism of other volunteers, interference in lessons on behalf of benefactors' own children, and excessive expectations about learning accomplishments.

The final component of volunteer management is recognition. When did the selective schools acknowledge the achievement of their benefactors? Sports day is over. The fall fair was a "blast." The library books are back on the shelves. A small child learned to read more readily. Toward the end of the academic year, the selected schools paused and gave thanks to their patrons. They recognized their works via mention in newsletters, plaques, lunches or teas. One school placed the volunteers' pictures on display.[47] Official thanks came from principals, teachers, and the students themselves. According to the volunteers, the acknowledgement was well received and deemed proper. One volunteer associated the respect shown to benefactors to a story her father had related about serving in World War I:

> The thing that you remember[ed] when you came back from an outing and before you dismounted was the command to *make much of your horses.* This would mean the recognition of the horses through patting. You don't eat until that horse has been fed. (vk47)

There may be a need to recognize the volunteer "horses," and not just at year's end. Several benefactors mentioned the appreciation of direct acknowledgement. Forms of thanks included certificates, books made by children, a volunteers' float in a local parade, reduction of costs for travel, free admissions to events on field trips, bouquets of roses, mention in newsletters, popcorn, and candy. One volunteer said,

> But do you know what's nicer than [the volunteer tea] is the teacher herself, the one that has the volunteer all the time . . . I'll find something in my cubby, just a little thank you note with something small. (vk61)

A teacher concurred when she mentioned how her school made the effort to thank its benefactors:

> We show our appreciation of them, which is all they require from us. It goes beyond just the Volunteer Tea at the end. It's throughout the year with thank-you's and "how are you doing?" making them feel at home and part of things and not an add on. (he31)

Personal and continual thanks may carry more weight than official acknowledgements.[48] When considered in terms of incentives for giving, the rewards offered to volunteers seem to be closer to affective benefits than utilitarian or normative as per Knoke and Wright-Isak's terms.

Recognition given to the school volunteers constituted another form of social capital. The thanks presented to them implied a social debt on the part of the school to its benefactors. Gratitude expressed by school personnel indicated that the jobs were well done and appreciated. It carried an implicit, positive evaluation.[49]

In summary, how were benefactors administered in the selected schools? Prospective volunteers were typically screened informally by principals. Administrators considered some persons unsuitable and so they discouraged or prevented them from becoming benefactors. Donors were then oriented to the school and asked to conform to norms that applied to school personnel as well. Acceptance of the rules constituted an increase in social capital since authority relations between volunteers and teachers were established. Principals and teachers attempted to match the interests of the volunteers with the needs of the school, taking into account benefactors' skills. Respondents believed that most volunteers required at least some training in order to perform effectively. That training was normally carried out on-the-job by teachers who also supervised the volunteers. Benefactors created some difficulties for school administrators, however. They were violations of confidentiality, lack of punctuality, and the safety of children while being transported. Although mentioned infrequently, the problems required accommodation or minor corrective action but no sanctions. Finally, the principals and teachers acknowledged volunteers' contributions either in a continual fashion or at the end of the school year. In this way, schools and individuals recognized their social debts to their benefactors.[50]

Principals of selected schools affirmed the centrality of voluntarism among their priorities and showed a considerable commitment to make their schools welcome places for parents and nonparents. Clearly, benefactors were made to feel at home but at some cost to the administrators' work loads and thus to the public resources of the school, as shown by the account of Great Lake Elementary. When parents and nonparents offered their services to selected schools, credit was often given to principals as the persons who were responsible for the high levels of voluntarism. They justified their belief in benevolence as being for the benefit of the children. The actions by individuals described in this chapter also raises some questions about the organization of voluntary public schools. Did the support staffs accept voluntarism? Did most of the teachers buy in? And what were the actions of parent groups? Let's find out.

Notes

1. One principal mentioned that not only did he seek more willing hands but that he wanted to find new people to offset the excessive ownership developed by long-term volunteers (sm43).

2. This sign was posted on a school in Ohio several decades ago. From Saxe (p. 31).

3. Forty percent of U.S. elementary schools report no volunteers. See Michael (p. 98).

4. See Becker and Epstein (p. 107) on principal attitudes, and Lortie (p. 200) on buffers between teachers and parents.

5. See Michael (pp. 98–99). This orientation may be similar to that of other managers who distrust volunteers. See Ilsey (p. 108).

6. An alternative explanation for the lack of volunteers is that parents and non-parents are unwilling to participate. Fortunately, there are some facts available that test the idea of reluctance. A broad sample of the American public taken in 1992 revealed that although 50 percent rated the overall performance of schools with a C, D, or F grade, 59 percent were willing to work as unpaid volunteers in schools! This group was comprised of public school parents, 72 percent of whom favoured voluntarism, and persons with no children in school, of whom 51 percent were willing to donate their time. These data come from the 24th annual Gallup/Phi Delta Kappa poll. All figures reproduced here are subject to a 4 percent sampling error except for the public school parent datum, which has a sampling error of plus or minus 7 percent. See Elam (1992, pp. 43–53).

7. A study of purposively selected schools in Ontario revealed that 24 out of the 39 school volunteer programs were initiated by principals. Other initiators included district special education departments, school board volunteer coordinators, or volunteers themselves. See Robinson (p. 6).

8. Some were too modest to admit that they were primarily responsible for the growth in numbers of volunteers even though others interviewees had ascribed the increase to their efforts.

9. Help was sometimes located in unexpected places. A few principals pointed out that families on welfare often had more time to give to schools than families with two incomes.

10. One instituted a baby-sitting service for all school events. Another "networked" in the community by attending funerals.

11. See Haughness (p. 96).

12. Other administrators do the same. See Epstein (1987, p. 125) and Swap (p. 119). Reflecting on sharing vision, Boulding states that "Integrative power often rests on the ability to create images of the future and to persuade other people that these are valid." See Boulding (1989, 0. 122).

13. Moles reviews many of the obstacles to parental participation that need to be surmounted. They include: restrictive custodial hours, clauses in teacher contracts, difficulty in setting meeting times, lack of parental transportation, and locked school doors (pp. 32–33).

14. See Chapter 6 for the teachers' views.

15. One volunteer commented: "The feeling here is . . . 'We want you here, you're welcome here, you're not in the way, you're not intruding, you're not causing a problem'." (vk49) A teacher remarked on welcoming parents of diverse backgrounds to try pumpkin carving initially: "The response was good. Some took the day off work to come. In this way, it's not too threatening for them; it's easy and fun." (rt60) Such successes were not difficult to document. See also Chapters 2.

16. A case study of a New York City School (P.S. 111) revealed a parent's room in which parents discussed personal and school problems. See Jackson (pp. 7–8).

17. Principals with volunteers may be more likely to be volunteers themselves. The time they spend in their communities may be high. See Ming (p. 51).

18. Administrators' time averaged 31 hours per school per year in a study that sampled 46 elementary schools. Some spent up to 100 hours. Principals of schools with 500 pupils spent an average of 55 hours per year in fund raising alone. Secretarial time was also considerable, averaging 44 hours per year. See Salloum (pp. 165–166).

19. Concepts of marginal utility and equilibrium appear to have some potency here. Several dissertations and masters theses are waiting to be undertaken on this topic.

20. In one study, notices to parents were found to be more common than school meetings or direct contact. See Goldberg. It is likely that many elementary schools use most of these devices to some extent. See Hancock (pp. 65 and 72). District-wide volunteer programs also use posters, newspaper articles, and advertisements on radio and television. See Michael, p. 96. Some schools have used social workers, bilingual aides, document translation, and other techniques to attract parents. See Johnson (p. 101). "Exemplary" secondary schools were found to make a similar effort in the study by Wilson and Corcoran.

21. Recall from Chapter 2 that parents of kindergartners were among the most willing volunteers.

22. According to Haughness, if a school has an volunteer coordinator other than the principal, then the principal's job may be confined to formalities such as welcoming volunteers (pp. 85 and 92).

23. For other evidence of the teacher-as-recruiter concept, see Hancock (pp. 65 and 94).

24. See Litwak and Meyer (pp. 38–40, 113, and 252–260).

25. The word-of-mouth technique constitutes a common way to persuade prospects to come and help and is method that is applied widely to attract volunteers in other fields. When volunteers in various fields across Canada were asked how they first became involved, 50 percent said that they were approached by someone in the organization to which they subsequently donated their time. See Duschesne (p. 70).

26. Public school volunteers are not that common, according to Michael, who report that 40 percent of elementary schools in the United states report no volunteers at all (p. 98.) Forty-six percent of schools in an English sample reported either minor or significant difficulty in finding volunteers (Craft, p. 156). Locating them may be even harder for secondary schools since 70% said recruitment was a problem in a U.S. study (Tierce, p. 176).

27. This person may make a calculation of the anticipated costs and benefits of contribution. When the costs are more than the benefits, he does not help out. See Coleman (1990, p. 247).

28. See Knoke and Wright-Isak (pp. 213–219). They suggest that churches are associated with emphasis on normative/affectual incentives. Perhaps schools resemble them more than political parties or trade unions that emphasize utilitarian/normative or utilitarian/affectual incentives in turn (pp. 231–234).

29. More specifically, benefactors said that they have an aim to gain some benefit for themselves or their child; they feel obliged to support the education of neighbourhood children; they know they can benefit from the positive feelings generated by friendship with others, particularly children.

30. This analysis waves aside the possibility that potential benefactors may not wish to profit from the work schools do or that they believe that effects of schools may do them harm. Not all avenues for encouraging parental support were used by the selected schools. One example was provided by a separate interview with the principal of an urban, Catholic, elementary school not included in the primary data. He explained that when students are enrolled, parents are asked to contribute time on a regular basis for certain tasks that they choose, such as bingo, school repairs, cafeteria, and work with school uniforms. The agreement is that they will help out "when asked." As a consequence, he said, "We are never short of people." He estimated there were ten to fifteen full-time parents on hand every day in his school of 270 students. Another example taken from interviews with personnel in six Catholic high schools revealed a similar arrangement. As a condition of their child's enrollment, parents were asked to make a commitment to a work participation program in schools in which fees were $800 per year and to donate further dollars where fees were higher. In two of the work participation program schools, the time contribution per student was high. Clearly, these Catholic schools had altered the balance between costs and benefits of parents. However, the parents were not volunteers as conceived in this study. They agreed to work some hours as part of what was owed for a year's education. Three of the schools actually appear to have accepted cash in lieu of labour. Consequently, the work participation agreement and the program of donations are examples of contracts or short-term exchanges and not examples of voluntarism.

31. The issue of contracts in charter schools (which are public schools) has been raised by Becker, Kakagawa, and Corwin, who found that 74% of charter schools in their sample in California required parental contracts while only 8% of neighbourhood schools did (p. 521). Again, contracts are examples of an explicit, two-way exchange relationship and are not examples of voluntarism which is defined as a one-way transaction in this book.

32. Research by Coleman and Schiller comparing public and private schools revealed that far fewer parents of public schools visited them, attended parent-teacher organization meetings, or acted as volunteers. Perhaps nonpublic schools are more knowledgeable about parental participation than public ones.

33. However, when custody constraints were in place, parents were denied access.

34. See also Carney (p. 20) and Hancock (p. 61).

35. Orientations are not carried out in all schools. Only fifty percent of volunteers in a district-wide survey said that orientation was always or sometimes provided. See Goldberg (p. 25).

36. For examples when the norms were not accepted. Note that the accepted norms were conjoint ones; they applied to school personnel and benefactors alike. The social capital constituted authority relations, mostly between individual volunteers and teachers. The social capital also had an information component. As a consequence of common interests, the benefactors permitted control of

their labours to be transferred to the teachers during the time when they were volunteering. See Coleman (1990, p. 65).

37. See Chapter 2 for more illustrations.

38. Exceptions to this practice were persons who were supervised by principals because they worked regularly outside classrooms and by those overseen by coordinators of mentorship programs. See also Haughness (p. 112). One study showed that although teachers probably undertake most of the training, volunteer coordinators also help with training when they are present. See Hancock (p. 65).

39. Many principals concurred with this view.

40. In one survey, most volunteers said that they were trained to their satisfaction. See Goldberg (p. 25).

41. The training contributed to the human capital of the volunteers as demonstrated in Chapter 3.

42. Schools in England reported that lack of confidentiality was a difficulty for 32 percent of them. See Cyster and Clift (p. 156). Davis found, from a telephone survey, that volunteer confidentiality was a key problem (p. 114).

43. Also addressed in Robinson (p. 12) and Hancock (p. 68).

44. Some volunteers complained that their supervising teachers had forgotten that they had agreed to work on specific days. One recalled, "Nothing is worse than turning up to volunteer and having the teacher say, 'I forgot you were coming today'. . . . This happened to me. I had lots of other things I could have been doing, but I was there for my child—who was expecting me to help—so I couldn't say, 'Well, I'll be on my way'."(sm51)

45. The example of the unsafe car is not one that constitutes a breakage of the school's explicit norms that apply to volunteers. Rather, it constitutes a disagreement between the school and parent as to what constitutes appropriate means to achieve common interests.

46. There is a certain irony worth noting in the principal's statement. His legal position was *in loco parentis*, which normally means that he stands in the parents' stead. In this instance, his duty of care required him to protect the children from their parents' shortcomings.

47. Awards programs may also be included. See Haughness (p. 116).

48. In the Haughness study, seventy-three percent of principals said that personal daily contact was their most important activity with regard to volunteer acknowledgement (p. 118).

49. None of the respondents expressed any wish to evaluate the volunteer programs, however. Perhaps because volunteers were organized quite informally in the schools in the primary data, no school personnel expressed the desire to assess their impact. See also Haughness (p. 119). Evaluation of volunteer programs is not common. See Michael (p. 37).

50. In contrast, data gleaned from unselected elementary schools in this study showed they had few volunteers; some had none at all. Quite possibly, a reason for their absence is that many principals found volunteers to be a bother. It is unlikely that the parents and nonparents did not want to help.

6

Voluntary Public School Organization

The significant influx of volunteer time was associated with changes in the organization of the selected schools and may have created a new relationship between the schools and their neighbourhoods. This chapter considers the interface between the volunteers and the paid personnel, a significant problem. Just how were the job interests of support staff and of teachers accommodated? The conditions under which teachers worked were altered when considerable donations of time were received. Were their burdens lightened or increased? The infusion of volunteers into the selected schools implied that not only were "many hands" added, but the hands were joined in structures called either a home and school organization (HSO) or a parent advisory council (PAC). The growth of HSO's or PAC's adds to the story of increased social capital between school and community as discussed in Chapter 3.[1] An examination of these developments, along with the alterations in the administration of selected schools documented in Chapter 5, deepens the understanding of such schools. In that light, this chapter concludes with a comprehensive definition of what constitutes a voluntary public school.

Voluntary and Paid Labour

As shown in Chapters 3 and 5, social capital was produced when volunteers and school personnel either worked together or just agreed to work together in pursuit of their common interests. However, there is another, less desirable effect that may occur when benefactors enter schools and lend a hand. Groups of school employees may object and assert themselves through their union contracts and grievance procedures to reduce or eliminate voluntary donations of time.

Respondents from some nonselected schools reported that, as a consequence of union action, there were no aides or tutors. Sometimes this absence was modified by the regularity of the voluntary contribution—while irregular donations were seen as acceptable, hours on a periodic basis were not. At other times, the problem was framed as an issue about the low level of training of volunteers compared to paid employees. Donations of time for classroom help and office clerical work were more contentious than those for special events and field trips.[2] Occasionally, a specific project was discouraged even in schools with volunteer programs, as noted in this example from a principal of a selected school:

> The parents wanted to put up the adventure playground . . . they wanted to dig the holes, put in the cement, erect the posts themselves and save money. We were told that that just wasn't legal for starters and it would be putting a person out of work. (ob48)

A support staff union in one district adopted a policy that there be no volunteers permitted in schools.[3] The policy may not have received acceptance because the union's members contravened it.[4] What were the responses to the opposition? Principals and parents tried not to threaten support staff members but persisted in supporting voluntarism. Even when district policies prohibited the use of volunteers in classrooms, principals found ways around the regulations.[5]

The divergence of views of what constitutes an appropriate amount of voluntarism may be understood in terms of the different interests of unions and schools. Although the support staff unions offered a number of reasons why use of benefactors should be restricted, their most salient one was the probability of job loss. Conversely, schools, trying to offer the most services for the least cost, appeared to prefer some voluntary labour over fully paid labour. Further, some school personnel and parents argued that many of the services could not be provided without volunteers, particularly under conditions of financial retrenchment. Under financial exigency, for example, the role of classroom aide was simply not funded and therefore could not be lost. These positions, when entrenched, produced an ongoing disagreement, particularly in unselected schools in "union towns."[6]

The clash between voluntary service and paid employment is an example of the difference between conjoint and disjoint authority relations.[7] Conjoint relations are binary; they are built from the coincidence of the interests of the school and its volunteers, as seen in Chapter 5.[8] In contrast, the interests of the school and its employees diverge (they are disjointed) because school personnel are paid—they work to some extent for money and not necessarily for the interests of the school. One of the outcomes of disjoint authority relations is that the superordinate (school) may not always act in the interests of the subordinates (support staff).

Consequently, some of the unions suggested that there interests were not being served when volunteers are asked to assume tasks normally undertaken by their membership.[9]

Teachers' Perspectives on Voluntarism

Some teachers, even ones in selected schools, feared volunteers. They were very uncomfortable with the idea of adult helpers, particularly in their own classrooms. One mentioned, "Some parents are very pushy and threatening to the teacher, challenging what the teacher does" (rt42). The perception of volunteers as intruders into the teachers' domain was asserted quite strongly on occasion.[10, 11] If the intruder metaphor was fully accepted by teachers, then very few volunteers would be observed in schools.

Willard Waller, who studied schools in the late 1920's, concluded that teachers and parents were "natural enemies, predestined each for the discomfiture of the other," because of their different interests.[12] According to Waller, the teacher "desires the scholastic welfare of children even at the expense of other aspects of their development." This interest is in conflict with that of parents, who view the total welfare of their children as paramount.[13] He developed a picture of social relationships that were primarily competitive and conflictual rather than cooperative.[14] Principals were seen as being responsive to parental wishes but parents were clearly outsiders. In Waller's school, there is no sense that parents and other citizens could work with teachers as natural allies in the "small society" of the school in the early decades of the twentieth century. Research undertaken during the 1960's by Dan Lortie found much the same gulf:

> My respondents project a clear sense of territorial proprieties. There is "teacher territory" and "parental territory," and leadership on school affairs rests with the teacher. Teachers, in sum, want the parent to be a "distant assistant." . . . The cooks do not work in the same kitchen. (Lortie, p. 191)

As shown by the Great Lake Elementary and examples in Chapters 2 and 3, teachers in this study experienced voluntarism quite differently, especially in selected schools. Most teachers did not consider volunteers to be meddlers as long as they were assigned only if desired and in a manner that protected teachers' job security.[15] One teacher in a selected school observed, "Usually, nobody wants them. I have let it be known I do, so the vice principal sends them to me. Other teachers feel they're too much trouble, but I find them so helpful" (rt56). This teacher then noted the reaction of her colleagues: "Since some of the teachers have now met my volunteers and had a chance to see them working; they all want a volunteer!" Teachers who actually work with volunteers demonstrate positive attitudes toward them, as shown by other research.[16] A few of the teachers interviewed said that they had become friends with their volunteers and knew them socially. Obviously, these relationships were far closer than Lortie's "distant assistant." Other teachers felt crowded, however, as one said, "On some days I feel I need my own space" (sp94).[17]

One of the reasons that many teachers viewed volunteers positively is the important contributions benefactors made to the teachers' work lives. A teacher in a rural school observed that her volunteers built puppets, helped with music and cooking, supervised a visit to a farm to see sheep sheared, and were drivers for field trips.[18] Sometimes, volunteers rendered expert assistance as in the instances of mentor programs. A teacher supervisor of a mentor program said, "With the exception of one, the response from the classroom teachers has been fantastic. . . . They know that there is no way that they can provide a service like that" (dn70). An illustration of expert assistance was provided by a volunteer who said,

> I was a music teacher before I left the profession to have my own children. I like to help the music teacher by playing the piano so she can devote 100% of her attention to the school choir. [Consequently,] she is able to enter the choir into a number of musical events. (ad33)

Clearly, some jobs were done that would have remained undone if volunteers did not do them. But other tasks would still have been assumed by the teachers.[19] What happens when teachers are relieved of some of their duties? As volunteers perform chores such as drills and student supervision, teachers appear to be much more able to give personal attention, lead groups, experiment, and plan instruction.[20] A few reported that their union contract was interpreted as requiring a clear demarcation between volunteers' and teachers' work. This outcome was shown by one teacher's comment: "You have to make sure that they are not doing any teaching. Teachers' union policy. They do reinforcement only" (rt48). Even though this respondent did not make clear just what constituted teaching as opposed to other instructional activities, most teachers interviewed just appeared happy to substitute other tasks for the ones assumed by donors.

Another potential contribution to teachers was that volunteers actually reduced their overall workload. If someone comes into your classroom and offers to take on some of your duties, it follows that you have less to do, except for that which you add to your role by choice (such as more planning). A few of the teacher interviewees agreed that their total workload had been decreased by volunteers. Several interviewees mentioned the expression, "Many hands make light work." They pointed out that some of their benefactors were ex-teachers who brought a good deal of knowledge and skill to their volunteer roles. However, other evidence from a district-wide survey of principals, teachers, and support staff members indicated there was effectively no change in teachers' workload as a consequence of benevolence.[21] Perhaps teachers just break even. Many principals and teachers, however, considered teachers' overall responsibilities to have *increased* because of the use of volunteers. While they generally endorsed voluntarism, they mentioned that the training and supervision of donors consumed time and energy. One principal noted, "It's extra work for the teachers in learning how to use volunteers effectively and how to use 'Mrs. Jones' specifically—a question of training that particular individual" (rt39). A teacher gave an example of the intensity with which she works:

> I explain exactly what to do; I model it for them. It does take a lot of time. I try not to overload them; keep it simple. I model everything, e.g., short and long vowels, "don't tell them the answers," and how to encourage the kids. I make it clear that I don't write a reference letter if they are not productive and consistent. (rt60)

Teachers recognized that volunteers improve their knowledge and skills over time, as shown by a teacher in a nonselected school:[22]

> Volunteers become very proficient at their tasks with experience. It takes a little time to structure and explain volunteer tasks especially when volunteers and teachers get to know each other and teachers recognize the strengths of individual volunteers. (ps49)

Some schools worked to establish a core of parents who became long-term benefactors and thus reduced the requirements for training. In some instances, the sense of care and commitment shown by teachers to volunteer parents was quite remarkable:

> Some volunteers need a lot of support. I once had a full-time volunteer who found the school a place of refuge. She had had difficulties and the school was a transition place for her. I wouldn't leave her alone with students but she was a great help. Another full-time volunteer was quite slow and therefore unemployable. She needed a place to go, to feel important where someone was relying on her. She was wonderful with the children and a help to me. . . . One volunteer with schizophrenia was in a transition home. She wasn't allowed to see her own children. My job as a teacher expanded. I didn't mind. It feels good to help someone and she was helping me. (sm50)

These responses are long way from Waller! The impression given by the interviewees was that the teachers' overall load had increased slightly as a result of welcoming donors into their classrooms. However, the extra demands were not resented; they were accommodated willingly in light of the benefits gained. When presented with the opportunity to do more for their students, the teachers acted upon it.

Extensive Organizational Efforts

The roles of administrators, teachers, and support staff are affected by the infusion of volunteers into a school, but so is the overall structure of the school itself. Groups of parents and teachers have been around for a long time and called by various names (parent-teacher association, home-school organization, parent consultative committee, or parent advisory council). While this structural appendage to schools has always been associated with resource acquisition (such as the proceeds from pie sales) and has always acted as an avenue through which parents could articulate concerns to teachers and administrators,[23] the home-school organization located in selected schools had more substantial effects.[24] Home-school organizations (called HSO's) took an active role in organizing volunteers and raising funds in many schools, as noted by a principal who said that his parent advisory committee members were

> central to all the volunteers in the school because they plan and carry out most of the volunteer activities. You're talking about the Hot Dog Day, which is routine every month, or what happens at Sports Day when they bring barbecues. They are responsible for major fund raising events in the school when they sell things at Christmas time or go to the casino. (ob46)

Another principal in a selected school illustrated the integration of his parental volunteers by acknowledging that he had three staffs: his regular teaching staff, his special teaching staff, and his parent staff (db70).

There were other implications from the presence of HSO's, most notably in the area of roles and decision making about school programs and the expenditure of monies raised. Most principals worked with their HSO's to assist their volunteer efforts. They also welcomed their HSOs' accomplishments and benefits from their donations, but roles and personalities sometimes intervened in complex ways. One volunteer observed:

> We raise the money and we'd like to have a say on how this money is being spent and that might not be what the school wants. It's understandable that . . . teachers might not agree. I don't think the laminator is important, but the teacher thinks the laminator is top priority. (ob48)

A principal reflected on the complexities and said, "Parent volunteers can be supportive but they can also be power-seeking" (rt51). Several administrators expressed the idea that a certain justice was served; the parents who generated the resources saw their children benefit.[25] The association between the resources generated and the decision making requested is corroborated by Epstein and Dauber's study of 171 teachers in five elementary and three middle schools in disadvantaged neighbourhoods. They found a remarkably strong correlation of 0.519 between voluntarism and decision making.[26] What is significant in terms of impact on the organization of schools is how the HSO's provided formal avenues for benefactors to exercise influence. Permitting volunteers to have a "say" moved the selected schools closer to their private school counterparts in which parents, who have responsibility for generating the resources needed by the schools, also have some control over their deployment.

Many respondents thought that the way HSO's were organized contributed to their success or failure to attract parental participation. Some HSO's suffered from lengthy meetings, formalities, and a lack of goals. Others engaged the teachers, used flexible agendas, and were integral to their school. A teacher observed one of the positive effects of HSO's or PAC's:

> Because of parent advisory council activities, teachers and parents find themselves working shoulder to shoulder, thus getting to know each other on a more personal basis. They find that they have more in common than just kids. (jr02)

Where parental participation was perceived to be high, the corresponding HSO's sponsored many events, engaged in telephone campaigns on behalf of their schools, had parent education programs, raised substantial funds, deliberately recruited volunteers, and were active in school decisions.[27]

Another organizational change that appeared to make a dramatic impact on the presence of volunteers was the institutionalization of the role of "volunteer coordinator" in the school itself. The effect is illustrated by the account of a parental volunteer who occupied the part-time, paid position:

> As coordinator of the noon-hour programs, I set up two sessions each year. I find [volunteer] staff, think of new ideas, liaise with the school to coordinate schedules and facilities, and stay aware of what is happening. Some of the instructors are parents who are paid to teach. I pay salaries, purchase some of the supplies, and trouble shoot. I'm always thinking about it and get ideas from the community centre flyers. It's very intense twice a year: August/September and then in January. I start phoning instructors at the end of August and then the meetings start in September. I photocopy the information package for parents. The registration takes place over three days, then the class lists have to be made and then I go every lunch hour for the first week. There are 14 classes this session and these programs involve over one-third of the students. Just about all the classes are full: clay, chess, gymnastics, computer, knitting, beading, Chinese knotting, piano, painting and

drawing, drama, and a lunch brunch (grade 1–3 students who make and each lunch together). The response is really positive. It's a big commitment. It takes time and tact and you have to stay cheerful and try to be fair. The program has been built up over the years. We get phone calls from other schools inquiring about our program. (sm41)[28]

This coordinator offered the possibility that a small amount of public dollars combined with a willing employee was able to generate a multifold response in the form of private resources. Since the role of volunteer coordinator was encountered only rarely in this study, the thought of "priming the pump" in this way requires some more evidence to substantiate it.[29]

The idea that public resources might be converted into private donations was supported further by a small number of district-wide volunteer programs encountered in this study. The Prime Mentors' Program was one of them. Its district coordinator worked as a liaison between all schools and community members while each school's district coordinator linked mentors, parents, and students directly. One of the school-based coordinators described her duties. Notice that her position is quite atypical within most schools.

I am responsible, as a liaison between teachers, parents, and mentors, to ensure that these groups come together in an actual event. For example, today I had a phone call from a parent making sure that there would be a place available for a meeting to happen with her child's mentor. Later in the day, I had a phone call from the mentor making sure that I had arranged for a meeting place. I also made sure that the student was prepared and organized and ready to roll. (volunteer, dd52)

While parents covered the cost of materials, students and mentors (who were often their grandparents' age) worked on special projects. There were about 20 pairs and the district coordinator reported a 70 percent success rate when asking for volunteers for the program. Aside from a few programs such as this one, there was little evidence of district efforts to organize benefactors.

It is possible to engage in grander strategies of intervention, to "prime the pump" in large jurisdictions. Districts, states, federal governments, or other agencies sometimes support initiatives designed to increase the extent of benevolence. Although these interventions are atypical in the spectrum of giving to schools, their presence demonstrates the extent and variety of programs that can emerge.

An overview of substantial programs designed to encourage volunteer participation was undertaken by the National Research Council and published in 1990 under the editorship of Bernard Michael.[30, 31] It describes the most extensive programs undertaken to that date. Some worked with volunteers at the school level while others restricted their aims such as help for latchkey children. Some were nonprofit organizations that depended on private revenues while others were internal components of their districts and are supported mostly by public funds. Almost all were located in large school districts; several of the programs were started with private resources and were initiated over two decades ago. The report shows "what can be done" with a substantial effort to impose structures to encourage voluntarism but it does not emphasize the results of the programs so the effects on social capital are unclear or unknown.[32] A further study of 88 notable school programs in three counties in southern California showed that most had a paid volunteer coordinator and kept records on present and potential volunteers. Interviews of personnel in selected programs revealed that most were started externally to their schools and many coordinators worked about 15 hours per month. Six programs resulted in time donations of 8.5 hours per student per year but again, the purpose of that study was descriptive rather than evaluative.[33] A number of other initiatives to increase parental participation of all kinds and not just voluntarism have been undertaken, most of them subsequent to Michael's review. They include the Comer process and the Accelerated Schools Model and are described by Susan Swap. She develops the True Partnership Model that requires a collaborative role for parents with strong leadership. It encompasses new policies and integrates educators, parents, and community representatives in a unifying mission.[34] All the programs altered the districts or schools by adding an organizational component. Whether financed publicly or privately, all were aimed at increasing community participation in schools.

Some of the organizational programs designed to augment voluntarism may be quite cost-effective. Corrine Hill sampled 20 programs judged to be outstanding by the National School Volunteer Program in 1977–78. They were characterized by a mix of funding sources, use of advisory boards and fund raising, extensive training for volunteers, their own newsletters, and yearly questionnaires. After determining the annual budgets, numbers of volunteers and hours of service, cost per hour of donated time, and the comparable cost to provide the service by aides, Hill concluded that the potential gain in dollar values ranged from 57 percent to 93 percent with an average of 81 percent.[35] If her data are correct, the economic payoff for the use of volunteers is substantial.[36] Clearly, many more studies of this order are needed to determine the cost-effectiveness of volunteer programs under a variety of conditions, particularly those that are not large-scale. But what do the changes in schools (and perhaps districts) imply for the relations between the school and its environment? The effect may be profound.

The School and Its Environment

The observations of Waller and Lortie are in contrast with the harmony between school folk and town folk just described. The researchers saw the public school as detached from its community rather than integrated with its neighbourhood. If a school is, indeed, separate, there is a useful model that may be applied to it. The school may be considered to be a bureaucracy with a distinct division of adult labour, governance by rules, and affectively neutral treatment of students.[37] The bureaucratic school has a relatively clear hierarchy of control, and boundaries that are not difficult to define.[38] Teachers are seen to have universalistic expectations of children; achievement and growth are valued highly.[39] If schools are seen largely as bureaucracies, then there is a clear separation between the school and its environment and particularly between the school and the families of those children who attend it. Joyce Epstein calls this bureaucratic view of schools the "separateness model."[40] Tony Bryk et al. describe a separate school. Notice how completely self-referential such a school is; its perspective does not extend beyond its perimeters:

> The vision of the "good school" from a bureaucratic perspective is captured in the ideals of progressive urban reformers who sought to create comprehensive high schools. Such institutions would be efficiently organized to serve large numbers of students of varied backgrounds and interests by offering specialized services and a diverse array of courses. Managing the multiplicity of organizational goals would require a large and specialized administrative staff. Social relations within the school would be formalized in accord with rational-legalistic norms. (Bryk, Lee, and Smith, pp. 137–138)

Coleman and Hoffer lay out the societal mission embedded in the same bureaucratic view as it applies in the United States. It

> sees schools as society's instrument for releasing a child from the blinders imposed by accident of birth into this family or that family. Schools have been designed to open broad horizons to the child, transcending the limits of the parents, and have taken children from disparate cultural backgrounds into the mainstream of American Culture. They have been a major element in social mobility, freeing children from the poverty of their parents and the low status of their social origins. They have been a means of stripping away identities of ethnicity and social origin and implanting a common American identity. (p.3)

When the school and its mission are described in these terms, it is not difficult to understand why persons outside the school, such as parents and other citizens, are not considered to be integral either to its daily functions or its long-term goals. Such an organization is designed to educate students and it does so under a set of norms that vary considerably from the social environment out of which students come, particularly their homes.

There is, however, an alternative to the bureaucratic model. Called "communitarian" by Bryk, Lee, and Smith, the school is seen as a collectivity with a shared ethos, informal and enduring social relationships, and diffuse roles. It is not a bureaucracy at all:

> The communitarian ideal, on the other hand, has a nostalgic flavor reminiscent of an earlier, simpler society where schools were small and organizational goals less complex. The curricular offerings were fewer in number, and a common experience for all students was emphasized rather than specialized services. Social relations were personal, and there was a natural deference to adult authority.[41]

Hoffer and Coleman present a similar depiction:[42]

> a school as an extension of the family, reinforcing the family's values. The school is IN LOCO PARENTIS [original emphasis] vested with the authority of the parent to carry out the parent's will. The school is, in this orientation, an efficient means for transmitting the culture of the community from the older generation to the younger. It helps create the next generation in the image of the preceding one.[43]

The essence of the communitarian school is its shared values (and norms), shared activities (courses and rituals), and shared social relations (ethics of caring and diffuse teacher roles) as shown in a landmark study by Bryk, Lee, and Holland entitled *Catholic Schools and the Common Good*.[44] They link the effectiveness of Catholic schools to their communal organization and decentralized governance.[45] As presented, the communitarian model accurately portrays many private schools. The mission of most schools that receive no support from the state is to serve the families and religious organizations that support them, although they also serve society at large.[46] Connections to the environment are not just desirable; they are required for continued existence. But are there only two models of schools, the public and private? Is there any other alternative?

Litwak and Meyer suggest an integration is possible between the public school and the community.[47] On the one hand, educators (as part of a bureaucracies as secondary groups), are able to provide knowledge of the curriculum, teaching skills, and resources for learning to schools. On the other hand, families (as primary groups) are suited to the provision of basic needs, initial learning, and fundamental values to children.[48] Litwak and Meyer insist that experts are required to handle uniform tasks and

nonexperts to perform nonuniform tasks.[49] Not only are the groups complementary, but each is deficient in the areas of contribution where the
other is strong. Furthermore, Litwak and Meyer explain how, in the integration of school and neighbourhood, groups outside the family may
play a significant role in the overall development of the child:

> Two important activities that neighbors are uniquely able to perform are
> nonuniform tasks which involve time emergencies, or those tasks based
> technologically on territory. To put the matter in the most common-sense
> terms, only a neighbor is in a regular position to tell a mother that her small
> child has wandered into the street. . . . Only children in the neighborhood
> can provide the immediate everyday socialization that young children re-
> ceive in their spontaneous play after school. These kinds of nonuniform
> tasks can not be handled by the larger kin unit because they are unlikely to
> live in the same neighborhood; they can not be handled by the nuclear fam-
> ily because it does not have sufficient primary group resources. (p. 127)

Litwak and Meyer's proposal permits the bureaucracy and primary
groups to perform functions to which they are suited, but also develops
linkages between them. Accordingly, they offered suggestions that
schools make use of persons indigenous to their neighbourhoods and
nonexpert knowledge in order to link schools with the people they
serve.[50] Their writing foretold the direction of later work regarding
schools and their neighbourhoods.

The most significant attempt at developing a perspective about the gap
between public school and community is the construction of the "overlapping spheres" model developed by Joyce Epstein. Basing her schema
on the work of Bronfrenbrenner, Leichter, Seely, Litwak and Meyer, she
establishes four major spheres of influence of student development:
schools, families, community groups, and peer groups. These spheres
have interlocking histories and contain individuals with many skills that
affect the education of children.[51] Epstein asserts that there are substantial
forces that influence the extent of overlap, most notably the philosophies,
policies, and practices of both the family and the school. Most importantly, they overlap by design. In contrast to the specialization of labour
associated with schools as bureaucracies (the separation model), the consolidation or overlap of spheres produces a generalization of labour in
which schools adopt some familial characteristics and families take on
some school attributes.[52] The comprehensiveness of Epstein's research offers guidance on how schools can cultivate the transformation of school-
community relations.[53]

In summary, a separation of home and school has been a hallmark of
bureaucratic schools. Within this framework, teachers and parents are

"natural enemies" as a consequence of their divergent interests regarding the child. Such schools are organized to be standardized, impartial, and have special knowledge to impart to students. They are state agents maintained by governments. The schools are not designed to serve the parents—they keep them at a distance. Emphasis is on the efficient delivery of educational services. Conversely, a nearly complete integration of home and school is the aim of a communitarian school. Rather than serve societal goals solely, its purpose is primarily to transmit ideas through emphasis on common values, a core curriculum, and shared activities. The school is an extension of the home and related institutions; its emphasis is on the integration of the child into community life. Litwak and Meyer recognized the that the bureaucratic nature of schools and the primary group character of families and neighbourhoods can each serve children well. Epstein's overlapping spheres model is designed to show how to hold public and private aspects of life together by effecting a generalization of labour and parental participation. Her vision and data show a connection of school and home based on the commonality of interests shared by teachers and parents. These three models bear an important relation to the voluntary public school.

What Is a Voluntary Public School?

A voluntary public school is one that is mainly supported by public funds but receives a substantial amount of its resources in the form of gifts. This definition clearly excludes schools that are strictly public (such as those with no contributions of time, dollars, or goods), and those that are strictly private (those not in receipt of any public aid). The meanings of "mainly" and "substantial" are deliberately left vague, except that most of the resources originate from public revenues via federal, state (or provincial), and local taxation while some of the support comes from gifts.[54] "Resources" is taken to mean the total supply of public money (and the labour, equipment, and supplies generated by it), volunteer time, and other donations upon which the school depends. Private resources that emanate from exchanges are not included in the definition; voluntary public schools may or may not gain support via fees, lotteries, or the sale of services.[55] Apart from their general sources of support, voluntary schools also share some particularly notable characteristics.

A voluntary public school receives many gifts. Some aid student learning directly such as tutorial time; other gifts assist in learning indirectly, as with teacher support and student transportation; still other donations help with special events. A few persons associated with the school give much; many give a little; many more give none. Although the value of the voluntary school's gifts is modest compared to its public funding, the total monetary equivalent is likely many, many millions of dollars when aggregated across the United States and Canada. The school's benefactors tend to be mothers who are employed part-time or not at all outside the home. Some patrons are single parents, senior citizens, or college students. They give in order to receive personal benefits (such as a sense of fulfillment or employment skills), out of duty to the younger generation, or because they enjoy the sociability of participation.

A voluntary public school is noted for its student achievement supported by the learning norm (students should apply themselves to their studies) and its solidarity between benefactors and children supported by the caring norm (students should give time to others). Its students are linked to their communities and correspondingly, certain community members are linked to their schools. The school is at least partly familial thanks to the presence of parents. While it receives gifts of physical and financial capital, the school is most strongly marked by its social capital, that is, the network of relations that support its students, school personnel, and community members.

A voluntary public school may be found in any neighbourhood. It may be located in a wealthier circumstances where parents participate almost automatically; it may be found in a poorer neighbourhood or in a context of varying ethnicities where barriers of language and tradition have been overcome so that community members donate their time actively. It may be situated where parental work and family lives do not permit much time for volunteering and it may be located in urban, suburban, or rural settings.

The principal of the voluntary public school makes extensive efforts to locate prospective patrons through various media. Teachers and volunteers are among the most active recruiters although their efforts are not always successful because of the free rider problem. The school offers incentives to donate time: personal benefit, sense of obligation, and potential friendships. Once benefactors are on hand, the school's administrators match them to the tasks to be performed. Donors are usually trained on-the-job by teachers and later thanked formally or informally for their contributions. Administrators ensure that volunteers are "made welcome" in the school. They spend extra time seeking gifts, and work to build relationships with others outside their school building.

Cooperation of support staff and teachers sustain the voluntary public school. Support personnel willingly work alongside benefactors; teachers perceive the contributions positively because the donors increase teachers' ability to instruct and they, on balance, appear to reduce work loads. The home and school organization (HSO) assumes key responsibilities for the administration of volunteers and establishes fund raising priorities with school personnel. Although a voluntary public school would not normally receive external assistance designed to attract benefactors, it may be connected to a district program which is designed to increase the numbers of volunteers who give their time to schools.

Where can the voluntary public school be placed with reference to the bureaucratic, communitarian, or overlapping spheres model? The school retains many of the elements of the bureaucratic model. Its basically hier-archical structure (with layers of administrators, teachers, and support personnel) is not altered. It is lodged in a school district organization set up to deliver a state or provincially mandated curriculum and to provide most of the resources needed by the school. Instructional and subject matter expertise largely resides with the teachers. Standardized adminis-trative procedures address uniform tasks, such as grouping students and monitoring their progress. Many universalistic expectations of children are upheld. But some aspects of the bureaucratic model are discarded. Rather than having a sharp separation between school and community, the school blurs the distinction considerably, particularly with the infu-sion of members of students' families. The services of these people are welcomed and their presence emphasizes the acceptance of at least some of the values of the community which the school serves. Rather than have all the resources of the school provided by taxation, aid also come from gifts freely given. Consequently, the neighbourhood context of the voluntary public school takes on a greater importance than the bureau-cratic model would imply.

The voluntary public school may also be compared with the communi-tarian model that gives rise to the communal school. There are many fea-tures that the two types of schools have in common.[56] The voluntary public school may be considered to be a small society in which school personnel, students, parents, and other community members participate.[57] Certain norms are emphasized and the lives of participants are more integrated through the construction and affirmation of norms that make up social capital, particularly for the young. However, the school is not fully a com-munal school, partly because it retains some public (and therefore bureau-cratic) elements. It is not simply an extension of its community; integration is by no means complete. Boards of public education and school district administrators have their say. States or provinces assume a governing role and exercise their mandates on a range of functions such as evaluation and employment. Most of the resources needed to sustain the voluntary public school come from outside its neighbourhood. It is still a formal organiza-tion and not a primary group. It is not strictly a creature of its context.

Thus, the bureaucratic and communitarian models may be used to un-derstand the voluntary public school—but only partially. As illustrated in this book, the school fits largely under the model of overlapping spheres. If the distinction between family and community is removed and the influence of peers set aside, then two spheres remain, school and community.[58] The voluntary public school exhibits a bridge between these two institutions—one a formal organization, the other an entity with primary group characteristics.[59] Existing neither as a "citadel in a foreign land" nor a simple extension of localism, the voluntary public school apparently resolves the tension between the public and the private and between formal and informal social structures. Its generalization of labour and community participation make it communal but its embeddedness within a larger organization and its external funding permit a degree of separation. Resources and controls come from two sources.

One of the objectives of this and earlier chapters was to provide some answers to questions: How is a voluntary public school created and maintained? What are its component parts? Who are the main actors in the school? Where may the school be found? When is voluntarism likely to occur? Some tentative answers have been offered. Yet, there is a persistent and intriguing question left unaddressed. What is the major contribution of a voluntary public school to a society? A more complete attempt to answer that question requires an expedition outside the realm of education into the greater panorama of ideas and conceptions about the fundamental natures of societies and human beings.

Notes

1. Throughout this volume, "community" refers both to the location of persons outside schools and the networks of relations that link people, depending on context of its use.

2. See also Goldberg (p. 20).

3. Lack of support for volunteers among teacher aide organizations is noted by Michael (p. 98).

4. In a district-wide survey, many support staff union members favoured the use of volunteers. See Goldberg (p. 21).

5. It would be interesting to know the reaction of principals' organizations to the use of volunteer administrators.

6. For further discussion on this debate, see Brudner (pp. 32–35).

7. See Coleman (1990, pp. 66–73).

8. Coleman's examples of conjoint authority relations include organizations such as communes and unions (pp. 66–73).

9. For a more extended discussion on how incompatible interests may produce conflict, see Coleman (1990, p. 73).

10. Michael mentions concerns about teachers being observed, volunteers' gossip, possible donor "butt-in" and potential conflict with teaching style (p. 99). See also Becker and Epstein (p. 109); Roberts (p. 34); and Smrekar (p. 37).

11. If the intruder metaphor holds, then the reaction of the part of some donors that teachers are seen as "gods" is understandable. See Roberts (pp. 35–36) and Lareau (p. 112).

12. See Waller (p. 68). Although Waller directed his inquiry toward secondary schools, his characterization appears applicable to elementary schools as well.

13. Further, Waller saw solidarity as confined to students and not shared across student, teacher, and parent groups.

14. See Waller (p. 40). The conflict may have produced negative experiences for students. Those experiences could form the foundation of later adult readiness to criticize public schools. See Willower (p. 29).

15. See Robinson (p. 10) and Streit (pp. 116 and 122).

16. A study by Davis of 246 elementary teachers in Sacramento generated a correlation of 0.345 between current use and attitude (p. 95). Past use was also associated with positive attitude more than lack of prior use (p. 98). Elements of the positive view may include learning from the volunteers and an absence of stereotypic judgements about the limitations of parental contributions. See Swap (p. 27) and Epstein (1990, p. 112).

17. It should not be surprising that teachers find a certain empathy for the volunteers in their classrooms. Perhaps that is because teachers are often volunteers themselves. According to the Canada-wide survey, 53% of teachers volunteered their services in some way during the previous year (See Duschesne, pp. 48–49). Teachers sometimes act as benefactors in their own schools as the unpaid supervisors of school clubs. They also work in fund raising events. One study revealed that the average teacher time in a random sample of 47 elementary schools was 17 hours per year spent on fund raising. By extrapolation, the total amount of private funds raised in British Columbia in 1983 was $14.8 million. Remarkably, that amount was equal to the pro-rated salaries paid to the teachers for their time; in other words, they had effected a dollar-for-dollar conversion of public money into private money. See Salloum (p. 165). An extensive study on educators' attitudes towards parental involvement showed considerable sentiment for their participation, though mainly in terms of their own children. See Chavkin and Williams.

18. See Chapter 2 for detailed gifts of time.

19. Flexibility seems to be required of teachers because they little influence on the lives of benefactors outside schools. See remarks on volunteer reliability in Chapter 5.

20. In short, there seems to be a shift to the tasks more central to teaching and instruction. See Robinson (p. 10), Hedges (p. 13), and Henderson (p. 151). Due to recent trends toward the integration of special needs and English as a Second Language children into regular classrooms, work load changes may have increased the desire to reduce the burdens of routine tasks.

21. See Goldberg (p. 23).

22. Remember that volunteers worked in nonselected schools as well as selected ones in which benevolence was emphasized. There were just fewer of them.

23. See Hancock (p. 72) and Robinson (p. 6).

24. Many of the sponsored activities were similar to those undertaken without formal home-school organizations, such as a touted annual "Halloween Howl" party for 1,000 students, family members, and friends (sm42).

25. One principal from an unselected school remarked about parents in this way: "Those who do, don't complain; those who don't, complain. Industrious people don't complain."(vw57).

26. See Epstein and Dauber (p. 294). This connection may be quite significant because it links resources and control.

27. This view of HSO's is supported by an interview study of 115 teachers in eastern Massachusetts. Johnson found that parents shared many responsibilities in their schools. (p. 97).

28. This coordinator, who recruited nonparents as well as parents and volunteers as well as persons paid for their services, was employed four to five hours per week.

29. Notice that most of the data discussed thus far have been based on schools that saw benevolence grow naturally—from the "grass roots," thanks to the initiatives of principals, teachers, and volunteers.

30. They included: Boston Partners In Education with a budget of $800,000 largely from businesses and foundations; Chicago Schoolhouse Volunteers, comprised of 80% parents with 11,263 volunteers in 1987–88; Dade Partners with an annual allocation of $80 per school that matching businesses and community organizations with schools; Dallas with each school having a volunteer coordinator; Montgomery County with a program that manages school volunteers and orients faculty; Los Angeles with a nonprofit group focusing on latchkey, dental and health programs; San Francisco School Volunteers, a nonprofit agency that manages volunteers and has a budget of $500,000; the Tulsa program that manages volunteers; and the Washington, D.C. program that attracts benefactors and has school volunteer coordinators. See Michael (pp. 47–87).

31. Programs were selected based on suggestions made by state and local coordinators of voluntary service organizations, including the National School Volunteer Program, the National Educational Association, the National Parent Teachers Association, the national School Boards Association, and others. Criteria for inclusion included administrative and policy-level support, written goals and objectives, availability of data, and operation for a least two years. The study was undertaken using 13 site visits lasting two days each by two to three investigators.

32. Actually, the report laments the paucity of formal evaluations even for student achievement (Michael, pp. 37 and 90).

33. See Carney (pp. 38–128).

34. See Swap (pp. 48–57).

35. The time per year per student ranged from 36 minutes to 15 hours, 23 minutes with a median of 2 hours 57 minutes. See Hill (pp. 107–115). Her study is an exceptionally fine dissertation.

36. Brudner also analyzed the costs and effects of volunteers and concluded that the benefits are several multiples of the costs (pp. 24–37).

37. The general conception of bureaucracy comes from Weber. Its application to schools is discussed ably by Bidwell (pp. 992–1008), and is amplified by Litwak and Meyer (pp. 58–60).

38. Parent-teacher organizations do not play a prominent role in the discussion of schools as bureaucracies; Bidwell only mentions parent teacher-associations twice (pp. 1011 and 1016).

39. "Universalistic expectations" means that children receive equal amounts of attention in school. Status is granted through academic achievement. See Lightfoot (p. 22).

40. See Epstein (1990, p. 101).

41. See Bryk, Lee, and Smith (p. 137–138). This conception arises from a study of Roman Catholic high schools undertaken by Bryk and Driscoll. They see them as having a system of values rooted in the home, a pattern of social relations that may be described as caring, and a common agenda such as a core curriculum, activities that teachers and students share, and special rituals (pp. 5–6). According to Bryk and Driscoll, study of the communal school has been neglected because of the dominance of the bureaucratic perspective (p. 184).

42. In their case, of private schools.

43. See Coleman and Hoffer (p. 3). They undertook a major study of high school seniors and sophomores that was sponsored by the National Center for Education Statistics. Their research, which included both public and various kinds of private schools, permitted them to induce two very general orientations or missions of education. In fact, they state that the aim of their book is to compare schools: those which are societal agents and those which are outgrowths of religious communities or extensions of individual families (p. 24).

44. By "shared," Bryk, Lee, and Holland mean that students and teachers agree on important values, undertake actions together, and interact meaningfully. Values and norms are also held in common with most parents.

45. See Bryk, Lee, and Holland (pp. 277–296).

46. Bryk, Lee and Holland also offer evidence that indicates the Catholic high school of the late twentieth century is a substantial contributor to society as well as to the individuals and families directly in contact with them. They show that Catholic schools are somewhat more successful at reducing social inequalities than are public schools (pp. 245–271).

47. They refer to an empirically-based theory of coordination. See Litwak and Meyer (pp. 7 to 10).

48. See Chapter 7 for a discussion of primary and secondary groups.

49. See Litwak and Meyer (pp. 7–12).

50. Litwak and Meyer (p. 113)

51. See Epstein (1990, pp. 102–104).

52. See Epstein (1990, p. 104). It should be noted that her schema is designed to bridge the institutions in a number of ways and so it is not restricted to voluntarism. Her arenas of overlap also include assistance with school work at home, parental participation in school governance, and community involvement of various kinds. Her model is supported by a followup study by Epstein and Lee.

53. The weight of the literature may be shifting from a belief in a "family deficiency theory" to the affirmation of an "institutional discrimination theory" when authors try to account for variations in school voluntarism in particular and parental involvement in general. Rather than focus on the paucity of resources in some homes, attention is shifted to the actions or inactions of the schools. See Ho (pp. 50–54).

54. This definition includes nonpublic schools that are supported partly by public funds in countries such as Canada.

55. Enterprise activities have the potential to generate considerable amounts of resources for public schools, particularly secondary ones. See Brown (1995).

56. See Chapters 2 through 6.

57. This sense of small society differs from Waller's, who confined his to the school personnel and students.

58. This modification is probably safer for elementary schools than secondary. The catchments for elementary schools can be small and so their students subject to less variation in backgrounds than their secondary counterparts. As for peer influences, they are usually seen as much stronger in secondary schools than in elementary

59. See Chapter 7 for a discussion on primordial institutions.

PART II

Generalizations
and Policies

7

The Voluntary Public School as
a Bridging Institution

This chapter reviews patterns of individual giving in light our background knowledge about community. Previous discussion has offered evidence that benevolence affects schools, both the persons in them and their organizational structures. To examine why schools undergo such transformations, this chapter places schools in their contemporary social context. That context is currently beset by tremendous conflict between traditional and modern institutions. The negative impact of that conflict is felt in the daily lives of nearly everyone in modern societies, particularly children. Does the voluntary school offer some hope for them? Can benevolence in schools provide a bridge to help resolve some of the conflict?

In order to probe the possibility that the voluntary public school works as a social "bridging" institution, this chapter begins with a discussion of the theories of individual benevolence. It is concerned especially with the influence of voluntarism on the development of a sense of community. Next, the chapter focuses on some theories about how schools and other organizations function within their environments. Finally, given the rift in contemporary societies, the chapter concludes by exploring how well voluntary public schools are positioned to act as bridging institutions between colliding parts of societies.

Individual Benevolence and Community Construction

Interviews revealed that volunteers gave to schools for many reasons, as shown in Chapter 2. They claimed that donation of time served as a substitute for paid employment and as a source of fulfillment and stimulation. They gained satisfactions from being in a teaching role. Some saw benevolence as a way to obtain knowledge about how their children's schools "works." Others were on the path to a political career. Some considered their volunteer time to be a duty to their own children or repayment for previous gifts of time to themselves. Many just enjoyed being with young people. For a number, the reasons for giving were transformed from initial concern for the good of their progeny to the welfare all the school's students. In this study, it was possible to group these responses into the desire for immediate or long-term benefits, the wish to contribute because of a duty to others, or the hope that affective relationships with adults and children could be achieved. This simple trichotomy permits some synthesis of the primary data but it invites a deeper analysis about the human impulse to give and the social effects that giving generates. To explore them in more depth, a good start is to consult Kenneth Boulding's writings on power, which he defines as "the ability to get what we want."[1]

According to Boulding (and Pitirim Sorokin before him), there are three kinds of power: destructive, productive, and integrative.[2] Use of destructive power is associated with coercion or threat behaviour and results in relationships such as master and slave.[3] Since compulsion was not mentioned in the reasons given for benevolence to schools, destructive power will not be considered further.[4] In contrast to destructive power, productive power arises out of exchange behaviour exemplified by roles such as buyer and seller. Rather than emerging from threat, productive power is contractual and involves reciprocal services; what is exchanged is what is produced. Certain elements of giving to schools are appropriately labeled as exchanges, particularly those in which returns are immanent and relatively certain, such as training for employment, useful knowledge about a school, and pleasures gained from proximity to children.[5] In contrast to destructive and productive powers, both Boulding and Sorokin assert that integrative power (or the power of love) is distinctive from the other two.

Integrative power arises out of respect or love.[6] One characteristic of love is that it is not seen as purposeful. As Sorokin says, "Each party gladly does and gives anything for the well-being of the other party. There is no bargain, no calculation of profits, pleasures, and utilities."[7] According to Boulding, a marked attribute of love is that it has the ability to generate loyalty, legitimacy, reciprocity, and identity.[8] However, he acknowledges that integrative power also has the capacity to create enemies, alienate people, and generate hatred; it can be divisive.[9] While no data in this study revealed that tendency, it seems that voluntarism may have the potential to worsen relationships across groups while it strengthens bonds within them.[10] Very simply, benevolence is neither coercive (against the will of the individual),[11] nor is it just an element of immediate exchange. Associated as it is with giving freely, voluntarism requires no direct or certain benefit. Benevolence, then, may be considered to be a form of investment in others so that the general welfare is increased and with it, the welfare of the donor.[12, 13]

As shown in Chapter 3, benevolence produced connections among all who were involved in it. Children became closer to their families, parents became more linked to other parents and to other children, and consequently all children received more "sustained attention." A learning norm was established as was a caring norm. Something of a trust relation developed between benefactor and child; it may have been symmetric or asymmetric.[14] Volunteers, apart from receiving individual benefits, also formed groups and became goodwill agents for their schools that enjoyed closer relations with their neighbourhoods. This depiction of the effects of school voluntarism suggests that giving to schools produces linkages, both of knowledge and of shared obligations. Richard Titmuss described the highly personal nature of such linkages in his study of donations of blood:

> Within all such gift transactions of a personal-face-to-face nature lies embedded some element of moral enforcement or bond. To give is to receive—to compel some return or create some obligation—either in the form of a similar or different material gift or in the overt expression of sentiment, pleasure or pain, manifested in physical acts of behaviour on the part of the recipient. No such gift can be utterly detached, disinterested or impersonal. Each carries messages and motives in its own language. (p. 210)

Social connections in the form of norms may even be born by an individual act of giving, as shown by Crenson's example of the solitary-street sweeper of Baltimore whose effort suggested that it was both possible and desirable to maintain a clean neighbourhood.[15] The inference that may be drawn for school voluntarism is that new norms are generated when people work together to pursue common goals. Clearly, voluntarism results in the establishment of "community" as defined by Robert Nisbet in this way:

> Community is the product of people working together on problems, of autonomous and collective fulfillment of internal objectives, and of the experience of living under codes of authority which have been set in large degree by the persons involved.[16]

This definition of community emphasizes its generative sense. It is a simplification, of course, from what is encountered if one takes a walk outside one's door.[17] Yet, Nisbet's definition reinforces the notion that community may be built from just the interests and resources of proximate people.[18] This generative aspect of community can be likened to the concept of social capital (the set of "social relationships which come into existence when individuals attempt to make best use of their individual resources" see Coleman, 1990, p. 300).

During the construction of community or social capital, other things happen. Loyalty is built both ways, particularly from the giver to the recipient.[19] Volunteers come to identify with the receivers of their gifts.[20] For Coleman, identification and its accompanying sympathy arise out of the common interests of the benefactor and beneficiary. The benefactor becomes an agent of the recipient.[21] Coleman explains identification by using the concept of "expanded object self." Persons give to certain others because their concept of self has been enlarged to include the recipients.[22] In this study, remarks made by the school volunteers appear to corroborate this "enlargement of self," particularly among those who showed long service. The effects of social capital were not restricted to identification of participants with schools, however. The rich networks of relations were used to produce not just sustained attention for students (another term for caring), but also the immediate delivery of physical capital (equipment and supplies for schools), provision of human capital (knowledge and skills offered by volunteers), and the development of further human capital (knowledge and skills learned by students). Social capital generated significant amounts of other kinds of capital for the benefit of children.[23] Which type of capital comes first? Evidence offered suggests that when school volunteers work together by donating physical and human capital, they develop social capital. In time, when a community has built a rich store of social capital, its capacity to contribute physical and human capital to its school is increased.

Gifts in the schools studied came mainly from individuals. Acts of voluntarism may have had an element of exchange associated with them, but they occurred most readily via expressions of love as agape and had no certain benefits to the giver. They were definitely not coercive. Their most significant outcome was an integrative effect—the generation of community or social capital in the form of norms that linked benefactors and receivers. Benevolence produced an identification of givers with recipients. The social capital generated by voluntarism resulted in turn in an increase in physical capital and human capital for schools. School benevolence affects schools directly. How do schools, as organizations, respond to voluntarism?

Organizational Action and Reconstitution

The proliferation of giving to schools and the resultant formation of community suggest that the environments that surround schools are mostly hospitable to them. Yet an examination of neighbourhoods reveals that benevolence can vary depending on the wealth that environments have to offer. One might suppose that parents in more affluent neighbourhoods have more frequent connections to schools than persons in less affluent settings. This general pattern was broken, however, by the existence of schools that were rich in physical, human, and social capital that served children in poor neighbourhoods. Certain schools in this study made persons from lower income backgrounds welcome and thus gained their benevolence. Similar conditions applied to neighbourhoods of varying ethnicities. Although barriers of language and tradition were in effect, some schools made an extra effort to encourage voluntarism among all the ethnic groups resident in their catchments. Two lesser factors were also evident, although their effects were not very clear. The first was the extent that parents were employed outside the home and the second was the school's urban, suburban, or rural location.

The neighbourhoods of public schools constitute an important source of all three forms of capital for the provision of education to students. Private physical and human capital are critical resources; social capital enables the other two forms to be supplied. If public funding is restricted (as indicated in Chapter 1), schools can either go without required resources or seek assistance beyond tax revenues. These independently generated resources can allow the schools considerable flexibility compared to schools which receive only public funding. The selected schools that sought resources from their neighbourhoods apparently recognized their dependence on environmental sources for support.

Resource-seeking behaviour on the part of organizations constitutes one of the main foci of a model of them called resource dependency. A tenet of the resource dependency model states that attention to environments is required for survival.[24] A direct consequence of the recognition of dependency is that "administrators attempt to manage their external dependencies, both to ensure the survival of the organization and to acquire, if possible, more autonomy and freedom from external constraint" (p. 193). Clearly, this is what the principals did. Note that the model accentuates the responsiveness to environmental conditions and sense of adaptation to new demands. Pfeffer projects a cycle of change that organizations follow as they engage in this kind of adaptive behaviour. It includes redistributions of power, administrative personnel changes, new actions and structures, and effects on the environment.[25, 26, 27] One of the most salient features of the resource dependency model is that

it assumes that organizational structures can be modified, and that they are subject to manipulation by participants who are attempting to improve their adaptation. The strategies we have reviewed presume the presence of decision makers who survey the situation, are confronted by alternatives as well as constraints, and select a course of action. They presume, in short, that organizational structures can be changed by *rational* [original italics] election processes. (Scott, pp. 203–4)

Very importantly, the resource dependency suggests that schools are behaving rationally as they adapt to their new environmental conditions. In effect, principals scan their neighbourhoods and undertake actions to address their resource deficiencies; hence, the school actively participates in the determination of its own fate.[28] This is a radical idea for public schools since they were established in order to be independent of their community contexts. It assumes not just that there is a degree of dependency, but that schools and communities are linked.

Richard Scott explains resource dependency by locating it within the open systems model of organizational theory. According to Scott, "The central insight emerging from the open systems model is that all organizations are incomplete: all depend on exchanges with other systems. All are open to environmental influences as a condition of their survival" (p. 179). He contrasts the open systems model to earlier models of organizations (rational and natural systems) which assumed organizations were self-contained and preoccupied with their internal affairs.[29] By comparison, the open systems model assumes that organizations are not only active participants in their contexts, they are undefinable without their surroundings. Heretical stuff. As such, organizations are neither masters nor slaves of their environments, but are inextricably connected to them. It would seem that Scott's open systems model well describes voluntary public schools whether they educated children in rich or poor neighbourhoods, in ethnically homogeneous communities or diverse ones. In that light, it is useful to examine what actions the selected schools a actually took to interact structurally to benevolence.

Voluntary public schools made special efforts to attract gifts, principally by the recruitment of volunteers. Administrators used many communication devices to invite them to schools; teachers made important efforts to overcome the reticence of prospective donors; current volunteers asked prospective benefactors to participate (failure of these efforts may be explained by the free rider idea since refusal may be very sensible from the perspective of the non-volunteer). Schools used three kinds of incentives (utilitarian, normative, and affectual) and matched them to the three kinds of individual predispositions to offer support.[30] The incentives constituted an organizational response to the need to receive commitments.[31]

Once inside the school, volunteers were screened and matched with tasks according to their interests. Benefactors were asked to conform to school rules and in some cases to be trained by teachers. Their commitment to norms was monitored and they were thanked for their work by school personnel.[32, 33] Were the benefits of benevolence worth the costs incurred in the selected schools? Principals and teachers initiated and facilitated their volunteer programs with noticeable increase in their work loads. They also affirmed that they were satisfied with the results. It is possible that they would continue to add to their volunteer programs until the marginal benefits equaled the marginal costs of too many volunteers to manage. But how were voluntary schools reconstituted to accommodate voluntarism?

Selected schools increased the amount of volunteer labour relative to paid labour. This shift occurred either because schools were unable to pay for labour or they preferred services from affine agents.[34] Teachers, who constitute the main labour component in schools, accommodated and endorsed the contributions of their volunteers, largely as a consequence of sharing common interests. To coordinate this functional shift in services and labour, voluntary public schools often contained an active structure, namely, a home and school organization. The HSO's assumed some control over both the administration of benevolence and the allocation of the resources generated from voluntarism. In this way, the selected schools appear to have resolved a central issue for organizations that depend on voluntary help:

> The strategic question facing all organizations is how to recruit participants and harness their associated roles and resources in the services goals (whether goal attainment or survival), while avoiding or minimizing the danger of becoming captive to participants' external interests or personal agendas. (Scott, p. 184)

Parents and others in the selected schools provided resources and were given a direct voice in what services were offered students. This change is an example of the shift from "global viability" (in which citizens make their general wishes known through school boards) to "reciprocal viability" (in which individuals' wishes are expressed to schools without an intermediary).[35] Resources and control were made to coincide more closely than before. The transition in viability was also given impetus in settings outside the sample schools in this study by the establishment of substantial programs, usually in large American cities, that generally encouraged the participation of volunteers. It is quite likely that the interventions were cost-effective for the schools.[36]

Schools have been conceived in different ways. Waller's accentuation of the separate interests of home and school produced his depiction of natural enemies, part of a bureaucratic model that had many features but in which hierarchy of control, specialization of labour, well-defined boundaries, and societal aims were central.[37] The antithesis to the bureaucratic model is the communitarian model of schools that emphasizes a common ethos, generalization of labour, caring, and family goals.[38] The overlapping spheres model of schools is a compromise, a synthesis of the two. This model balances what are believed to be the strengths of the bureaucratic with the virtues of the communitarian.[39] Voluntary public schools fit nicely under the rubric of overlapping spheres.[40] It is worthwhile to probe where the overlapping spheres model for schools may be located within the more general perspective of organizational theory. Ronald Corwin offers his mutual adaptation framework for organizations which emphasizes environmental relationships over internal properties. He suggests that

> organizations can be best understood as components of a larger context. . . .
> [They have a] fundamental relationship with the environment. . . . An organization is a coordinated collectivity which is comprised of autonomous units, each with an adaptive structure, multiple normative systems, and permeable boundaries.[41]

Corwin's framework and definition incorporate previous discussions in this book on organizational subparts (administrators, teachers, etc.), environmental adaptations (pursuit and accommodation of volunteers), normative systems (among volunteers, students, and teachers), and very permeable boundaries (the participation of volunteers in organizational life).[42] After examining an extensive number of rival organizational metaphors and many ways that organizations develop ties to their environments, he asserts that

> Organizations are not merely impersonal, adaptive organisms. They have been deliberately created and they can be adapted. Once in motion, organizations can influence their environments and control the way in which their structures become adapted.[43]

Unlike the definitions of bureaucratic or communal schools, this definition is distinctive because it suggests that schools (and indeed, all organizations) are subject to rational control by persons and furthermore, it posits that schools adapt and affect their environments via mutual accommodation. Optimism wins this round![44]

So, voluntary public schools in this study deliberately altered their structures to incorporate benevolence.[45] Neither strictly bureaucratic nor communal, they fit within the model of overlapping spheres. They are also compatible with the large-scale mutual adaptation framework of organizations. The schools viewed themselves as largely integral to their community environments. What characteristics of those environments did they have to address?

Two Social Galaxies

All of social space may be divided into two parts. One of the earliest thinkers who wrote about this bifurcation was Ferdinand Tonnies, a German author who observed that there were two basic forms of human association. He labeled the first one "Gemeinschaft." It is close to the concept of community in that it exists in nonutilitarian relationships. It refers to bonds such as those formed within families and friendships which exist as "ends in themselves."[46] Actions within this realm are governed by love, understanding, and custom, directed by what Tonnies called the "natural will."[47] In contrast, there is "Gesellschaft." This term is ascribed to calculated relationships. All things, including people, are viewed as means to ends, hence, contracts are based upon results alone. The roles most closely associated with Gesellschaft are those of businessmen or politicians who appear to care little for the people with whom they deal. Actions in this realm are guided by measures of wealth or power based on the "rational will."[48] Tonnies' elegant statement of what I call the two social galaxies remains the conceptual basis of more current thought.[49]

The distinction between Gemeinschaft and Gesellschaft closely resembles the difference between primary and secondary groups.[50] Eugene Litwak and Ivan Szelenyi emphasize the tasks performed within primary groups, which are face-to-face, permanent (ascribed), affective structures. They consider secondary groups to be wholly instrumental. For instance, the nuclear family undertakes tasks that require few adults while extended kin help with commitments that are long-term but not usually face-to-face. Friends provide close bonds with long-term involvement, while neighbours do everyday jobs such as aid in the socialization of the young. Litwak and Szelenyi insist that these primary group roles are neither interchangeable nor can secondary groups substitute for them.[51, 52]

While Litwak and Szelenyi describe the two social galaxies, the most compelling depiction and exposition of them may be Coleman's. He sees the construction of primordial institutions (families, clans, communities, and religious organizations) as based on simple relations between two persons at a time, such as father and son or king and vassal. These relationships are self-sustaining and extend like building blocks to larger structures. Community thus grows from principal relations between persons and forms a natural social environment.[53] In contrast, modern corporate actors (such as businesses, governments, and schools) are not self-sustaining but dependent upon third parties (e.g., the roles of customer, server, and owner of a business). Unlike simple relations, these complex relations do not require binary personal obligations and expectations as mechanisms for social success. Rather, they invoke complicated manoeuvres to attain the satisfaction of all three parties and thus, the continuation of complex relations is much more involved than simple ones.[54] Modern corporate actors provide a social environment analogous to the constructed physical environment in which human beings live.[55]

Elements of school voluntarism may be seen in light of Coleman's understanding of the two social galaxies and how they function. Using his nomenclature, much of voluntarism emanates from primordial institutions such as families. The relations are mostly simple and exist between volunteer and student or benefactor and teacher. Roles are diffuse rather than strictly delineated. Givers identify with schools. Schools become somewhat familial. Students receive a measure of care. To some degree, community is constructed as persons work together on common aims. But voluntarism also takes place with a modern corporate actor, the school, which is based on complex relations. The school takes actions to encourage benevolence; it also reconstitutes its structures by sharing control so that it augments its resource flows. The school is further embedded in a network of other modern corporate actors that affect its behaviour. Both primordial institutions and corporate actors are rationally constructed social structures, that is, they are human inventions based on norms and knowledge. They can work together toward mutual interests. As described, the alliance between the primordial and modern corporate actors sounds quite harmonious and positive for communities and schools, but that is not the relationship advanced by the foregoing writers.

The thinkers who have analyzed the two social galaxies have stressed two themes. One is that there is extreme tension between these two realms of social interaction. The authors speak of antithetical conditions, allegiance to the two worlds, and their outright incompatibility. This conflict stems largely from the divergent functions they perform.[56] Individuals often find themselves adrift between the two galaxies, their lives pulled to both at once. The other theme is that there has been a unidirectional shift over the last 500 years from the dominance of primordial institutions to the near-supremacy of modern corporate actors today, although the authors note that aspects of primary groups or primordial institutions persist.[57] For example, Hewitt remarks that

> modern society has disrupted, transformed, and in many cases simply destroyed the organic communities of the past, but it has not eliminated those human tendencies that were satisfied within those communities. Organic communities provided places where traditional activities could be rewarded, where diffuse obligations could flourish, where a stable set of affective ties could develop between people who were linked to one another as whole, concrete, and particular persons and not only as social roles. Such organic communities are inherently difficult to sustain in the modern world, and in important respects they have simply vanished, but the human propensity to construct and to live in a world of concrete particularity, of contact with whole persons and not simply with roles, endures. It is a fundamental part of our being—not something that culture or society may capriciously discard. (pp. 119–120)

This quotation offers some hope that communities will not be completely overtaken by "modern society." But Coleman is less optimistic. He believes the functions of primordial structures are unraveling as their tasks are taken over by modern corporate actors.[58] The evidence he cites includes the removal of parents from the home and the reduction of family time together, indicating a loss of social capital as children are isolated from their families. Modern corporate actors, such as schools, substitute for the care given to children, but their concerns are only for part of the child, not for the whole child. Coleman notes that the shift from primordial to corporate structures involves an change in incentives as well:

> primordial social organization [generate] the incentive structure that brings into being actions on behalf of another, norms, trustworthiness, and other components of social capital. The constructed social organization purposively created by governments and other modern corporate actors undermines that existing incentive structure (by encouraging free riding) and does not generate a comparable replacement. . . . Incentives (for example, the incentive to care for particular others) are supplied through extrinsic means, ordinarily a wage payment for professional services (for example, those of a teacher, nurse, or day-care attendant). The knowledge of how to use these extrinsic rewards to bring about interest in, attention to, and care for others is weak. (Coleman, 1990, pp. 653–4)

He maintains that the interests of children may be better served by primordial institutions than by modern corporate actors because of their different incentive structures. When the social space of children is dominated by modern corporate actors, a consequence is the depletion of social capital for children, who, like "poor little rich kids," may be wealthy in physical or human capital, but destitute in sustaining relationships. Who claims responsibility for the social welfare of the child?[59]

School voluntarism stands as an important exception to the well-asserted conflict between the two social galaxies of societies. One selected school, Sawmill School, serves as an example of the substantial integration between primordial and modern corporate institutions. Sawmill school enrolled 84 children in kindergarten to grade seven with five teachers. It is located in a small, rural community that has modest, well-maintained homes and a sense of isolation although it is within 15 minutes travel of a larger town and less than an hour and a half of a small city of one quarter million people. At Sawmill, there were eight to ten regular volunteers and 45 other benefactors. Some brought toddlers with them. Others were grandparents and uncles. Benefactors made a quilt with the help of students and teachers. It was raffled for $700. Two more quilting bees were planned. Donations from teachers and others were converted into coinage for a money tree that was raffled for $500. Pancakes were served on Winnie-the-Pooh's birthday. At Christmas, poinsettias were sold, wreaths made, children given stockings and a turkey dinner was provided for all students at lunch time. Benevolence thrived in other ways. Older students phoned the homes of absentees in the safe arrival program and Community Night saw the school kilns opened to pensioners and others. The reaction of the students was seen to be very positive. They became accustomed to the presence of their parents. A volunteer recalled her son's request, "Stop in at recess and say 'Hi,' Mom!" She observed that "they notice when you're not there" (db87). Much of this social capital was crafted deliberately by the principal. He established the parent's advisory council and initiated an open door policy in which parents were welcome to come to the school at any time. This change (from a previous understanding that parents were not welcome) was designed to give community members a sense of ownership and make the school "a place where the kids want to go" (principal, db92).[60] Linkages with the rest of the community were also a priority of the principal. All teachers lived in the small town. The principal chaired the local recreation association which held summer and winter programs for adults and school-aged students, and was active in bowling, curling, hockey, softball, and the summer swim regatta. When discussing the role of school personnel, he claimed, "You're one with the community" and described the school-town closeness as "familial" (db92). However, it is important to remember that while Sawmill School built its bridge and promoted integration with its community, it maintained its status as a modern corporate actor. Sawmill School taught a provincial curriculum, was constrained by union contracts, and was financed by provincial dollars. Considerable control remained at the school board and district offices where many decisions about school staffing and equipment were retained.

Unlike the pattern in general society that indicates the near-supremacy of modern corporate actors, voluntarism provides the school with an interinstitutional bridge between primordial structures and the large corporate actors. School voluntarism in particular can foster a remarkably cooperative relationship between the family and community on the one hand and school on the other. Rather than increasing the segmentation of children's lives, benevolence augments the social capital available to children by multiplying the time they spend with members of their communities. *The child is claimed.* Unlike many public schools, voluntary schools may have succeeded in reversing a social trend evident for several centuries, at least temporarily. As one volunteer said,

> [Benevolence] makes the school more open. It makes new parents feel more comfortable. Having parent volunteers in the school gives parents, who can not come to help, a sense of security because they know that there are familiar parents present to help with their children. By including members from the local community hall (who no longer have children attending the school) in special school events, there is a bridge between the school and the community. (sp91)

The "intergalactic bridge" is not a one-way link between the hearth and the outside world.[61] It is not used to describe the public school's role as a catapult from private life within Gemeinschaft and primary groups to the public business of Gesellschaft or secondary groups. Rather, the bridge is a *pathway* crossed and recrossed by many persons in both the school and community. Naturally, the supports of the bridge are the benevolence of the hearth and the response of the school.[62] It is even possible to consider voluntarism as exercised in public schools as a new microsocial institution. Neither strictly ancient nor quintessentially modern, this bridging institution may be the harbinger of social inventions to come as conceptions of the two social galaxies are transcended.[63]

This outcome of harmony between the two social galaxies may be reassuring but it still does not explain fundamentally why voluntarism comes into being. Why do people give and why do schools respond? Some of the most basic reasons for giving and responding are contemplated in Chapter 8.

Notes

1. See Boulding (1989, p. 17).

2. See Sorokin (1954, p. 76) and Boulding (1989, pp. 24–25).

3. Boulding notes that gifts such as tribute can be given through fear (1989, p. vi).

4. Even in cases in which persons offered reasons associated with conformity to norms of duty or repayment, there was no indication that they felt compelled to act against their wills. Unlike the decision to pay school taxes, the choice to give was not made under any conditions of threat. The compulsion in the case of school taxes comes ultimately with the seizure and sale of property for claims.

5. Boulding admits to an "integrative factor" in exchange behaviour (p. 28). Sorokin does not. He considers exchange to be impersonal, as shown by his example of the free prostitute and customer (p. 76).

6. The two authors disagree on the nature of this love. Boulding's idea of love is close to agape (love of humanity), while Sorokin's is nearer to romantic love or devotion (as in husband and wife, close friendship, or mother and child). See Boulding (1989, p. 25) and Sorokin (1954 p. 77).

7. See Sorokin (1954, p. 76). Note that lack of purpose is contrary to the idea that people are rational beings.

8. These words are similar to many of the effects of voluntarism, such as the creation of affine agents and the construction of norms.

9. See Boulding (1989, p. 25).

10. Sorokin does not admit to any divisive effects of love. His book is very much in the style of a grand theorist, being more synthetic than analytic, more inclusive than focused, and morally assertive. Boulding's work, in contrast, is concerned mostly with giving from the point of view of "an economist gone soft." While his generalizations are rather extensive and his personal values most evi-

dent, Boulding is largely preoccupied with the effects of integrative power through grants and the need for the world to appreciate them.

11. See Sciulli (p. 774), for an analysis of the meanings of voluntaristic action.

12. The notion of investment is supported by Wuthnow's work on compassion, in which he acknowledges gifts as an investment of time and energy. See Wuthnow (p. 90) and Boulding (1989, p. 115). Boulding suggests that the amount of giving by one person is governed by the theory of utility maximization in which the marginal utility to the recipient is balanced against the marginal cost to the giver (1981, p. 5).

13. Note that the concepts of investment and marginal utility make giving a purposeful act, contrary to Sorokin's view.

14. A symmetric trust relation entails reciprocity to the benefactor; an asymmetric one implies a later obligation to repay the gift to another person. Thus, the longer the time before repayment, the more likely that the trust would be asymmetric.

15. She said, "'In the beginning, I swept both sides of the street on the block all by myself. Depending on the way I felt, some days, I would work my way down to Ducatel Street (two blocks away). I was trying to get a message across—to show people what was possible." See Crenson (pp. 202–03).

16. See Nisbet (p. xv). Note that his definition is not restricted to conditions of voluntarism.

17. As Getzels notes, community may be conceived in a relatively complex way: "One is no longer an integral part of a single, all-encompassing community—of *the* community, but a member of communities—of communities within communities. . . . One may think of communities as groups of people conscious of a collective identity characterized by common cognitive and affective norms and values, and may order the variety of communities from those where the collective identity is most dependent upon a particular geographical locality to those where it is least dependent, although of course such ordering is approximate and the categories will overlap. Thus, one may be a member simultaneously of a local community (e.g., a particular neighborhood), an administrative community (e.g., a particular school district), an instrumental community (e.g., a particular professional group), an ethnic community (e.g., a particular national or racial group), an ideological community (e.g., a particular religious or sociopolitical group stretching beyond the local, administrative, instrumental, or ethnic communities)." (p. 117).

18. Boulding, by contrast, shows that giving can transcend community as in his reference to an intergenerational grants economy in which parents support children who repay their parents (or others) at a later time. His example is one in which the caring norm operates on a large scale. See Boulding (1989, pp. 119–120).

19. See Coleman (1990, pp. 108–111).

20. Boulding calls this phenomenon "conversion," (1989, p. 31), and Hewitt suggests that identification with a community helps to locate the person within the larger society (p. 129).

21. See Coleman (1990, p. 158).

22. See Coleman (1990, p. 518).

23. See Chapter 3.

24. See Pfeffer (p. 192).

25. See Pfeffer (p. 203).

26. Data from this study support these predictions, particularly with regard to principal behaviour and the development of home-school organizations.

27. The resource dependency approach also fits well with Wayne Hoy and Cecil Miskel's model that shows different levels of environmental complexity and environmental change. When the complexity is high and the change unstable, extensive integration with the environment is in order. See Hoy and Miskel (pp. 69–71). Another related perspective is organizational learning as advanced by Argyris and Shon and also by Levitt and March. Inspired by work on learning by individuals, organizational learning focuses both on how the internal workings and environments contribute to their growth. While adaptive behaviour is a component of learning, there is little emphasis on resources or conflict. For a review of organizational learning see Cousins. The need for schools to collaborate with their environments may be growing. See Young and Levin, p. 203).

28. See Scott (p. 115).

29. See Scott (pp. 21–22).

30. See Knoke and Wright-Isak (pp. 231–234). Note that utilitarian incentives promise a return in the near future. According to Knoke and Wright-Isak, the incentives are derived from the predispositions.

31. See Knoke and Wright-Isak (p. 231). Although their examples are voluntary associations and not public schools, they hypothesize that the amount of resources received is proportional to the extent of the incentives and the longevity of the organization is believed to be enhanced by the use of all three incentives rather than just one (Knoke and Wright-Isak (pp. 242 and 245). They acknowledge that their conceptual scheme considers organizations as open systems (p. 4). The topic of incentives is also a major concern of Olson, whose book is a landmark on voluntary organizations, particularly lobby groups. Although he made a persuasive case for the centrality of utilitarian incentives, he excused small groups (such as volunteers in a single school) from his analysis (pp. 1–2).

32. Why were principals and administrators able to gain the volunteers' acceptance of school and classroom norms? Recall that the benefactors' interests were the same as the school's—the educational and social welfare of the students. The volunteer was acting as an affine agent for the school. Consequently, most of the norms (most of the time) were considered to be legitimate. Norms are the social analogue of individual purpose. See Coleman (1990, p. 287 and p. 292). They formed the basis of an authority relation between the school personnel and the volunteers in which the volunteers surrendered control of their labours for a period of time. Note that the norms of conduct in the school were not the same as the norms generated among the volunteers and the students (the norm of learning and the norm of caring). Under affine conditions, the need to impose sanctions is rare and so the norms are effective. See Coleman (1990, p. 266). This agreement did not take place when persons who were invited did not volunteer their services. They may be considered free riders because others contributed when they benefited in part.

33. A few volunteers became zealots who devoted a great amount of time to school affairs. Their zeal is explainable by the kinds of positive rewards they re-

ceived for working toward common goals. The cost of their efforts was smaller than the combination of satisfaction of their own and the schools' goals. See Coleman (1990, p. 274). Coleman's prediction is that such zeal will more likely occur when the social network is more closed, that is to say, high in social capital (1990, p. 278).

34. Coleman (1990, p. 161).

35. See Coleman (1990, pp. 426–435 and 442–450) on optimizing organizations' internal structures and the changing concept of the corporation.

36. Financial costs and benefits were considered on their own since the production of social capital was not a part of the calculation of outcomes.

37. See Bidwell (pp. 992–1008).

38. See Bryk and Driscoll (p. 184).

39. See Epstein (1990, pp. 102–104).

40. Voluntary public schools also share a kinship with some organizations outside of education, particularly nonprofit organizations. Some authors support a compromise position between public and private organizations. Galaskiewitz focuses on the idea of a grants economy based on donations that result in hybrid organizations that produces collective goods as governments do but distribute services as a result of voluntary decisions (p. 210). Weisbrod considers nonprofit organizations to exist because neither governments nor the marketplace can provide all desired services. He suggests that nonprofits have the advantages of greater flexibility than governments and greater trust than private enterprises. Naturally, nonprofits depend on either voluntarism or exchange for their survival (pp. 18–45).

41. Corwin (p. 6).

42. There is no intention to discuss Corwin's categorizations here. It is sufficient to state that his substantial review of organizational theory has led him to a framework that is largely compatible with the description of a voluntary public school in this monograph. For more thoughts on coordinated activities, adaptive structures, permeable boundaries, normative systems, and goals, See Corwin (pp. 6–21).

43. Corwin (p. 21).

44. See Corwin (pp. 135–137).

45. See Guthrie for an historical account of management changes in education. He suggests that structures of management build on each other; they are evolutionary (p. 226).

46. Tonnies believed that the peasant's calling typified Gemeinshaft since most elements of his world, even his livestock, were not merely the means to a living (p. xvii).

47. He associated with women and young people as well as village life and holy orders. See Tonnies (pp. 22–23, 223 and 270.

48. Tonnies associated this with men, old people and particularly economic or scientific man in city life. See Tonnies (pp. xviii and 271).

49. See Fischer on the impact of urban and rural environments on personal networks.

50. Their definition is based on the works of Cooley and Worth.

51. See Litwak and Szelenyi (p. 471). Uneasiness with the roles of secondary groups is also articulated by Robert Nisbet who associates their ascendancy with

alienation in which individuals are not part of a social order. He says that alienation is from important anchors in the life of individuals. It is from the past, from one's social identity, from physical place and property, and from the community. He associates the centralization of power away from primary groups with individualism (pp. viii to x).

52. The contrast between community and individualism is a rather similar discussion as that between community and society. See Bellah, et al, who call for a return to community. Both comparisons are addressed in the work of John Hewitt, who suggests that human beings are drawn to each of communal and individual pursuits. On the one hand, personal identity is defined in relation to the self and a societal mode of participation. It stems from modernity which is based on role relations that are specific rather than diffuse (pp. 115, 118 and 170). On the other hand, social identity, grounded on diffuse role relations, links a person to a community, perhaps best exemplified by the family, which is ". . . a social unit that gives us a paradigm for experience, for our whole approach to social life."(p. 120). Also see Hewitt on families (pp. 169–170). Furman and Merz provide a review of the relation between the Gemeinschaft / Gesellschaft conflict and educational reform.

53. See Coleman (1990, pp. 43 and 546).

54. Coleman uses the term "actors" to denote both persons and modern organizations but they are not acting in the thespian sense. Both are conceived as purposive and entirely real.

55. See Coleman (1990, p. 610).

56. See Tonnies (p. 272), Litwak and Szelenyi (p. 465), and Nisbet (p. 280).

57. See especially Tonnies (p. 272) and Litwak and Szelenyi (p 465).

58. See Coleman (1990, p. 585).

59. See Coleman (1990, pp. 597–609).

60. Two parent volunteers spoke highly of the open door policy. Not only did they feel most welcome as volunteers, but they were encouraged to be in the school and enter classrooms. They perceived teachers to be very supportive of their presence and contrasted their experience in the Sawmill School with the chilly climate of previous schools.

61. See Bryk, Lee and Holland and also Furman and Merz.

62. See again the definitions of voluntarism and the voluntary public school in Chapter 2.

63. See Coleman's remark that the modern corporate actor may not be the ultimate form of social invention (1990, p. 552). Also note his call for new institutions that are proximate to natural persons and assume some of the responsibilities currently accepted by the state (1990, pp. 657–8).

8

Some Theories of Voluntarism

The human propensity to give to others has intrigued people for some time. Why do we do it? Do we, like lesser animals, have a genetic disposition? What causes them to help each other? Does their behaviour offer some insights into our own? Perhaps people have an inclination to donate their time because they are fundamentally selfish; they are hoping for a reward when they engage in apparently altruistic acts. "To give is to receive." Perhaps not. Humans have been known to give when there is no prospect of return in their lives. Does the existence of altruism indicate that people are actually irrational? Are they slaves to the norms that govern their behaviours? What general explanations of all human behaviour (and therefore giving) are available? After some tentative answers are provided, the general development of benevolence and its response is sketched.

Sociobiology and Helping

There are many examples of altruism in the animal kingdom. Although giving among animals could be defined to include the care of young by their parents, it usually focuses on services provided by nonparents or helpers in what are called cooperative breeding systems.[1] For instance, members of jackal groups feed the young and nursing females, guard the pups, groom them and teach them to hunt. White-fronted bee-eaters have helpers who attach themselves to a single nest, excavate it, defend it, feed the female, incubate the eggs, and serve and care for the fledglings. Breeders and helpers exchange roles during their lifetimes.[2] Does altruism exist among other life forms? This question has been pursued in the studies of ants undertaken and compiled by Bert Hölldobler and Edward Wilson, who provide more examples.[3] They note that ants have a group of nonreproductive workers who serve as builders, foragers, and defenders for the colony. For instance, the Idaho Harvester foragers embark on long and dangerous searches in which they face drowning and have a short life expectancy. Another type of ant engages in the suicidal defense observed in honey bees. When the guards are provoked, they burst their insides and release a sticky substance to trap attackers.[4] Suicidal defense introduces an important idea: benevolence requires some sacrifice, if not of life, then certainly of time.[5] So animals, birds, and insects demonstrate altruism. But why do they?

Whatever explanations are advanced, sociobiologists require them to fit within the general framework of the theory of evolution. One set of assumptions is called *reciprocity*, in which acts of giving among nonrelatives are returned at some future date.[6] The fitness of the reciprocal altruists is enhanced. Unfortunately for this explanation, not all giving (which is offered at some cost) is returned.[7] Another set of reasons rotates around the kinship of helpers and receivers. *Kin selection* goes some distance to explain why relatives help, particularly in the rearing of the young.[8] Self-sacrifice may be the best way to preserve one's genes. Observing kin selection among ants, Hölldobler and Wilson suggest that "[b]y reducing personal survival and reproduction, workers nevertheless increase the survival and reproduction of genes they share with other members of the colony by common descent. Individuals suffer, but the colony flourishes and so do the genes (including the altruistic genes)" (p. 180).[9] This explanation becomes the most plausible when the family is the unit of selection, as was suggested by Darwin. So ultimately, the genes are selfish even when the behaviour is not because the fitness of the family is increased. Wilson muses about kin selection in human families:

> Do the emotions we feel, which in exceptional individuals may climax in total self-sacrifice, stem ultimately from hereditary units that were implanted by the favoring of relatives during a period of hundreds or thousands of generations? This explanation gains some strength from the circumstance that during most of mankind's history the predominant social unit was the immediate family and a tight network of other close relatives. Such exceptional cohesion, combined with detailed kin classifications made possible by high intelligence, might explain why kin selection has been more forceful in human beings than in monkeys and other mammals. (Wilson, 1978:153)

This explanation suggests that any volunteers, and most particularly school volunteers who are engaged in work with the young, are following their primeval inclinations to help their genetic kin.[10] In doing so, they offer assistance to all those within their social unit, e.g., their community. The weaker explanation, that of reciprocity, may also be relevant. It indicates that people may help each other in the way that animals do with the prospect that assistance will be returned at some future date.

These explanations of altruism have encountered some skepticism within the general nature-nurture controversy. Perhaps biological factors

are feeble compared to the cultural influences that account for human behaviour.[11] For example, reciprocal altruism has been attacked because it is
just too easy to be a free rider.[12] The explanation of selection fares worse.
Barry Schwartz suggests that because people are rational and therefore not
bound by biology, kinship is social rather than biological. Humans make
choices in ways that animals do not.[13] Alfie Kohn, a psychologist, agrees.
He observes that we help others that are unrelated to us and we help
strangers without expecting help in return.[14] His conclusion is that sociobiological explanations are entirely deterministic; they just do not stand up:
"most of what is human and prosocial does not seem to fit into either inclusive fitness [related to kin selection] or reciprocity theory, and it cannot
be made to fit even if we sit on the suitcase and tie it up with rope" (Kohn,
1990:217). Schwartz concurs when he says that there is no inflexible link
between behaviour and genes in humans.[15] The critics insist that Homo De-
terminus died in the prison cell of his genes. Critics of sociobiology see volunteers are not just busy bees or sacrificial ants or willing horses pro-
grammed by their genetic codes but as social beings that want to be
benevolent. It would be premature to dismiss the work of the sociobiologists entirely, however. Quite possibly, school volunteers who sacrifice
their time to work with children are responding to some instinctive direc-
tive to help. Future studies may illuminate further links into the relations
between altruistic behaviour in humans and other life forms.

Egoism and Altruism

If sociobiological explanations are not sufficient to explain voluntarism, it
may be useful to explore benefactors' motivations. Do they give primarily out of egoism or altruism? Obviously people give to others with little
prospect of reward.[16] Although giving can be infectious, the answer does
not rest with the rewards of giving. Kohn observes that some persons
misinterpret the rewards of giving anyway. He suggests that, if we give
to our own work, then intrinsic interest in the task takes precedence over
money received.[17] If we give to others and we are rewarded, then

> we tend to assume the reward, and not altruism[i.e., intrinsic interest in giv-
> ing], accounts for our having acted as we did. If we do not see ourselves as
> altruistic, we are less likely to act prosocially once the extrinsic reward for
> acting that way is withdrawn. . . . Conversely, encouragement to think of
> oneself as a generous person—an appeal not to self-interest but to genuine
> altruism—seems to be the most reliable way to promote helping and caring
> over the long haul and in different situations. (Kohn, p. 203)[18]

The possibility that altruism may not be rewarded suggests that neither
benevolence nor malice have any basis in rationality since both would

seem to require a purpose based upon self-interest.[19] This logic has a certain attractiveness because altruism has no apparent goal.[20] Since it is not undertaken to benefit the actor, it does not depend upon the means-ends linkage that is integral to rational behaviour.[21] If the assumption of rationality is made, then people do act rationally in the interests of others.[22] Persons may pursue the benefit of a group just as rationally as their self-interests. For instance, they maintain friendships or trust relations.

Altruism is clearly conceived not as a state in itself but as the absence of egoism, e.g., behaviour based on calculating self interest. Kohn points out that the axiom of egoism (self-interest as the sole reason for action) is the prime assumption underlying neoclassical economics, exchange theory in sociology, and public choice and game theories in political science.[23] They cannot stand without it. Consequently, altruism is ignored in these fields of study and egoism is assumed.[24] Homo Avarus (the greedy) is king.[25] Economists in particular are forced to assume that benevolence always produces some kind of extrinsic personal payoff:

> when pleasure does result from generosity, it need not have been—indeed, probably was not—the point of the act. But egoists are unable to show that pleasure always *does* result; they cannot make sense of prosocial actions that bring no apparent satisfaction to the actor—unless, of course, they fall back on the question-begging assertion that some sort of satisfaction *must* have been present or the action would not have taken place. [original italics] (Kohn, p. 210)

Here is relatively complete description of the villain, Homo Economicus:[26] He can always express his preferences (say what he wants). He always desires more of what he wants, prefers lower prices to higher, has stable preferences which are transitive,[27] consumes more goods or services until the rule of diminishing marginal utility kicks in, acts on the basis of complete information and is completely rational. A rather calculating character! Although this model provided by Barry Schwartz may be useful, there are many aspects of human behaviour that do not fit this idealization very well. People cannot always express their preferences. Sometimes, they desire expensive items over cheap ones. Often, they lack complete information with which to make choices so they "satisfice" rather than maximize their utilities.[28]

Perhaps egoism, with its reliance on rationality, may have come to be an unsuited explanation for all human behaviour and thus has crowded out altruism, which may be misconstrued as unreal or very rare.[29] The idea of crowding is intriguing; it is possible that people are naturally altruistic and unnaturally self-interested, much like saints. This thought is expressed by Collard, who says "it is not that selfish men sometimes appear to behave unselfishly, but that unselfish men sometimes appear to behave selfishly" (Collard, p. 112, also quoted in Kohn, p. 238). If altruism is assumed, then explanations based on self-interest are useful but quite incomplete—they cannot explain the spectrum of human behaviour.[30] Anthony Downs suggests that

> [I]n reality, men are not always selfish, even in politics. They frequently do what appears to be individually irrational because they believe it is socially rational—i.e., it benefits others even though it harms them personally. . . . In every field, no account of human behavior is complete without mention of such altruism; its possessors are among the heroes men rightly admire (Downs, p. 29, also quoted in Mansbridge, p. 90).[31]

From this overview, it is easy to conclude that Homo Economicus is a failure, a self-consumed, ultrarational, pathetic individual with limited usefulness for understanding the behaviour of the rest of us.

Altruism exists and is a frequently encountered interpretation for giving; it is not exceptional. It does not require a guaranteed reward for the giver. Altruism may be rational in the long term, particularly if rationality is not seen as serving solely self-interest. Rationality may serve other-interest as well. Sociobiology and classical microeconomics both depend on strict self-interest to explain human behaviour and thus they attempt to explain altruism using self-interest. Thus far, their explanations fall short. Either egoism and altruism may serve as the basis for voluntarism, but when are the reasons for benevolence based on self-interest and when are they altruistic? A more complete understanding of benevolence requires an answer. The next section demonstrates some ways in which this problem has been tackled.

Normative Action and Benevolence

This section considers some attempts to explain altruism and benevolence as well. It is important to note that they are not explained using the same grounds. Altruism has been defined as concern for others without reference to reward, while benevolence, as encountered in this study of school voluntarism, is associated with three predispositions to give (rational choice, normative conformity, and affective bonding). After hacking up Homo Economus, Kohn proposes four categories of reasons for giving. Self-gain is the first, in which direct benefits occur to the giver. A softer version of self-gain is the second category in which an individual giver achieves the avoidance of guilt or relief of vicarious distress. The third is unselfish aid simply to help someone else. And a fourth is prosocial action that is empathic in which the giver identifies strongly with the receiver. Prosocial action is "neither egoistic nor altruistic. It is a function of the relationship itself" (Kohn, p. 246).[32] In his typology, it is clear that the pair of reasons for giving (versions of self gain) can be understood as grounded in self-interest (ego-ism). The second pair of reasons is social. Unfortunately, Kohn does not say why these four categories exist and so his typology of giving remains un-substantiated. However, his categories of giving intersect with ones from work on compassion based on case studies and surveys.[33]

Although compassion differs from voluntarism in that it suggests not just caring but some sacrifice on the part of the benefactor and suffering on the part of the recipient,[34] the possible reasons for compassionate giv-ing are very similar to ones suggested for altruism. Wuthnow's gently-stated argument is essentially this: persons who engage in compassion-ate acts accept an old expression, "What goes around, comes around."[35] Eventual repayment of kindness is a clear possibility; people are depen-dent upon one another. Wuthnow acknowledges the objections to his po-sition, such as the lack of close connections among people, the existence of free riders, and the absence of exact calculation. However, he counters that compassion need not depend upon equivalent value (as in ex-change), that it permits connections outside of intimate circles, and that it helps to construct group identity.[36] Yet, he observes, "We do not have to reap the rewards personally to know that we are all better off" (Wuth-now, p. 300). It is likely that compassion can bridge barriers of ethnicity and social status, perhaps because "compassion symbolizes . . . a com-mitment to those who may not be able to reciprocate, an acknowledge-ment of our essential identities as human beings, and a devotion to the value of caring itself" (Wuthnow, p. 301).[37] Although his research is more descriptive than theoretical, Wuthnow shows how participants in com-passion account for their giving behaviour. While self-interest plays some part, his respondents reflected a wider view of common welfare in which their individual futures were embedded. He states:

> it appears that individualism does not necessarily contradict holding altru-istic values and engaging in a wide variety of caring and community-service activity. . . . The most compassionate in our midst, it appears, have not be-come caring individuals by giving up their individualism. . . . those who be-lieve most intensely in the importance of pursuing their own self-interest in these ways seem not to be any less oriented toward caring for others than those who attach less importance to their self-interest. (p. 23)

Wuthnow's incorporation of self-interest into acts of compassion for oth-ers is supported by Titmuss' study of blood donation to anonymous re-ceivers. His interpretation is:

> social gifts and actions that carry no explicit or implicit individual right to a return gift or actions are forms of "creative altruism" (in Sorokin's words). They are creative in the sense that the self is realized with the help of anony-

mous others; they allow the biological need to help to express itself. Manifestations of altruism in this sense may of course be thought of as self-love. But they may also be thought of as giving life, or prolonging life or enriching life for anonymous others. (Titmuss, p. 212)

Titmuss, Wuthnow, and Kohn thus posit quite similar orientations regarding acts of benevolence. they do not exclude self-interest entirely as a motivating factor and they all acknowledge that "pure" altruism exists since even the love of strangers may be returned some day.[38]

A similar approach to understanding why people give is the trichotomy offered by Knoke and Wright-Isak. It was used to order the categories of reasons for voluntarism as articulated by school volunteers and others who observed them.[39] The three-part division included rational choice (the egoist position), normative conformity (close to altruism), and affective bonding (which may be defined as pleasure and is therefore egoistic, yet it is entirely social).[40] Like Kohn and Schwartz, Knoke and Wright-Isak are willing to criticize rational choice.[41] Unfortunately, they do not offer any corresponding critiques of normative conformity or affective bonding. They conclude that no single kind of predisposition is sufficient to understand support of voluntary organizations. Knoke and Wright-Isak provide no fundamental basis for their trichotomy except to point out its well-established historical roots. That omission is also evident with Kohn's categories of altruism and with Wuthnow's partial explanation of compassion.

The debate on egoism and altruism may be intriguing but not really illuminating. Self-interest, which is damned by Kohn, Schwartz, and others, is acknowledged as an important part of benevolence by Wuthnow and Titmuss. Knoke and Wright-Isak incorporate both dimensions and add one more. Can everyone be right? Ample description and cases abound but what is needed is a good theory of voluntarism. Is there a theorist in the house?

For more progress to be made, it may be necessary to look beyond the discussion of voluntarism thus far and contemplate all social behaviour in order to provide an adequate explanation for benevolence.[42] One field of study that address social action broadly overlaps sociology and economics. A prominent writer in the domain of "socio-economics" is Amatai Etzioni, who has undertaken extensive work in order to build an encompassing theory of social behaviour that transcends the boundaries of the two disciplines. He addresses the problem of the limitations of economic man as discussed in the previous section and then adds one important criticism. Etzioni states that rationality in people is unnatural because acting rationally requires considerable effort, including the search for effective means to achieve goals, and the development and maintenance of resources to undertake the search.[43] The implication is that it is easier for most of us to act irrationally than rationally. Etzioni offers examples of irrational actions such as care for others, return of lost cash, responses in distress, civility, and cooperation without pay.[44] He groups the irrational bases of social behaviour and calls them normative-affective factors, thus losing the distinction of the two categories made by previous authors. For him, they are compelling predispositions for behaviour, since

> *normative-affective factors shape to a significant extent the information that is gathered, the ways it is processed, the inferences that are drawn, the options that are being considered, and the options that are finally chosen.* (original italics, Etzioni, 1988, p. 94)

The normative-affective factors are seen to interrupt logical-empirical (rational) factors.[45] In fact, he claims that logical-empirical choices are only allowed by normative-affective factors and most decisions made by people are effected on normative-affective grounds. Personal values enter into decisions and in some instances, logical-empirical criteria become unthinkable in light of normative-affective criteria. There is a sense of the sacred here.[46] Etzioni's statements are powerful arguments for the existence and effects of normative and affective predispositions on social behaviour,[47] including voluntarism. His work suggests that benevolence may be the result of individuals' sense of obligation and their affective ties. It may also be a consequence of utilitarian motives.[48]

What is to be done with these two giant dimensions of social life (normative-affective and logical-empirical), now that they have been acknowledged? Etzioni's response is that people seek not just individual pleasure, but also action that is moral.[49] He advances the "I &We" paradigm to describe social behaviour may be analyzed:

> The I&We paradigm does *not* hold that people simply internalize their society's moral code and follow it, impervious to their own self-interest, or allow it to be defined by the values of their society. The position is (1) that individuals are, simultaneously, under the influence of two major sets of factors—their pleasure, and their moral duty (although both reflect socialization); (2) that there are important differences in the extent each of these sets of factors is operative under different historical and societal conditions, and within different personalities under the same conditions. Hence, a study of the dynamics of the forces that shape both kinds of factors and their relative strengths is an essential foundation for a valid theory of behavior and society, including economic behavior. (Etzioni, 1988, p. 63)

Thus, Etzioni seeks to put all social action within a dynamic complex of desire to achieve pleasure and act morally.

Clearly, social behaviour is governed by two large factors—"codetermination" is the word he uses, yet the notion of codetermination is disquieting. Etzioni wants individuals to make free choices but he says that both consequences and principles determine human behaviour. It is difficult to see how people are both free agents to choose and prisoners of their values at the same time.[50] Why do we decide to obey some norms rather than follow our own objectives?[51] Why do we act selfishly some times and generously at others?[52] A further problem with the I&We paradigm is that it addresses mainly how society works today, not how it came into being. The two dimensions are already in place; there is no indication of why they were formed. That means that the establishment of social capital, such as that formed via benevolence found in schools, may not be as usefully understood using this theory as their ongoing behaviour might be. In order to focus more closely on the origins of voluntarism and its consequences, it is useful to turn to the work of another writer who presents a different paradigm. It is Coleman's theory of rational choice.

Rational Choice and Voluntarism

Coleman has formulated an economic theory of social behaviour that helps to explain voluntarism observed in schools and its response. While not initially tailored to school benevolence, it aims to provide insights into how and why much of human social action takes place[53] and how social institutions are constructed.[54] Before it is applied to benevolence in general and school voluntarism in particular, it is necessary to examine the basic components of the theory.

At its core, this explanation of social order contains just four elemental concepts at the micro level. First is the individual actor that Coleman calls a "natural person." This actor is seen as initially separate from other humans.[55] Second, there are resources, defined as all the goods and services available in the world, apart from actors themselves. Resources include the services (or labour) provided by natural persons.[56] Third are the interests in the resources that natural persons possess. While interests include ones relevant only to individuals, they also encompass ones pertinent to the welfare of others.[57, 58] The actions taken by natural persons reflect the fourth concept in the theory—control, which is the authority to make decisions about specific resources. Control is considered to be the genesis of social action because whenever two natural persons are considered, each may have interest in the resources controlled by the other.

A most remarkable assumption is added to the four elements of actors, resources, interests, and controls. Coleman ascribes rationality.[59, 60, 61] The assumption of rationality implies that human beings are able to construct some of their social circumstances. While natural persons are influenced by their environments, they are not bound by them. There is no room for Homo Sociologicus (man driven by norms) in this theory.[62] Social determinism does not exist.[63] The axiom of rationality is also carried over to corporate actors which also have interests in the control of resources.[64, 65]

Coleman's explanation of social phenomena, called rational choice theory, forms a basis of understanding of a great deal of human behaviour. Social contracts are formed between natural persons when they come together and agree to certain benefits and responsibilities with regard to each other's resources. That means they may trade partial control of their own resources for partial control of the resources of the corporation with the knowledge that there is a net benefit to them. Their interests are served.[66] Yet, interests are not seen as *solely* self-serving. Society does not consist of independent individuals with only selfish interests. Rather, interests are generalized.[67] And persons live in a world of very real social structures. They may be invisible but they are not imaginary.[68]

As indicated, people come together when they recognize they have common interests (or objectives). They may not transfer even temporary control of their own resources, however, unless they recognize that their objectives will not be achieved without the aid of each other. This is an important component of the theory: other people are needed to achieve one's own interests.[69] Coleman sums up the origins of social relations in this way:

> Actors are seen as beginning with resources over which they have some (possibly total) control and in which they have interests. Social interdependence and systemic functioning arise from the fact that actors have interests in events that are fully or partially under the control of other actors. The result of the various kinds of exchanges and unilateral transfers of control that actors engage in to achieve their interests is . . . the formation of social relationships having some persistence over time. (1990, p. 300)

In the schools studied for this volume, examples of social transactions are those in which volunteers and students engaged. They may have been relations of trust. The norms governing volunteer and student transactions may have been invented "from scratch," and appeared to arise spontaneously in the way that rational choice theory suggests.[70] Examples of one-way or unilateral transfers of control may be seen when volunteers surrender the authority over their labours (for a period) to school personnel.[71] These transfers of control may all be interpreted as generated from the contacts between rational actors, as indicated in the quotation. Yet, norms that prescribe or proscribe behaviour of school volunteers and school personnel may not have their inception at the school. Rather, they may emanate from district policy and then be accepted (or not) by the participants. Regardless, the transactions (agreements) are the products of rational thought. There are also occasions in which norms governing benevolence to schools arises inadvertently. Most readily observed as a consequence of the work undertaken by volunteers toward a major school event such as a spring fair or the construction of an adventure playground, the solidarity (including norms and knowledge, that is, all of social capital) generated appears to be a byproduct of the pursuit of common interests. Coleman asserts that because the social capital is shared widely, it is not created in a deliberate way, but that it tends to arise in conjunction with other activities.[72]

Three conditions should be noted concerning the existence of contracts between volunteers and schools (or the persons within schools). First, contracts are pursued by the parties until the extra benefit received is no longer greater than the extra costs incurred.[73] This rule helps to explain the degree of contribution that any volunteer makes. Second, the services produced are not shared (completely) with others except for those who participate. Another way of saying the same thing is that the benefits of contracts are not fully public;[74] there are not too many free riders. If there were, then participation would no longer serve the interests of just the participants and would probably be viewed as too costly.[75] This contingency suggests that persons who do not have contact with a voluntary public school may not benefit greatly from the benevolence it receives. The final condition for contracts is that natural persons and corporate actors are required to communicate their interests and strategies to each other. Physical proximity and a common language logically enhance this communication.[76]

When contracts are made and control of resources is transferred as a result of natural persons and corporate actors working together to pursue their common interests as rational beings, social capital is created. Such is the case for volunteers and schools. Although social capital is defined primarily in terms of norms, it also incorporates extensive knowledge about persons and their backgrounds. The label "community" may be applied to those networks of volunteers, school personnel, and children. But such social linkages are not just the products of shared labours; they may also be viewed as resources that enables interests to be attained. Children and school volunteers, in particular, may be able to achieve their short and long term interests much more completely when they enjoy the sustained bonds that connect each of them to others.[77] Homo Voluntarius triumphs![78]

As a consequence of these deliberations, it seems fair to conclude that rational choice theory has provided some strong grounds for understanding school benevolence. Volunteers are indeed acting rationally when they donate their gifts and construct networks of social relations in schools. But the general report card on rational choice theory has been written. Rather than embrace the theory uncritically, let's see how it stands relative to some other general explanations of social behaviour in order to clarify rational choice further.

Rational Choice and Other Theories

The explanation of rational choice is part of a family of perspectives called exchange theory. This section examines some of their general features. Then a few standing criticisms of rational choice theory are reviewed in order to acknowledge its weaknesses. Some rejoiners are considered. Other large-scale perspectives on social action are noted briefly and some contrasts are made with rational choice. Since rational choice theory survives this test, its application to the phenomenon of school voluntarism is reaffirmed and its links to institutions are reviewed.

Rational choice theory is a close relative of earlier work on social exchange by George Homans and Peter Blau who based their statements on ideas from economics and behavioural psychology. They used the concepts of marginal utility and reciprocity as motivators for behaviour; rewards were generalized far beyond money; they observed that interactions from exchanges produced norms.[79] Others who applied ideas from classical economics even more directly were Anthony Downs and Olson.[80] The prevailing assumption behind these works was an instrumental or calculative rationality that was based on both evidence and logic.[81] Exchange theories, therefore, share the assumption, of purposive individuals:

> These individuals are inventive and forward-looking, have a mind which can evaluate what goes on and are endowed with willpower and the ability to make choices. Furthermore, they make intelligent choices, maximizing gains and cutting losses, and are not merely pushed around by culture or other people. (Collins, p. 353).

A rather positive statement! Rational man and his habits have incurred considerable amounts of criticism, however. Critics argue that such rationality pertains primarily to mostly monetary aspects of life. Such a view may acknowledge too little of the complexity of what humans take into account when decisions are made and leaves important components of effort, love, or advice almost unmeasured.[82] In general:

> theories that make individuals primary tend, at the extreme, to become open-ended, solipsistic [focusing solely on the self], and voluntaristic approaches in which the entire world is renegotiated in every social interaction. They are excessively subjectivist or posit abstract conceptions of human "nature" which are invariant across time and space—like utility maximization. (Powell and Dimmagio, p. 241)

This emphasis on utility constitutes one of the major criticisms of social exchange and by implication, rational choice theory. People are assumed to recalculate the costs and benefits of their actions almost daily when they probably do not.[83] The costs of being rational may be high.[84] Another severe criticism of exchange theory is its apparent inability to explain elements of injustice and conflict that seem to be outside the purview of choice.[85] In a world in which all acts are rational, even behaviour based upon malice and hatred must be explained from the point of view of the rational individual actor. Furthermore, Coleman's treatment of natural and corporate actors suggests that social capital is wholly positive, leaving the reader to wonder if negative social capital also exists. In fact, negative social capital may consist of those relationships between people based on antipathy, fear, and pain; perhaps not all social capital is advantageous to natural persons. Still another concern about exchange theory is its omission of values. While values may be assumed to operate through individual or corporate interests and be implied by norms, rational choice theory is silent on how they might come into being or how they may influence behaviour. These criticisms of the theory, taken together, seem rather substantial.

The problems of the lack of realistic assumptions, avoidance of attention to negative features of social life, and the omission of important determinants of social behaviour originally led sociologists to reject economic man in favour of a *"less rational actor driven by norms, values, and beliefs."* (original in italics, Ritzer p. 416). Exchange theory was just too positivist and individualistic. Despite this rift, one of the few statements that sociologists agree upon is that "there is a distinctively sociological way of looking at the world. It holds that the key to understanding social life lies with the analysis of groups, rather than individuals" (Hechter, p. 2). But even that safe-sounding assertion is in doubt.[86]

Partly because of these dissatisfactions with exchange theory, sociological theorists have developed a number of rather general alternatives to exchange theories. Three are mentioned very briefly here, along with a few of their drawbacks. The first is a set of normative explanations. Their proponents assert that social order depends upon rules that become internalized and, in turn, set both goals and the means to achieve them.[87] Since both goals and means are largely established, there is almost no room for individual decisions; this suggests that the normative approach is overly deterministic. Further, there is often no clear basis for why certain norms emerge or why some groups are more solidary than others.[88] A fair portion of Etzioni's I/We paradigm is grounded on this normative model, as is Kohn's reference to childhood experiences and the assertion that people give because they believe it is the right thing to do.

The second alternative explanation is labeled functionalism. It may be seen as a variation of systems theory, which was invoked in part in Chapters 5 and 6 when the school response to voluntarism was considered. Functionalism studies the relationship between the smaller and larger parts of social systems;[89] an offshoot is its consideration of organizations as organisms. While the need for organizational adaptation is stressed, one deficiency of functionalism is its assumption of one-way influence of environments on organizations.[90] More importantly, this alternative assumes there is an associated harmony that suggests that all parts of social systems function well. Units are explained in terms of the purposes they serve. As Collins states, functionalism "tends to justify whatever exists" (p. 56). Emphasis is placed on the positive contributions of institutions to societies and there is little acknowledgement of either self-interest or conflict.

The third alternative to rational choice is a set of structural theories that address how societies generate conflict and injustice.[91] The structural theories explain social change by showing how interests of oppressed groups coalesce under certain environmental conditions and seek to remedy the uneven distribution of resources. Unfortunately, stability is not very well explained by these theories and in some cases, the incidence of solidarity is overestimated. Collective action on the part of one group may be at the expense of another.[92, 93, 94]

In addition to the particular deficiencies noted, the three alternatives to rational choice theory present rather inexact tools for analysis. They are often expressed largely as taxonomies. However, a theory requires much more than a set of categories to constitute an explanation. It needs both elemental and constructed terms and it requires a description of relationship among them. Rational choice theory does not have this defect.

Clearly, the competitors of rational choice theory have their deficits, as does rational choice theory itself. Despite the criticisms laid against it, however, this theory affirms that the study of individual's behaviours in groups and the assumption of rationality are compatible: people are seen not as bound by their social conditions, but as thinking beings who find their way in life by making informed decisions. In order to understand why individual and corporate actors do that, their interests must be ascertained. They build social structures to suit their purposes and thus construct elaborate social worlds around them. Corporate bodies are seen as real as motor cars and have major consequences in the lives of individual persons. If institutions do not serve natural persons well, they can be altered and even reinvented. As such, rational choice theory unabashedly begins from a focus on individual actors in order to understand group behaviour.

Coleman's emphasis on traditional social structures (such as the family, clan, community, and religious organizations) and his concern about the negative impacts of modern organizations (such as businesses, governments and non profit institutions) may be misinterpreted as an endearment of primordial actors.[95] It is correct to say that Coleman's theory offers a critique of the impact of deliberate progress and its attendant changes on our social environment. Coleman could be called a conservative in the best sense of the word; he could also be labeled a "social environmentalist." Since one of its aims is to be relevant to current times, rational choice theory seeks to "make sense" of many daily social phenomena. For a Weltanschauung, it's not a bad try.[96] There is, of course, a simple pragmatic test of rational choice theory; its efficacy may be judged from the accuracy of its predictions of human behaviour.[97]

The brief review of some other theories helps to place rational choice theory in perspective. While its limitations are acknowledged, its special strength is its ability to explain why individuals act and how social structures are built, major components of this study of benevolence in schools. An alternative to mainstream sociology and economics, rational choice theory falls under the rubric of economic sociology. The two disciplines have much to offer each other; their borders may become diffuse.[98] For instance, Etzioni discards egoism and classical rationality, embraces the normative/affective aspects of human behaviour, and emphasizes community. Coleman upholds egoism and classical rationality, attacks simple individualism, and emphasizes social structure. Perhaps the next century will see a kinder, gentler economics? A more coherent sociology? Like two giant clipper ships crossing courses in a stiff gale, these two premier perspectives are off on remarkably similar missions; one to "sociologize" economics, the other to "economize" sociology.

The Dynamics of School Voluntarism

This chapter has presented some of theories concerning the origins of giving behaviour and has emphasized rational choice theory as a useful tool for examining voluntarism. Now the time has come to paint a broad picture of voluntarism in schools. That picture, supported mainly by rational choice theory, is not a precise set of patterns but is instead a general topography of the processes that may characterize benevolence in education.

There are three general levels of the topography. The first contains natural actors that make up the building blocks of social structures, including parents, other community members, children, principals, teachers and support staff; in this study the volunteer was featured. The second level comprises corporate actors and includes families, schools, and communities. Here, voluntary public schools were emphasized. A third level, the societal one, encompasses primordial actors (such as the family, clan, community, and religious organizations) and modern corporate actors (such as public education, health care systems, and welfare structures).[99]

PREDISPOSITIONS → GIVING → SOCIAL CAPITAL

FIGURE 1   *The Dynamic of Individual Voluntarism*

Although the data are limited in scope and the conceptualizations always open to criticism, the following dynamics emerged.

The first dynamic level is volunteer action. Benefactors (as natural actors) are purposive individuals who have resources to offer. They come with the hope that the school may help them gain knowledge or skills or social bonds to assist themselves or their children. They also arrive because they believe that "what goes around comes around" so that their works with children will contribute to a better life for all.[100] Volunteers with willing hands arrive at the school door without coercion; characteristically, they see a coincidence between their interests and those of children and school personnel. Consequently, the benefactors are willing to surrender limited control over their resources (their labours) and may enter a "cycle of immersion."[101] They offer small donation of time and if their interests are realized, they donate more gifts up to the point of zeal in a few cases. Each natural actor reaches an equilibrium. Satisfactions are realized and individuals come to identify with the persons and groups to whom they have given their resources. Norms are either generated or accepted and thus social capital is created. This dynamic is summarized in Figure 1.

Some minor dynamics also occur at the individual level.[102] (1). Students become aware of voluntarism. They receive guidance and social support (partly from the norms of learning and caring) and thus become linked to their benefactors. (2). Individual administrators act to communicate the school's interests to prospective volunteers, partly by emphasizing the three incentives to give.[103] Principals select volunteers, match them to tasks, exercise general supervision and recognize their works in what may be called a managerial cycle.[104] (3). Teachers encourage volunteers, train, and supervise benefactors. As a consequence of the volunteers' contributions, teachers' instructional roles alter.

The second dynamic level is the voluntary school's response to individual benevolence. The school is a rational modern corporate actor that facing discrepancy between the resources it receives and the resources it requires. Recognizing that its interests (the educational and social welfare of the students) are shared by volunteers, it embarks on organizational processes designed to enhance gifts. Voluntary public schools *make welcome* persons of disparate backgrounds of wealth and culture, largely overcoming barriers of low income, language, and tradition. The school's perception of volunteers changes from intruders to helpers. Norms of authority are invoked. Some control is gained over the labours of benefac-

DEFICIENCY → RESPONSE → COMMUNITY LINKAGES

FIGURE 2   *Voluntary Public School Response*

tors; some control is lost with the formation of a new group inside the school. Issues of work, such as the desired number of volunteers and the balance between paid and unpaid labour, are resolved. The school becomes a place of somewhat diffuse roles; it is more familial and less bureaucratic; it benefits from increased physical and human capital. Most profoundly, its store of social capital in the form of linkages with families and its community increases. It cares; it becomes a *school with heart*. Figure 2 summarizes the processes.

Another minor but critical process that accompanies the school's response is the formation of solidarity among the volunteers. As a consequence of working together towards common interests, this group coalesces and invents or affirms rules of behaviour, such as the learning norm and caring norm. Connections across families, community members and students are established.[105] The social capital generated within the group is sufficiently strong for its members to become affine agents of the school. They also come to have a voice in school affairs and use their social capital to augment the school's resources further.

The third dynamic operates at the societal level.[106] What does individual school benevolence and its organizational response imply if generalized? A few hundred years ago, primordial institutions were the only ones that served natural persons. Rich in social capital, they sustained humanity for hundreds of thousands of years. Modern corporate actors were then invented to provide service to natural persons on a large scale. While they have been successful with new technologies and forms of service, their present domination has diminished the role of primordial institutions and especially the extent of social capital available to natural persons. In recent times, modern corporate actors which provide public services have found themselves with insufficient resources to pursue their interests. Consequently, some of them have recognized that their productivity and even their survival may depend upon their willingness to accept gifts (an essential grace) from natural persons who are members of primordial institutions. One group of modern corporate actors, the selected schools in this study, acted on this realization in a clear manner. Not only did they helped to solve the problems of resources and control, they generated networks for all participants, both natural persons and corporate actors.[107] Further, the schools transformed the character of the modern corporate actor from a bureaucratic structure to a partly voluntary one. One way to express this adaptation is to say that voluntarism has provided a bridge, a pathway for millions of persons, situated be-

| PRIMORDIAL INSTITUTIONS | MODERN CORPORATE ACTORS | BLENDED INSTITUTION |

FIGURE 3   *Societal Pattern of Voluntarism and Its Response*

tween primordial institutions and modern corporate actors. Another way is to suggest that voluntarism helps to produce a new type of institution that is a blend of the other two social galaxies (primordial and modern corporate). Either way, there is a break in the pattern of near-supremacy of modern corporate actors and an affirmation of primacy of natural persons who have altered the social structures that are designed to serve them. Figure 3 outlines the pattern.

Although the dynamics have been sketched on three separate levels, there are vertical influences among them, as shown by the ability of the home-school organizations to recruit benefactors, for instance. These dynamics begin on the individual level and build upward. There is also no doubt that actions taken on the societal level have effects at the organizational stratum and at the locus of natural persons.

This inquiry has, thus far, presented primary data, secondary data from many sources, and a variety of theories that stem mainly from organizational theory and economic sociology. I have attempted to show how voluntarism works, where it comes from, and what its effects are in terms of theoretical directions that are relevant to the phenomenon. Many authors would consider their work finished at this point, but I do not. I believe such an investigation should offer some directions for educational policy. Since the chief aim of educational research is to be ultimately relevant and useful, the next chapter contemplates what social actions might be undertaken if school benevolence is seen as desirable.

Notes

1. Emlen (p. 302).
2. Emlen (p. 303).
3. See Hölldobler and Wilson (pp. 179–180).
4. Hölldobler and Wilson (pp. 179–180). This act gives special meaning to the expression "spill your guts."
5. Sacrifice of life on the part of school volunteers is not impossible to imagine, however. Field trips occur in which volunteers are required to chose between their own safety and that of young students in dangerous traffic conditions.
6. Vampire bats cooperate. Acorn woodpeckers stay at home and help when the prospects for maintaining their territories worsen. Arctic plunder fish guard unrelated eggs.
7. See Emlen (pp. 330–332) and Drickamer (p. 576) for an application of the prisoner's dilemma game here.

8. Kin selection is not the selection of kin. It is defined as "selection mediated by interactions among kin." (as opposed to species selection). See Hölldobler and Wilson (p. 180).

9. They use the example of an ant's sacrifice for her sister, since her sister carries her genes.

10. Presumably, genetic predispositions toward giving vary and that is why some humans give more than others.

11. Drickamer (p. 583).

12. See Schwartz (p. 110).

13. See Schwartz (pp. 182–201). Reductionism is apparent if the generalization from animal behaviour to human behaviour is too strong, See Drickamer p. 66.

14. See Kohn (pp. 214–215).

15. See Schwartz (pp. 317 and 320).

16. Giving may be a human predisposition that is (or is not) built in during childhood. According to Kohn, when children's needs are met, they are freed to be open to the needs of others (pp. 67 and 87). But why socialize children to be giving? Why do children seek to help? Kohn says, "Helping is like lying: one finds it difficult to stop with just one generous act"(p. 204).

17. See Kohn (p. 201).

18. Kohn urges us to accept the explanations of benefactors at face value, insisting that when people say that they care about and want to help others, that is exactly what they mean (pp. 23 and 229).

19. See Kohn (p. 211). Kohn's book is one of the most remarkable I have read. His expression and content can move a reader both to laughter and to tears.

20. Jean Hills suggests that altruism may be conceived as giving in which the interest is in the giving itself (private correspondence).

21. The description of human behaviour as rational is closely related to the definition of reason provided by the Shorter Oxford English Dictionary: "The mental faculty . . . which is used in adapting thought or action to some end;" (p. 2495).

22. See Kohn (pp. 211, 220, and 225). Etzioni also indicates that ". . . there is no necessary connection between the self-serving goal and the efficient use of means."(p. 146) as does Mansbridge (p. ix).

23. See Kohn (pp. 185–187).

24. Schwartz asserts that these disciplines show people as greedy and selfish "by their very natures"(p. 312). "The disciplines in question have mistakenly treated the particular social conditions in which we live as representative of the universal human condition. As a result, they have mistaken local cultural and historical truths about people for natural laws"(p. 312). He demonstrates the mutual support of the three disciplines in this way: Economists say people are self-interested; critics say no, their behaviour is socially determined. Economists turn to sociobiologists who say that animals pursue self-interest; critics say no, genetic determination is overblown. Behaviourists say that observed flexibility and diversity is governed by self-interest; critics say that behaviourism can't generalize to people. So behaviourists turn to economists who say that people are self-interested. Schwartz says this is how the self-interest assumption becomes an apparent fact rather than a moral matter. For him, science is just too limited; human nature is actually human nurture (pp. 316 and 317).

25. See Kohn (pp. 181–182).

26. It is abstracted from Schwartz (pp. 68–74).

27. Transitivity of preferences means that there is a definite, noncircular order to his wishes.

28. These are just some of the objections advanced by Schwartz (pp. 152–162).

29. Kohn's example is Mother Teresa (pp. 197–200).

30. See Mansbridge (pp. ix and 90) who calls for inclusive modeling.

31. Apart from his emphasis on the heroic, Downs is in accord with his predecessors. Adam Smith separated interests, social, and unsocial passions. Others acknowledged the anonyms of self-interest such as animosity, enmity, and even cruelty as well as affection, attachment, and love as prime reasons for human behaviour (pp. 268 and 279).

32. See Kohn (pp. 239–240).

33. See Wuthnow.

34. Compassion frequently implies that aid will be given for the benefit of others in need and that suffering may be shared. Perhaps this is why compassion is associated with charity. See the Shorter Oxford English Dictionary (p. 458).

35. A Native colleague, Richard Atleo, Hereditary Chief of the Ahousat on the west coast of Vancouver Island, challenged the idea that "what goes around, comes around" is simply a belief in the way societies work. He asserted that the proposition was testable; his heritage told him that persons who act on that assumption should ultimately benefit more than those who do not. An intriguing thought worthy of a dissertation.

36. See Wuthnow (pp. 293–299). His argument matches the early experiences in the lives of volunteers in this study were an important factor in giving. Wuthnow contemplates a number of narrow reasons for caring, including pleasure, therapy, growth, and reciprocity (pp. 86–117).

37. Note that his summary statement is supported by many of the results reported in Chapters 2 and 4.

38. See Titmuss (pp. 238 and 239).

39. See Chapter 2.

40. They acknowledge that this three-part division is founded on the work of David Hume. See Knoke and Wright-Isak (pp. 273–275). Their trichotomy is also reflected in Adam Smith's thoughts mentioned in the last section which showed that affective bonding may include negative "passions."

41. For instance, Knoke and Wright-Isak also point out the violations of the free rider principal (p. 223). They acknowledge that Olson's work provided a major insight into how voluntary organizations are required to induce commitments based on personal payoffs (p. 221).

42. Knoke and Wright-Isak's framework is a good start.

43. See Etzioni (1988, pp. 151–157. He also links the use of rationality to particular zones in society in which science, technology, and public administration are prominent [He suggests this association is what is called modernization]. Tonnies would probably agree. See Etzioni (1988, p. 152).

44. See Etzioni (1988, pp. 51–59).

45. Just why the logical dimension is empirical and the normative-affective one is not is unclear.

46. See Etzioni 1988, pp. 93–105 and pp. 67–82.

47. Etzioni's distinction may be questioned, however. Jean Hills points out that rationality can be considered a normative standard, perhaps new to some peoples who have not experienced modern economic development (private correspondence).

48. These affirmations fit well with the data presented in Chapter 3.

49. See Etzioni (1988, p. 83).

50. Recall that the reason why the sociobiological arguments were largely discarded was because of the problem of determinism.

51. For instance, why did Oskar Schindler decide to help his Jewish workers in the movie *Schindler's List?*

52. Mansbridge raises a similar question—when are we acting morally and when are we acting stupidly (p. 137)?

53. See Coleman (1990).

54. As will be shown, social constructions are derived from the behaviour of individuals. See Coleman (1990, pp. 17–18).

55. See Coleman (1990).

56. Since the approach to voluntarism in this book highlights individual actions and resources as major components, the potential relevance of the theory is already apparent.

57. Coleman remarks that the basis for society would hardly exist if individuals did not at least appear to act in the interests of others. See Coleman (1986, p. 311).

58. Although the theory does not say where actors' interests come from, their postulation suggests that if they can be determined, then not only are they connected to certain resources, but that the social behaviour of actors will be linked to them. Just how interests are revealed is not stipulated by the theory. Interests are assumed to be evident to the actor, so one way to uncover them is to ask.

59. The weak assumption here is that natural persons are purposeful, but also rationality, meaning that natural persons not only have a set of ends to achieve, but reasonably good methods for selecting means that will attain those ends. The essence of Coleman's argument for human rationality is that most people are rational most of the time, although he notes a number of exceptions. See Coleman (1990, pp. 13–15).

60. Actions are conceived to be coherent, maximizing, and sometimes far-sighted. See Hechter (p. 30).

61. Rationality implies that individuals tend find relatively efficient ways to achieve their ends that consist of control over resources (and events).

62. For a further discussion on the tensions between Homo Sociologicus and Homo Economicus, see Boudon.

63. Coleman's aim for all of social science is understand behaviour from the point of view of the rational actor (1990, pp. 16–18).

64. The simplest corporate actor consists of two natural persons, each of whom has interests initially controlled by the other and who agree to shift the location of the control. They form a basic social system and thus spark the inception of a society. For preces of the theory of rational choice, see Hechter (pp. 30–39) and Ritzer (pp. 411–416 and pp. 491–492).

65. Thus schools, as modern corporate actors, may be interpreted as acting rationally in the pursuit of resources when they make volunteers welcome and are successful at attracting and retaining them.

66. See Coleman (1990, p. 341).

67. Simmel asserted the same idea: "Strictly speaking, neither hunger nor love, neither work nor religiosity, neither technology nor the functions and results of intelligence, are social. They are factors in sociation only when they transform the mere aggregation of isolated individuals into specific forms of being with and for one another—forms that are subsumed under the general concept of interaction. Sociation thus is the form (realized in innumerable, different ways) in which individuals grow together into units that satisfy their interests. These interests, whether they are sensuous or ideal, momentary or lasting, conscious or unconscious, causal or teleological, form the basis of human societies."(p. 40–1).

68. See Coleman (1990, pp. 300–301).

69. See Coleman (1990, p. 33).

70. As one teacher mentioned, "The children have come to expect that other adult in the classroom."(ps49).

71. In a sense, they "join up." Most appeared to do so when the costs of contribution were low; they may benefit later when their needs are high, as suggested by Coleman (1990, p. 309).

72. See Coleman (1990, pp. 312–3 and 317). It is also possible that this kind of construction of social capital may only appear to be inadvertent. Principals of schools often encouraged substantial projects involving volunteers not just to pursue common interests for the benefit of students but also to produce a set of linkages among those who participated.

73. his condition is the simple limit of production of services when marginal benefit equals marginal cost.

74. This condition means that the externalities do not overwhelm the private benefits.

75. The benefits may be called excludable jointly produced goods. See Hechter (p. 10).

76. See Hechter (p. 33).

77. See Coleman (1990, p. 300).

78. I know that my Latin teachers would not approve of the frivolous use of labels such as Homo Voluntarius but their use helps to convey meanings that other nomenclature would not.

79. See Collins (pp. 339–343). The capability to account for social order may be the greatest strength of rational choice theory. See Sciulli, p. 161.

80. See Hechter (p. 8). They departed from behavioural psychology at this point since people are conceived as conscious entities.

81. See Etzioni (1988, p. 144).

82. See Collins (pp. 354–356).

83. Gary Becker's Treatise on the Family is an example. See Munch (p. 160).

84. See Etzioni (pp. 139–140).

85. See Collins (p. 354). Coleman makes the point that injustice is almost always claimed from outside the sphere of the participants (1990, p. 53). As indicated by Sciulli, existing distributions of power are taken as given (regardless of

its variation) by rational choice theory (p. 165). For instance, according to exchange theory, slavery does not exist; it is simply the better of the two alternatives, bondage or death. Are power relations actually voluntary? Perhaps not. See Munch (p. 139).

86. And yet, if the assumption is made that theories based on individual behaviour cannot explain social order, then there is little point in pursuing rational choice theory. See Hechter (p. 7). Coleman has shown the idea that sociological explanations should start with social groups rather than individuals to be completely wrong (1990, pp. 17–18).

87. See Hechter (p. 4). Normative explanations are associated with the works of Emile Durhkeim and Talcott Parsons.

88. See Hechter (p. 20).

89. It is associated with the work of Robert Merton

90. See Morgan (p. 74).

91. They are associated with the works of Karl Marx.

92. See Hechter (pp. 9 and 25).

93. See also Friedman and Hechter.

94. Unless the data on voluntarism were to be expressed in conflictual terms, it is difficult to see how this perspective would apply to them.

95. His stress on the small scale in social life is an arresting examination of social progress which many will find disturbing

96. Some of these reactions to Coleman's theory appeared initially in a book review. See Brown (1994).

97. This criterion was supported by Downs (p. 21).

98. According to Swedberg, *"the border line between two of the major social sciences is being redrawn, thereby providing new perspectives on a whole range of very important problems both in the economy and in society at large.* (original italics) Maybe it will even become possible again—as in the days of Adam Smith, John Stuart Mill, and Karl Marx—to get an analysis of central social problems that is informed by both economics and sociology."(p. 5).

99. Note that they are generally based on rational choice theory and its derivations.

100. Note that Knoke and Wight-Isak's three dispositions of rational choice, normative conformity, and affective bonding all become rational interests in Coleman's theory. Natural persons choose to obey norms or to seek affective relations.

101. Some free riders may never enter this cycle.

102. These lesser themes are very important aspects of voluntarism but they are possible only because of volunteer action.

103. The three incentives are utilitarian, normative, and affective, matching the three predispositions.

104. They contribute their personal resources toward voluntarism until their marginal benefits approximate their marginal costs.

105. Trust relations between benefactors and recipients constitute an example.

106. While not studied directly in this volume, some inferences regarding the societal level may be offered since some of its organizational elements were investigated.

107. See Chapter 1 for the three problems facing public education.

9

Educational Policy:
Macro and Micro

This volume has considered, in turn, both experiential and conceptual aspects of voluntary public schools and the social consequences of benevolence. Together, their discussions provide compelling arguments that benevolence and voluntary public schools should be cultivated. This chapter continues the discussion by considering the roles of voluntarism in the face of governmental provision of education and addresses concerns about the "match" of government mechanisms to levels of need. Governmental provision was designed to equalize educational opportunity. Would factoring in voluntarism mean injustice for a fair segment of the population? Perhaps, but perhaps not, depending on the moral position one takes. And what would voluntarism imply for school resources and control? Issues of resources and control (which were argued to be major problems at the inception of this inquiry) are integral to proposals for substantial administrative changes in education. This chapter describes the main suggestions for reform in educational governance briefly and compares voluntarism with them. Benevolence is found to have some features in common with them and also some distinctive characteristics. A glance backwards in time reveals that voluntarism is not a new idea in education. Actually, governmental support of schools is a much more recent phenomenon than benevolence. If voluntarism is seen as a good idea for public schools, then certain policies could be undertaken schools, districts, and states or provinces to foster its growth. Some of these are presented. Finally, an overall vision of voluntarism for education is advanced.

Government and Benevolence

As observed in Chapter 8, modern corporate actors have assumed control over many services once offered by primordial institutions. For example, the provision or support of health, education, and welfare services by various levels of government is the status quo in North America and many countries world-wide. Governments have displaced the provision of services by primordial institutions—a shift that one writer calls the "crowding hypothesis."[1] Some time ago, de Tocqueville warned about the United States, "The more government takes the place of associations, the more will individuals lose the idea of forming associations and need the government to come to their help"(p. 487). He was referring to what is now called social capital and spoke against its depletion.[2] But social capital has not vanished; it exists especially in parts of society where modern corporate actors do not dominate.[3] Still, social capital is affected by governmental action, particularly the ability for individuals to make decisions on matters that affect one's work or personal life. Control of resources has drifted from natural persons to corporate bodies. Coleman's offers an arresting description of this problem:

> Thus a person living in a large city, working for a large firm, belonging to a large union or professional association, and having some interest in political affairs receives many benefits in the form of money, services, and other resources, but at the cost of having little control over those events which interest him. The individual in modern society has surrendered control of many of the activities of daily life to those corporate bodies that service him. (1986, p. 459)

As corporate actors, governments have positive intentions but their efforts are sometimes ineffective. They constitute a poor substitute for primordial institutions which are much more closely controlled by individuals.[4] When services are not provided as desired, people begin to see governmental provision as unattractive. Lack of viability may stem from the diverse demands that citizens make upon governmental agencies that really are just suited to providing uniform services.[5] Viability breakdown may also occur when the cycle of accountability (say from elector to politician to bureaucrat) is too large, rather than small enough to link pairs of natural persons (for instance, mother and daughter).[6]

Governmental institutions are also facing a crisis caused by a paucity of resources. This difficulty stems mainly from the desire to reduce public debts. Additionally, economic downturns reduce resource availability because tax revenues available for public spending are lowered. Budget reductions, accompanied by continuation of the desire to maintain services, enhance the call for volunteers and gifts of all kinds.[7] Perhaps as a consequence of the inability of governments to provide many services, voluntarism has blossomed across a broad spectrum of society, including public safety, justice, the arts, recreation, religion, health care, transportation, agriculture, welfare, business, the environment and the military.[8]

One estimate suggests that 20 to 30 percent of all volunteer programs are associated with the public sector.[9] In fact, even as the public finds governments ineffectual, volunteers are deeply involved in the "co-production" of services with governments. Is voluntarism as a means to provide services just a romantic ideal?[10] Some think not:

> Voluntarism evokes so many negative feelings and connotations that it is important to underscore the fact that much of the new interest in voluntarism is not in restoring a situation in which the wealthy bestowed charity on the grateful poor, but in sustaining and strengthening patterns of what might better be called self-help. (Glazer, p. 136)

> Real sympathy, a warm heart, unquestioning friendship, all-forgiving love—these free gifts of 'good neighbors' can hardly be granted by official agencies. These gifts are in the long run possibly more valuable than any number of dollars or material goods supplied. In this role the social functions of 'good neighbors' are perennial and immortal. Their forms may change; their substance remains unchangeable. (Sorokin, p. 16)

Such positive assertions about benevolence should be tempered, however. First, voluntarism sometimes serves just as a "fill in" for actions where governmental services and markets leave off.[11] That means there may not be sufficient capacity to sustain the needs of millions of people through benevolence alone. Second, benevolence is susceptible to favouritism, and so there is a risk that some in need will not benefit. Thus, voluntarism is not wholly complementary to the provision of services by other means.[12]

A discussion of voluntarism as it applies to all government services is beyond the scope of this book. However, it is fitting to mention its role in addressing the problem of equality of educational opportunity. To understand how voluntarism does this, it is first important to establish some understandings of the ideal of social justice. John Rawls observed that social justice is achieved through equal opportunity; as such, justice must involve support for the least advantaged. In the context of education, his ideas place all persons on the same footing; family influences on a child's opportunities are discounted. He envisioned a central authority to carry out the redistribution of wealth. This view of justice was challenged by Robert Nozick, who argued that justice constitutes entitlement or benefit. In contrast to Rawls, Nozick asserted that people should benefit from the results of their own labours and not be compelled to give to others.[13] How, then, do policy makers find compromise, and balance justice as equality with justice as benefit? In education, the implication is that schools should manifest both egalitarian and entitlement principles in order to be properly just.[14] Is there pragmatic way out of the conflict? Art Wise suggests that schools should get on with the job of education while governments should ensure equity.[15] If that is the case, then voluntarism is seen as a local matter and governments have the responsibility for the redistribution of wealth on the large scale. Somehow, the particular must be balanced with the universal.[16]

However, issues of justice are not the only ones facing schools at this time. As noted in Chapter 1, two others dominate many discussions and both, in turn, are strongly influenced by voluntarism. They are the issues are resources and control.[17] The problem of resource amounts is severe for many schools. Not only do they face fewer resources because of diminishing public tax bases, they also compete for available monies with other deserving public agencies. As shown in this volume, the resource problem is reduced by the incorporation of volunteers into schools. Public schools simply have more physical capital under conditions of benevolence.

The problem of control is also vexatious because many school personnel believe that they have the authority to allocate resources in the best interests of their students and many parents wish to have more authority in their neighbourhood school's affairs. According to the data gathered and reviewed in this book, school voluntarism provides at least a partial answer to the authority issue by either offering new resources for school personnel to control directly, or by giving resources that fall under partial control of persons who work in schools. The latter resource control is shared with parents (often organized as home-school organizations) who have a voice in how the resources are to be allocated. Some authority is theirs. But voluntarism should be understood in relation to other proposals for administrative change in education as well. Let's consider three of them.

Other Proposals for Administrative Change

There have been many attempts during the last several decades to change the way educational services are delivered. Many of the proposals have been forgotten or set aside, leading critics to suggest that "reform" comes in cycles but carries very little impact with it.[18] The cyclic observation may be applied to administrative changes in education specifically, most of which coincide with similar movements in the larger society[19] At the current time, there are three serious initiatives under way. Each has its strong proponents and a modest number of critics. They deserve some scrutiny since they have the potential for widespread implementation.[20] The initiatives are school choice, school-based management, and the affirmation of nonpublic schools. Each is considered here in the light of three comparative characteristics: the control problem, the resource problem, and the capacity to produce social capital.

The inspiration for school choice plans comes from the idea that public schools are overregulated and underproductive.[21] The extent to which they are rule-bound is seen as a large factor in their apparently low performance, particularly relative to nonpublic schools. Since most rules stem from the present structure of school districts, school choice advocates recommend a change in the authority base which would "free" schools and permit parents to select them. Presumably, this plan would raise the levels of student achievement. John Chubb and Terry Moe have laid out this argument in a persuasively-written book that considers the limited evidence available and concludes that a market mechanism is the key to school reform. Their proposal would work something like this: parents would be given vouchers equal to the value of a year's education for their child. They would select a school and surrender the voucher to the school, which would redeem it from the state. Schools would allocate the money as they saw fit. Since their survival would depend upon parental demand, schools would ensure that their programs were attractive to parents. They would compete with other schools and thus stress excellence in instruction and achievement. Minimal regulations and record-keeping would be retained by the state and funding would be fully public.[22] As mentioned, this proposal would require schools to compete in an educational market.[23] Parents are consumers and schools are producers of learning. Here, Homo Economicus is chasing Homo Bureaucraticus.[24]

While a lot is known about competitive markets in a variety of fields, little is known about how they would actually function in public education.[25] This is because they are almost nonexistent. Most nonpublic schools are not profit-making, so they do not provide suitable objects of study. Very few experiments with voucher plans have been undertaken. One revealed that parental preferences were based more on proximity than academic quality.[26] However, the evidence is not yet forthcoming on several key issues, such as the charges that vouchers will lead to greater segregation of races and social classes, result in the decline of the common core of values that public schools teach, or produce high costs when complexities such as tuition variations based on income. Most importantly, so far, school autonomy combined with client choice has not been shown to produce higher academic achievement.[27] Large-scale commitment to substantial voucher plans constitutes a great deal of faith at this time since the promised outcomes may be quite modest.

The most evident manifestation of school choice is the movement for charter schools in the United States and Canada. An option available in some jurisdictions, charter schools are typified by their distinctive missions, relative freedom from school district regulations, and complete public funding. They are prohibited from charging tuition, selecting their students, and religious instruction. They are also required to teach the standard curriculum, to have a board of governors, and to be strictly accountable to the agencies that grant their charters. Unfortunately, the amount of information on charter schools is very modest as a result of their recency. Early reports indicate that they tend to be small in size, are often designed to serve "at risk" students, and are characterized by hard work in order to establish them.[28]

How does the school choice option address the issues of control, resources, social capital? Arrangements of parental choice do focus on the control problem directly. These options would shift control of schools from district central offices to parents, who would play a consumer role. Schools would be authorized to make many key decisions, particularly about personnel and programs. However, parental choice would not augment the amount of public resources available to schools which operate on the value of the vouchers handed to them. Apart from tuition allowed in a few plans, market-driven schools will have no formal way to solve the resource problem. Would they encourage voluntarism and enterprise and thus increase the store of social capital available for the students, participants, and school personnel? Maybe. If a precarious, market-sensitive existence combined with a downturn in available tax dollars, market-based schools would have the incentive to generate social capital using some of the means observed in the selected schools in this study.[29]

School-based management is another initiative that has inspired educators and policy makers. The main reason for its attractiveness is that it addresses the problem of school regulation by central offices. Its aim is to give schools both the authority and responsibility for the education of children. Embodying the word "empowerment," parents, teachers and principals believe that if they control the resources available to schools and establish their directions, then students will benefit from increased learning.[30] The proposal works in one of two ways, depending on the role of parents. If parents *are not* involved directly, then authority to make critical decisions about personnel, equipment, maintenance, utilities, consultant services, and supplies is devolved to principals who consult with teachers.[31] If parents *are* involved formally, then a policy council is established that contains representatives of parents and teachers, inter alia. The council is authorized to set school policy and may be able to hire or fire the principal.[32]

Fortunately, there is a small but growing literature addressing reflections on and experiences with school-based management.[33] It certainly solves the problem of the inability of schools to make important decisions. Schools have the authority to spend their lump-sum budgets within reasonable limits. They are also held accountable for their expenditures in various ways. Whether they actually increase student performance remains an open question, although the satisfaction of parents, students, and employees appears to increase.[34] Three problems are apparent, however. Firstly, the hopes for empowerment held by teachers and parents may be subverted by principals who are required to serve two masters (their school council and their school board).[35] Secondly, adoption may proceed superficially so the scope of decisions permitted to schools is highly restricted.[36] Finally, the threat of recentralization is very real for districts that implement school-based management hastily.[37]

Does school-based management solve the problems of control and resources while generating social capital? It certainly tackles the control issue and resolves it by providing flexibility of decision making at the school level. Just who makes what decision is determined (sometimes ambiguously) by the form of school-based management adopted. The resource problem is another matter. Nothing in the structure and function of school-based management is designed to augment shrinking public resources. Only by turning to enterprise or voluntarism will a school be able to increase its resource flows. As for social capital, there may be some generated if parents take an active part in school governance, but otherwise, there is no mechanism in place to increase the linkages among students, parents, community members and school personnel.

The alternative of private and parochial schools is the third major administrative option available in education. Unlike the two other proposals, nonpublic schools present a highly diverse set of variations in their structures and purposes.[38] Catholic schools and others with a religious orientation are communal, but some of them are poor.[39] Independent schools are often well supported financially and have unique missions. Saturn schools are new; we know little about them except that they function as business firms in an educational market. While nonpublic schools outside the United States usually receive government aid, virtually all within North America and abroad are supported by tuiption along with the voluntary contributions of parents and other community members. It is easy to see why nonpublic schools may be considered as extensions of the families of the students who attend them. Parents who wish for familial influences to continue in school often find nonpublic schools to be compatible with their interests. As C. Arnold Anderson once said, "Parents want their children to be educated *up but not away*."[40]

Parochial schools, along with independent ones, achieve a sense of community among their students and teachers. Many include parents and others in their networks.[41] Along with a strong normative structure, they show somewhat higher levels of student achievement than public schools.[42] One of the factors that contributes to the construction of community is that parents select specific schools over others partly because they want their children to attend a school with other students whose backgrounds are similar to their own. Hence, these schools are genuinely schools of choice.[43] As a result, these schools may not always advance the interests of the state. Some of them may be faulted for their provincialism since their students remain isolated from persons of other religions, races, cultures, or income levels. One consequence is that the society may be divided further; another is that some avenues of social mobility through education may be blocked for disadvantaged groups. Educational opportunity may be rendered unequal although justice as benefit is served.[44]

How does the disparate array of nonpublic schools answer the problem of control, the issue of resources, and the challenge of constructing social capital? Again, control is exercised by headmasters in conjunction with boards of parents. The schools are autonomous or almost so. They usually conform to state curricular and evaluational regulations, but aside from these, nonpublic schools are free to fashion their own missions and accept the consequences of both their achievements and their mistakes. As for the resource problem confronted by the public sector, nonpublic schools are affected by variations in business cycles and by the numbers of students who select their schools. Many are most adept at finding resources via voluntarism and enterprise.[45] What about social capital? Some nonpublic schools, particularly parochial ones, appear to be highly successful at generating and maintaining networks of relationships that sustain their students and community members.[46]

Taken together, how do these three proposals compare to voluntarism in the areas of control, resources, and social capital? The three major policy options (choice, school-based management, and nonpublic schools) share one feature. They all address the control issue squarely and resolve it by placing authority to make many important decisions at the school level with some degree of parental influence. By comparison, voluntarism also solves some of the control problem through local agreements and retention of school-level decision making about resources that come as gifts. The three proposals face the issue of resources rather differently. Choice may encourage private resources to be acquired; school-based management does not necessarily attract them; private schools depend on them. Schools operating under one of the three options may not always seek private resources but when they do, they use voluntarism or enterprise as the mechanism.[47] As for social capital, the three administrative structures provide rather distinct outcomes. Schools of choice and decentralized schools (operating under school-based management) may or may not generate modest amounts of social capital, depending on how their parents and community are involved.[48] Some will grow rich and some will remain poor in social linkages to their neighbourhoods. Nonpublic schools appear to offer the most promise for the development of social capital because of their dependence on the people they serve and their missions that they hold. They make extensive use of voluntarism and enterprise.[49] In one sense, benevolence may be seen as a necessary component or potential element of the three options simply because it is an avenue that produces resources, alters control structures, and generates norms that bind persons who participate in it. In another sense, however, voluntarism may be regarded as an entirely unique alternative to the three because it has some distinctive aspects. It is evolutionary rather than revolutionary and may be found in schools outside the three policy options, as shown by the selected public schools in this study. Actually, as a feature of schools, benevolence has existed in education for a long time. Let us now consider briefly an historical overview of its role in schools.

A Glance Backwards

The donation of gifts to schools is not new at all. During the distant period from 1480–1660, when English kings and queens ruled their colonies in North America, 437 schools were established in England at a cost of £449,000.[50] They offered free tuition for boys who could not afford the fees. There were also 487 scholarships created from donations of £145,000, including some for grammar school students. The scale of giving was significant for the time, as was the proportion of donations directed toward schools compared to hospitals and other causes. What people were the source of the gifts? The largest benefactors were usually London merchants while the group that gave the next largest amounts consisted of tradesmen. A total of 35,000 donors are on record; a few gave only a penny while the average was £117.[51]

Why would people who lived about the time of Elizabethan England offer their money to schools? The merchants' wills and deeds of gift revealed they believed that their patriotic duty was to support the schooling of forthcoming generations in order to reduce the effects of poverty and offer children the skills needed for a changing world. Jordan gives this account:

> Thus scores of London merchants of humble provincial birth, who had won great wealth, when they came to set their worldly affairs in order, bethought themselves of the poverty and ignorance which had all but overwhelmed them. This explains, as they themselves so frequently confessed, why so many of them ordered the founding of a free school or a great scholarship fund in the home parish with which they had had few if any ties for a full generation. They remembered their own youthful hardships, the narrowness of the margin of their own emancipation, as they set out in poignant personal terms the motives which impelled them to make their foundation, sometimes quite unwisely, in that particular parish, as if to ensure for ever opportunity for boys not unlike themselves in this remembered corner of England. (p. 281)

Perhaps the learning norm and the caring norm were in effect four to five centuries ago.[52] During the interim, many of the schools that were estab-

lished in that period either closed or were absorbed by the public education system now in place. Voluntary provision gave way to statutory provision but the organizational structure of English education today still reflects the benevolence of the past.[53] England, however, was an old-world
society. Conditions of life were different in the North American colonies.

Long before de Tocqueville's observation of voluntarism, there was a
spirit of benevolence in America. John Winthrop, the Puritan leader,
stressed the need to care for others. Cotton Mather encouraged voluntary
associations to "do good." Benjamin Franklin, in "Poor Richard's Al-
manac," advocated self-help for the society of his time with the aim to re-
lieve suffering.[54] Alexis de Tocqueville, writing in the 1830's, observed
that such foundations resulted in a strong condition of benevolence:

> Americans of all ages, all stations in life, and all types of disposition are for-
> ever forming associations. . . . Americans combine to give fetes, found semi-
> naries, build churches, distribute books, and send missionaries to the an-
> tipodes. Hospitals, prisons, and schools take shape in that way. . . . In every
> case, at the head of any new undertaking, where in France you would find
> the government or in England some territorial magnate, in the United States
> you are sure to find an association. (p. 485)

Note that schools are among his examples. He wrote only four pages on
voluntary association. Moreover, he did not analyze his information much
or document his examples extensively. According to one critic, de Tocqueville was selective in choosing his facts and biased in his views that
Americans were simply transplanted English people.[55] Still, weaknesses in
his scholarship did not stop him from striking a chord of explanation and
empathy among his readers regarding the nature of life in America. Other
examples of benevolence included the actions of travelers on stage coaches
in fending off robbers in colonial days, the formation of Sunday school societies in 1791, service on early school boards circa 1825, and work on the
Underground Railroad around 1850.[56] One of the earliest examples of
school voluntarism was shown by the Old School House in Mount Holly,
New Jersey. It was constructed in 1759 by 21 citizens who bought the land.
While the schoolmaster was paid by parents who could afford the tuition,
other children attended for free.[57] A "public school" in the New England
colonies of the time was a school that depended on fees and taxes but also
received gifts from parents and other citizens to sustain it.[58]

Elwood Cubberley described four types of philanthropic schools that
existed between 1800 and 1900. The Sunday School Movement, which had
originated in England, was assumed by the churches in the United States.
Its main idea was to pay women to teach poor, working children reading
and to offer religious instruction on Sundays. City School Societies, no-

tably the one in New York, were established to attract donations for those children who had no opportunity for instruction.[59] Thomas Jefferson is said to have given $200 as a subscription to the society in the City of Washington. Some schools were established by wills. A third type of philanthropic school resulted from the Lancastrian Plan with its method of teaching by student monitors. This was said to be highly economical and successful in its time. Finally, there were the Infant School Societies, which also depended on voluntary contributions and out of which primary schools emerged.[60] These schools changed when the methods of school support evident until 1900 ceased. After that time, the mix of voluntarism, enterprise, and taxation shifted towards increasing support via public funding. Let's consider some of the reasons for the transition.

The origins of what is called public education in America are evident in the ideas of Thomas Jefferson. His arguments may be summarized in this way:

> a free society devoted to achieving the natural rights of its citizens can be maintained and tyranny prevented only if the people in general are well educated. Wise laws will be made and well administered only if the capable persons have equal opportunity to achieve a liberal education without regard to wealth or social status. Therefore, all children should have a chance at education at public expense . . . all free children were to be entitled to free tuition for at least three years and as much longer at private expense as their parents wished. (Butts and Cremin, p. 93)

The novel idea that all free children were entitled to attend a school without charge removed the authority of the family and community to educate the child as they saw fit and transferred that authority to the state which could require schools to be established with public funds.[61] From this basis, the general pattern became clear:

> Financial support for education has come increasingly from public funds and taxation rather than from private sources of endowment, gift, or tuition. Such public funds have been raised from larger and larger units organized for taxing purposes. The proportion of funds raised by local districts, towns and counties has declined, and the proportion raised by the states and the federal government has increased. Again, the common values of the general welfare have led to the necessity of providing equal educational opportunity for all children despite the inequalities of wealth represented in the several districts, counties, or states. It has been increasingly recognized that poorly educated citizens anywhere are a threat to the common welfare everywhere. Inequality among local units in ability to support education should not be allowed to stand in the way of the need for good education for all. (Butts and Cremin, p. 564)

There is no sense from Butts and Cremin that private support for education had any particular standing when compared to equal educational opportunity.[62] Education was just too important to be left to small groups.[63] Sources of support were seen as wholly substitutable; a tax dollar was as good as a dollar freely given. State funding was believed to be as viable as community support for schools. This assumption is part of the writings of Cubberley, whose work in school finance during the early decades of the twentieth century did much to advance the cause of "free" education. He decried the lack of provision of schooling to all during the eighteenth and nineteenth centuries and asserted his vision for the twentieth:

> Theoretically all the children of the state are equally important and are entitled to have the same advantages; practically this can never be quite true. The duty of the state is to secure for all as high a minimum of good instruction as is possible, but not to reduce all to the minimum; to equalize the advantages to all as nearly as can be done with the resources at hand; to place a premium on those local efforts which will enable communities to rise above the legal minimum as far as possible; and to encourage communities to extend their educational energies to new and desirable undertakings. (Cubberley, 1905, p. 17. Also quoted in Johns and Morphet, p. 207)

This statement suggests that Cubberley was not searching for absolute uniformity in the provision of education. Rather, he was willing to tolerate differences and also to encourage local initiative. Two of Cubberley's contemporaries, also advocates for free public education, sounded the same theme of state provision with local addition:

> The state should insure equal educational facilities to every child within its borders at a uniform effort throughout the state in terms of the burden of taxation; the tax burden of education should throughout the state be uniform in relation to tax-paying ability, and the provision for schools should be uniform in relation to the educable population desiring education. Most of the supporters of this proposition, however, would not preclude any particular community from offering at its own expense a particularly rich and costly educational program. They would insist that there be an adequate minimum offered everywhere, the expenses of which should be considered a prior claim on the state's economic resources. (Strayer and Haig, p. 173. Also quoted in Johns and Morphet, p. 210)

Both works reflect a tolerance for local initiative to supplement the state base for education. Cubberley's coverage of private support of schools in his book is an interesting mix of factual statements and judgements which suggest he held private sources in low esteem. It is difficult to know from his presentation if his concerns about private support were allowed to filter out other evidence concerning them. However, he does convey the sense in which a variety of private means supported schools. Cubberley seems to indicate that private support, without state provision, results in low educational quality and unequal access to schools. The public basis of school finance of Cubberley, Strayer, and Haig dominated thought on educational finance for most of the twentieth century. Actually, the main thrust of their ideas was implemented in the applications of educational finance systems throughout North America.[64]

The use of hindsight is an easy way to criticize the fervor of Cubberley, Strayer, and Haig. While their vision has produced public provision of schooling with an important measure of equal opportunity, it is possible that by removing the requirement that community members participate in the establishment and maintenance of schools, much social capital was subtracted, particularly for the students. Students and others gained but they lost.[65, 66] As the twenty-first century approaches, the current method of supporting schools fully with public funds becomes questionable. One historian reflected on public education in Canada at mid-century (1957) in this way:

> The persistent movement of public education . . . has been and still is regarded by interested people with mixed feelings. To many in the present century it has been the inspiring march of progress. To others it has been more like a reckless sortie from the fortress of established values. (Phillips, p. 605)

It is possible that neither the interests of the students nor of society are served by public schools supported exclusively by taxation. If this is true, then there are some policies to consider in order to shift the balance between public provision and private contributions through benevolence.

Specific Policies for School Voluntarism

The transfer of resources from one actor to another with no certain return, and a concurrent positive interest on the part of the giver for the welfare of the recipient constitute a phenomenon that has the potential to become a powerful force within public education.[67] This potential leads naturally to the contemplation of policies to augment voluntarism that are naturally directed at increasing the number of voluntary public schools. Recall that voluntary public schools are mainly supported by public funds but receive a substantial amount of their resources in the form of gifts.[68] This section describes some interventions designed to increase benevolence and thus address the problems of resources and control faced by public education today, as well as enhance learning and the creation of much-needed social capital. An increase in benevolence is desired to transform public schools from citadels into institutions in which parents and community members are welcomed. Fundamentally, the schools may be altered so that they serve the interests of natural persons more readily than they do today.[69]

What can public schools do on their own initiative to encourage voluntarism and transform themselves into voluntary schools? Several actions were reviewed in some detail in Chapters 4, 5, and 6. Principals (in particular) can recruit prospective volunteers actively by communicating with them. Adaptations of the three incentives (personal benefit, sense of obligation, or sociability) can be used to attract benefactors and overcome the free rider problem. Regardless of socio-economic or cultural backgrounds, volunteers can be "made welcome."[70] Once on site, benefactors can be integrated into school affairs through matching with tasks, training, supervision, and recognition and thus start cycles of involvement that may lead them to become affine agents of the school. While support staff members can provide assistance in benefactor involvement, teachers can work with volunteers and thus change the metaphor of the parent from intruder to helper. If a home and school organization is established, it can assume some of the responsibilities of volunteer management and offer direction on how to allocate donated resources.[71]

What can public school districts do to increase the level of voluntarism in their schools? Although schools are the location for benevolence, boards of education can do much to facilitate or impede giving. Genuine acceptance and approval of benefactors is considered to be necessary for the continued existence of volunteer programs established by districts.[72] Programs can take the form of initiatives for particular groups, such as the one called "Off Our Rockers," which provided senior volunteers to tutor first grade children, a grandparents' day in elementary schools, and an "older neighbour" day.[73] Programs can be designed to provide inservice training to principals, teachers, and support staff on the potential and use of volunteers in schools. Such training allows school personnel the opportunity to share experiences and build a knowledge base.[74] The creation of a district volunteer coordinator position would be one way to support the inservice education requirement.

Districts also have a good deal of potential impact on voluntarism through the mechanisms by which they allocate resources to schools. Particularly when faced with retrenchment and personnel layoffs, boards could invoke what I shall call the "90/10" rule. This rule suggests that public monies maintain 90 percent of school resources while up to 10 percent is supported through gifts. The 90 percent could include salaries and benefits of school administrators, teachers, and support staff (including a school volunteer coordinator), along with major capital outlays such as building renovations. The 10 percent could include: a) supplies such as texts, writing, cleaning, teaching, office, and library books, b) equipment such as computers, copiers, science, physical education, music, furniture, and telephones, c) labour such as minor renovation, minor construction, office, library, teaching aides, student supervision, and some maintenance, and d) services, such as for field trips and special presentations. Notice that these categories of resources are not just extras or "add-on's." Supplies, equipment, and nonprofessional labour are necessary for schools to carry out their missions of learning. This suggested policy makes voluntarism essential to schools and not a luxury.[75] There might be some schools that would claim correctly that they would not be able to raise nowhere near the 10 percent of the required resources through gifts or enterprise. If their cases were persuasive, then compensatory allocations could be made.[76] Naturally, the 90/10 rule would require compatibility with all collective agreements that it affected.

The establishment of volunteer programs and the use of the 90/10 rule may not, in themselves, be sufficient to sustain voluntarism at the district level. Boards would need to use some tools available to them to support benevolence. They consist of the rewards of personnel placement and promotion. Principals and teachers could be recognized for their abilities to attract and maintain high levels of benevolence in their schools along with the usual criteria. School administrators are known for their responsiveness to district policies and their implications for career advancement.[77] Actually, the placement of personnel who have strong track records in building school volunteer programs into schools that are situated in contexts challenging benevolence is a way to compensate for the unequal private resources available to certain schools.[78] Again, commitment to voluntarism at the district level becomes an important factor in its success. If these three policy suggestions of district-level volunteer support programs, resource allocation mechanisms, and reward structures are implemented, then schools should be able to recognize the opportunity, take organizational action, and generate important amounts of physical, human, and social capital.

What could states, provinces, and nation-states do to enhance school voluntarism? The history of action to increase benevolence is much more extensive for private organizations than public ones. The Parent Teachers' Association (PTA) was founded in 1897 and is now the largest voluntary organization in the United States. A significant advance was made by the Public Education Association when it received a grant from the Ford Foundation to establish the National School Volunteer Program. Seventeen large cities started or enhanced programs in this way in 1964. The United States Department of Education maintained an office of volunteers for two years from 1970 to 1972. Today, the leading organization in support of school voluntarism is the National Association of Partners in Education, a nonprofit society.[79] There are also reform projects under way that involve benevolence. Most noteworthy is the Institute of Responsive Education's League of Schools Reaching Out in the United States, a national strategy involving a cross-section of schools which is designed to enhance parental involvement and increase the academic and social success of children. Its support comes from foundations.[80, 81]

Actions by states to increase voluntarism have been modest. One of the earlier efforts was the establishment of an Office of Citizens' Affairs in North Carolina during 1970–71. Its aim was to place an adult for each 13 children in primary classrooms. The Florida Education Act of 1975 is regarded as the lighthouse effort, however. It provided training for volunteers and matching funds for school volunteer programs.[82] The survey undertaken by Michael revealed that among the states, Florida maintained the strongest legislative commitment to volunteers, having included estimates of 2,000 schools in programs with 140,000 volunteers.[83]

It would not be difficult for states, provinces, and nation-states to establish programs to encourage voluntarism. After all, they hold the legislative responsibility for education and most of the purse strings. But new programs are not considered favourably in times of retrenchment or debt reduction. If there are not millions in spare cash in state coffers, what can be done? Voluntarism may be enhanced through the normal resource allocation channels. If only one percent of all available revenues was made available to school districts as funds for voluntarism, the boards and schools could deploy them to amplify the amount of donations already being received, perhaps by a factor of two to four. For instance, if each school had a part-time volunteer coordinator (a person indigenous to the neighbourhood), the amount of benevolence could be magnified. This suggestion corresponds to the 90/10 rule for school districts. It means that the allocation of public funds could be used to generate private resources. It also implies that school finance may be conceived as three-tiered with provision at the state, district, and school-site levels. If states and provinces were to offer basic funding for educational equity, districts added some dollars, and neighbourhoods were asked to contribute a further reasonable percentage to school operations, then the benefits of voluntarism could be realized by most public schools. Persons who conceive of public education as fully public may find this proposal shocking. That is partly because public schools have seldom asked for direct help. Yet, if elected officials and educational administrators pointed out the public obligation to support schools through voluntarism, the public's view of the institution would change.[84] As one teacher said, "We need to be honest, . . . we need their help in educating their kids" (he26). People of all predispositions would offer their help to public schools.

The suggestion that the public should cooperate directly in support of "their" schools may not always be welcomed, however, as the following anecdote illustrates:

Public School 41, located in Greenwich Village, was notified on November 7, 1997, that because of cutbacks from the district office it would forfeit one Grade 4 teacher, thus increasing the class size in the remaining five classes to 44 students each. The parents, many of whom were professionals, met and raised $45,000 through voluntary contributions in one weekend. They presented the gift to the school, both to save the teachers' job and to keep the class size constant. The New York City Chancellor intervened, however, ordering the parents to take back their money since other schools in Greenwich Village and elsewhere in the city did not have all have parents with such deep pockets. The parents met, notified the *New York Times,* informed the radio stations, and filed a court case enjoining the Chancellor from removing the teacher. After all, the NYC Public Schools had raised millions from private donations, including $150M from the Annenberg Challenge, a gift from billionaire Walter Annenberg, though that money was under the control of the Central Board and Chancellor. The $45,000, however, went directly from the parents to the school and its teacher and therefore was not subject to the Chancellor's direct authority. Publicity became so intense that the Chancellor compromised: the parents had their money returned and the district superintendent was ordered to pay the teacher out of public funds.[85]

It may be expected that persons who hold strong egalitarian views or those whose power is threatened may speak and act against proposals which embody voluntarism, despite its generally beneficial outcomes. Yet, these difficulties may be overcome since benevolence achieves certain aims deemed to be very positive for schools. They include a union of schools with their neighbourhoods and communities—a condition which was ignored until recently. Thus, educational finance, which has been directed toward the elusive goal of student equity for 100 years, can accommodate another goal—the enhancement of community. The implementation of some of all of these specific policies towards fostering benevolence in education would result in bonds between schools and neighbourhoods within a framework of district and state support.

The Vision of Voluntarism

Voluntarism is a good thing, according to a number of traditional sayings. We have been exhorted to do good by giving to others for hundreds and even thousands of years as shown by the quotations from the Bible and other sources in Table 9.1.

It is quite likely that many persons are influenced by the Biblical teachings even if they are not practicing Christians. People in more modern times have added their views on voluntarism's effects and have also exhorted us to give to others. See Table 9.2 in which the morality and beauty of voluntarism are reflected in the quotations from leaders and writers.

Notice that both ancient and modern voices reflect many of the themes encountered in this volume. Giving is desirable. Giving is noble. Giving is

TABLE 9.1   Some Traditional Statements on Benevolence

"Go and do thou likewise." (Luke 10:37. Taken from the story of the Good Samaritan)

Be "kindly affectioned one to another with brotherly love." (Romans 12:10)

"And now abideth faith, hope, charity, these three: but the greatest of these is charity." (1 Corinthians 13:13)

"Charity suffereth long and is kind; charity envieth not; charity vaunteth not itself, is not puffed up." (1 Corinthians 13:4. "Vaunteth" means boasting or bragging. This statement is sometimes paraphrased as "love is patient, love is kind, it does not boast.")

"And though I bestow all my goods to feed the poor, and though I give my body to be burned, and have not charity, it profiteth me nothing." (1 Corinthians 12:3)

"He who wishes to secure the good of others, has already secured his own." (Confuscius)

"He only does not live in vain, who employs his wealth, his thought, his speech to advance the good of others." (Hindu Maxim)

"He gives not best who gives most; but he gives most who gives best. If I cannot give bountifully, yet I will give freely, and what I want in my hand, I will supply in my heart." (Earl of Warwick)

"Give freely to him that deserveth well and asketh nothing; and that is a way of giving to thyself." (Fuller)

an act of free will. Giving is smart. Giving unites us. As the second millennium comes to an end, there is hopefulness in North American society that a sense of community may be regained. While there is always the possibility that such a wish may be based on nostalgia or utopia, the desire for more social capital in the lives of individuals is grounded in the realization that our social structures could serve us better than they do today.[86]

The untimely death in 1997 of Diana, Princess of Wales, drew attention to our admiration for acts of giving. While her adulation was based on a number of her attributes and accomplishments, one of the recurrent themes that arose when people were asked why they mourned was her concern and work on behalf of the world's less fortunate people, particularly the children. Similarly, Mother Teresa's passing in the same week accentuated a similar sentiment and the need for action. The rest of us do likewise. Act by act, a great many individuals (mostly in their own quiet ways) engage in simple giving behaviour.[87]

When taken together, volunteers contribute to a process of social reconstruction that may be very significant when we look back half a century from now. We may think of this time as "the great reclamation," in

TABLE 9.2   Some Quotations on Giving from Modern Times

"The truly generous is the truly wise; And he who loves not others, lives un-blest." (Home)

"They who scatter with one hand, gather with two, not always in coin, but in kind. Nothing multiplies so much as kindness." (Wray)

"Give what you have. To some one it may be better than you dare to think." (Longfellow)

"The conqueror is regarded with awe; the wise man commands our respect; but it is only the benevolent man that wins our affection." (Howells)

"Nothing but what you volunteer has the essence of life, the springs of pleasure in it. These are the things you do because you want to do them, the things your spirit has chosen for its satisfaction. . . . The more you are stimulated to such action the more clearly does it appear to you that you are a sovereign spirit, put into the world not to wear a harness, but to work eagerly without it." (Woodrow Wilson)

"In every community . . . we need a program for voluntary action by the people, not just government action for the people—many problems can be tackled right at home; human and social problems like education . . . through the organization of voluntary effort. Nothing can melt such human and social problems faster than the willingness of one individual to involve himself voluntary in helping an-other individual overcome his problems." (George Romney)

"[Compassion] enriches and ennobles us, even those of us who are neither the care givers nor the recipients, because it holds forth a vision of what a good soci-ety can be, provides us with concrete examples of caring that we can emulate, and locates us as members of the diffuse networks of which our society is wo-ven." "Above all, compassion gives us hope—both that the good society we envi-sion is possible and that the very act of helping each other gives us strength and a common destiny." (Wuthnow)

which human beings reaffirmed the primacy of their primordial institu-tions. As the environmental movement had its inception in a few ideas and acts of a few decades ago, so the movement that might be called "so-cial environmentalism" now grows from small beginnings.[88] Although some changes in the social environment are considered to be beneficial, there is also the need to preserve social structures that have been devel-oped over the course of three million years since the time of Lucy, one of the world's first humans.[89] If we wish to change or replace institutions, then we must look to the long-term impact those changes have on our so-cial well-being as members of the human race. Such social environmen-talism resembles "natural" environmentalism in that both contain actions that are undertaken "for the good of others." There is some evidence that the movement has been started on a wide scale. Called "communitar-ian," it is dedicated to strengthening the social environment in which we

live. A balance of rights and responsibilities, affirmation of primordial institutions, and the desire to avoid both puritanical excesses and the police state are some tenets of the communitarian promise.[90] There is a spirit
of "can do" among individuals and small groups.[91] As we look around
for ways in which to "run" our world, we are reminded by Boulding's
maxim: "The stick, the carrot and the hug may all be necessary, but the
greatest of these is the hug" (Original in bold, p. 250).

If benevolence ennobles life, then what promise does school voluntarism hold? Observations of benevolence in public schools in this book
show that the path of voluntarism is one route to achieving greater connections among human beings. Perhaps no group is more important than
the younger generation (an oft-stated remark). As Alan Pifer, former
president of the Carnegie Corporation of New York said, "Not only are
they our future security, but their dreams and ideals can provide a much-
needed renaissance of spirit in what is becoming an aging, tired, and dis-
illusioned society. In the end the *only* thing we have is our young people.
If we fail them, all else is in vain" (original italics, quoted in Hobbs, pp.
1–2). Since we want our children to possess a sense of community,[92] what
better way to guide them than to demonstrate our benevolence to them?
Ernest Boyer, former United States Commissioner of Education, held
strongly to the potential of school voluntarism:

> I believe that every school can be enriched by volunteers, and every child be
> helped by those who care. Moreover, I believe that every volunteer *can* be
> spiritually rewarded by sharing time and talent with the school. The beauti-
> ful genius of volunteerism is this: happily, it springs not from coercion, not
> from compulsion, not from legislation. . . . The genius and the beauty is that
> it springs from the vitality of the human spirit and from the conviction that
> if we have faith and hope and love, we can make this a better world. (from a
> presentation to the National School Volunteer Program annual conference,
> Arlington VA, February, 1978)

This belief is quite distant from practices of the past in which schools
posted signs saying "NO PARENTS BEYOND THIS POINT."[93] As public
schools become more like private schools,[94] perhaps we may speak of re-
generation rather than reform of public education.[95] The wish is to build
Gemeinschaft within Gesellschaft.[96] Even Willard Waller, who accentuated the gulf between teachers and parents, thought that children would
benefit greatly if strong ties developed school and home.[97]

While there is no question that school voluntarism poses some problems (bees come with the honey), *the state can pay the bills but it can't love a
school.* What kind of educational institutions do we want for our children
at the start of the next millennium? Can they be schools with heart?

Notes

1. See Weisbrod, who compares governmental, nonprofit, and private sectors and asserts that they are imperfect substitutes (pp. 103–106).

2. Governmental provision is only one way to destroy social capital. Others include individual self-sufficiency and individual mobility. See Coleman (1990, pp. 316–318).

3. See both Bender and Warren on community.

4. The assertion that governmental agencies serve people sometimes rather badly may be generalized. Coleman suggests that all modern corporate actors (not just governments, but also businesses and nonprofit institutions) actually have a parasitic character. See Coleman (1990, p. 634).

5. See Weisbrod (pp. 25–28) and Douglas (p. 47).

6. See Coleman (1990, pp. 429–433).

7. See Kramer (p. 252).

8. Voluntarism is almost omnipresent. For a total of seventeen areas and many examples, see Ellis and Noyes (pp. 315–337).

9. Many initiatives are associated with state offices of volunteerism and federal initiatives such as the Peace Corps in the United States. See Brudner (pp. 3–17).

10. The return to a golden age of voluntarism is disparaged by Kramer (p. 252).

11. See Salamon on failure (p. 109).

12. See Salamon on the fit between institutions and the services they provide (p. 113).

13. There is therefore no need for public education since it violates the benefit principle. See Glazer (pp. 156–165) and Coleman (1986, pp. 365–367 and 374). Although these views of justice are conflicting, most of us may be said to subscribe to both to some extent.

14. Voluntarism with its gifts freely given becomes one avenue for the benefit principle to be effected. Enterprise is another means.

15. See Wise (p. 203).

16. See Peshkin on the attempt to preserve human dignity and well-being on the one hand, and national integration and justice on the other (p. 201).

17. Conceptually, these problems are linked since control means the authority to make decisions concerning resources. The problem of the reduction in social capital does not receive as much attention as the issues of resources and control.

18. See Cuban, Murphy and Hallinger (p. 4), and Chubb and Moe (pp. 6–23).

19. The best example may be the push for cost accounting (misnamed efficiency) that was well documented by Callahan.

20. A strategy of investigation, debate, and thorough understanding of changes for schools prior to extensive attempts at application might break the inevitability of the cyclic pattern.

21. There are many dissatisfactions associated with public schools and many of them may give impetus to proposals for school choice. See Elam, Rose, and Gallup (1996).

22. See Chubb and Moe, pp. 186–229. A host of variations and issues come to mind from this short description, but they are not addressed here. See Chubb and Moe, Boyd and Walberg, and Clune and Witte, Cookson, and Coons and Sugarman.

23. They always compete to some extent and students always choose schools. However, competition and deliberate parental/student choice would be enhanced under this plan.

24. Note that there is a certain disassociation in voucher plans: control is placed in parents' hands as private consumers but the resources they possess are public because monies are raised through tax rolls.

25. See Cooper (1993) for different manifestations of choice in education.

26. This plan paid public money to private schools. See Erickson (pp. 94 and 98).

27. See Elmore (p. 40).

28. The Education Commission of the States and Center for School Change reports that the average size of charter schools was 140 students, that their mission was often one of a multidisciplinary curriculum, technology, or back to the basics. Two case studies of charter school establishment show that both had the advantage of considerable parental cooperation and solidarity, according to Raywid.

29. Note that since the schools in this inquiry were almost all elementary ones and since voucher plans are usually aimed at secondary schools, the basis for generating social capital would most likely be enterprise more than voluntarism. Enterprise is based on immediate, two-way exchanges while voluntarism is based on one-way transactions. For a fine guide for mostly enterprise activities for schools, see Knight (1993a). If the schools of choice were elementary schools, as charter schools often are, then voluntarism would probably be a critical source of physical, human, and social capital to them.

30. See Brown (1991), Knight d(1993b), and Caldwell and Spinks.

31. See Brown (1990) for an assessment of the arrangements in Edmonton, Canada. This version of school-based management is closely akin to divisionalization in large corporations. For an extensive and insightful analysis of divisionalization, see Mintzberg.

32. See Knight (1992) for developments in England and Wales, Caldwell and Spinks for the Australian variation, and Hess for the story on how Chicago adopted school-based management.

33. See Brown (1991), Hannaway, Wohlstetter and Buffett, and Caldwell.

34. See Brown (1990).

35. See Malen and Ogawa.

36. For instance, only equipment and supplies rather than personnel decisions may be authorized.

37. See Brown (1991 and 1992).

38. See Boyd and Cibulka, Devins, and James and Levin.

39. See Bryk, Lee, and Holland on Catholic high schools and Hostetler and Huntington on Amish education.

40. Original emphasis. This remark was made in a class on the sociology of education at the University of Chicago in 1970. There were no reactions among the graduate students; perhaps most had been educated both up for occupational advantage and away, socially *and* geographically, from their parents. I wonder what their parents' reactions might have been.

41. See Coleman and Hoffer (p. 23).

42. See Chubb and Moe (p. 181) and Bryk, Lee, and Holland (pp. 245–271).

43. They are communitarian in Bryk, Lee, and Holland's terms.

44. Bryk, Lee, and Holland conclude that Catholic high schools are bridging institutions, but in a different way than public voluntary schools (pp. 316–318). While Catholic high schools are seen to provide a bridge upon which children tread from the home to the larger world as they grow older, voluntary public schools offer a double pathway upon which many persons travel from the school to the community and back.

45. Catholic high schools and single-focus magnet high schools typically have considerable parental involvement. See Bausch and Goldring.

46. See Bryk, Lee, and Holland (pp 297–304). They characterize Catholic high schools as having a common curriculum for most students, a communal organization, decentralized governance, and an inspirational ideology. In contrast to religious schools, others that rely solely on tuition and government aid probably possess less social capital.

47. Either they attract gifts or they engage in exchanges such as fees for services.

48. Again, they do so via voluntarism and enterprise.

49. Not much has been said about enterprise in this book, particularly regarding the construction of social capital. Enterprise, or exchanges based upon two-way transactions that render relatively certain returns, can produce social capital as people work together. But there are some elements of enterprise that do not foster the construction of norms at all. Examples are fund raising at casinos, investments, or other activities in which there is almost no social aspect. In general, voluntarism is more likely to result in social capital than enterprise is. See Brown (1993).

50. See Jordan (pp. 287–329).

51. Many gave small amounts; some gave a lot. See Jordan (pp. 337–340).

52. See Chapter 3.

53. See Owen (p. 597).

54. See Bremner (pp. 8–19). He reminds us that the Native peoples were the first philanthropists in North America and that not all philanthropy was solely for the unfortunate (p. 3).

55. See Eisenstadt (pp. 229–273).

56. See Ellis and Noyes (pp. 50–95).

57. See Ellis and Noyes (p. 26).

58. Butts and Cremin (p. 53).

59. Katz considers the New York School society to be an example of what he calls "paternalistic voluntarism," which he described as a class system of education (pp. 25–27).

60. See Cubberley (pp. 121–137).

61. See Butts and Cremin (p. 103).

62. Katz makes this point strongly when he labels rural community complete support and control of schools as "democratic localism." (p. 32).

63. See Mort and Reusser (p. 73).

64. See Johns and Morphet (p. 206).

65. See Crowson on the growth of public education with the centralization and consolidation that resulted in the reduction of neighbourhood control from the 1800's onwards (pp. 25–28). See also Lutz and Merz (pp. 12–33).

66. For an overview of contemporary educational finance, see Cibulka.

67. This is the definition of voluntarism or benevolence offered in Chapter 2.

68. As defined in Chapter 6.

69. This hope of transformation comes with a paradox, though. It is possible to provide excessive amounts of rules that, ironically, interfere with the process of building institutional bridges. An important point to remember is that voluntarism cannot be legislated. It can only be encouraged.

70. As Epstein and Daubler report, such programs become "equalizers" by encouraging the involvement of parents who would not otherwise participate on their own (p. 290).

71. Other authors have made similar recommendations. Coleman and Hoffer indicate the need for parent meetings and school-wide events to increase intergenerational closure (pp. 237–239). Epstein's six-part model, which is normative, indicates how linkages are to be built through family involvement, use of special scheduling to involve benefactors, and invitations to the community to attend school functions (1990, pp. 113–116). Michael et al suggest that volunteers be provided designated rooms, written guidelines, tailored training, and special thanks. They stress that teachers should not be coerced into accepting volunteers and that their reasons for not using volunteers be acknowledged as legitimate (pp. 90–99).

72. Michael et al indicate the need for support at the top policy level. Changes in superintendents and boards may imperil a volunteer program (p. 100).

73. See Michael (p. 67) and Hill (pp. 86–89).

74. Three guides which includes advice on how to set up a volunteer network is Batey's Parents are Lifesavers: A Handbook for Parental Involvement in Schools, Pawlas' School-community Relations, and Decker's Home-school-community Relations.

75. It is likely that another 10 percent could be supported with enterprise activities, such as the sale of goods and services and the collection of fees. See Brown and Bouman. Most nonpublic schools in British Columbia are sustained on a similar regimen. They typically receive only 50% of the funds that a comparable public school receives in the same school district.

76. The criteria to be applied to have more than 90 percent public support would need to be clear. They would probably include indicators such as parental income and parental recency of immigration.

77. McLaughlin also recommends the approach as using norm-based pressures to encourage inventive strategies for parental involvement (p. 157).

78. Naturally, such a criterion would need to be integrated with present policies of transfer and placement.

79. See Michael (p 16).

80. See Davies.

81. See Kraznow on working with teachers in the Schools Reaching Out Project.

82. See Hill (pp. 69–75).

83. See Michael (pp. 26–27).

84. I contend that this shift needs to take place to ensure that public schools remain viable. Parents, in particular, can no longer assume that even basic public education is provided entirely at taxpayers' expense.

85. From Bruce Cooper, via private correspondence.

86. See Glazer (p. 104) and Hewitt (p. 131 and p. 237). Community, with its aid and its ties, remains important to us all (p. 237).

87. Actually, Wilson (1993) observes that it is not everyday good deeds that capture public attention in the media. Rather, savage behaviour is considered newsworthy and people are shocked accordingly. Therefore, he asserts that compassion is the norm and inhumanity is the deviant behaviour (p. 2).

88. I know the world does not need another "ism," but these two words were the best I could find to describe the conception. Environmentalism is mostly concerned with the preservation of the natural environment, in part because human beings are seen to benefit in the long term from a natural environment that is not greatly altered from its primordial state. Better health, biodiversity, respect for all forms of life, minimization of unnatural impact are some of its aims. The word "social" is added to consider similar goals but applied to the social surroundings in which people live.

89. See Johanson and O'Farrell.

90. See Etzioni (1993, pp. 1–15) and Etzioni (1996) in which he affirms the need to achieve a societal balance between individual autonomy and order, thus giving more impetus to the communitarian ideal. Resurgence in the concept of community is usually attributed to MacIntyre and Taylor. See Bell for an articulation of the liberal-communitarian debate.

91. See Lappe and DuBois.

92. See Goodlad (p. 338).

93. See McLeod (pp. 146–148).

94. See Swanson (p. 229).

95. See Bryk (1988, p. 257).

96. See Sergiovanni (p. 14).

97. See Waller (p. 69).

Appendix:
The Research Method

Any document in the social sciences that purports to be more than simply a "think piece" based on arguments requires that evidence be brought forward in order to support its generalizations, however tentative they may be. Consequently, the credibility of that evidence is an important consideration in the overall evaluation of the veracity of the account and the weight of its conclusions. The evidence in this volume stems from two kinds of origins. One source, referred to as "primary," is the data set specifically based on voluntarism as found in certain public elementary schools in British Columbia.[1] The other source constitutes facts and generalizations used to understand voluntarism, first, in schools scattered around the world and second, outside of the institution of education altogether. Although the contexts of the studies varied considerably from the circumstances of the primary data, their recurrent themes were used to provide empirical checks against the patterns shown in the prime sources. Section by section, the "data chapters" presented evidence first from the primary data and then from secondary sources. When both primary and secondary sources were in general agreement, generalizations were proposed. This appendix offers the background of the primary data, outlines how the primary study was conducted, and discusses some of the basic premises on which this inquiry was founded.

The Questions and Interviewees

Data were collected during the period 1989–1994, usually in principals' offices or school classrooms, but occasionally in volunteers' homes. One interview was carried out in a car. Notes were written or taped, depending on the preferences of the interviewer and interviewee. Assurances of anonymity were given (but not of confidentiality).

This set of standard questions was asked (parentheses indicate probes):

1. What tasks do volunteers perform in your school? (tutoring, supervision, transportation, clerical work, fund raising, special events, lunch programs)
2. Please describe your average volunteer. (age, sex, child in school, employment, income level, ethnicity)
3. Why do your volunteers help out? (to assist own child, to learn skills, feel obliged, for companionship)

4. How are volunteer recruited for your school? (incentives, mechanisms)
5. How are volunteers organized in your school? (processes, roles and responsibilities, problems)
6. What effects do your volunteers have? (on children, volunteers themselves, contribution to the school, relations within the school, school relations with the community)
7. What factors influence volunteer participation in your school? (organization, leadership, neighbourhood characteristics, district policies)

Notice that the questions are presented in an order from those requiring more descriptive responses to those asking for more reflective answers. That design gave the respondents the opportunity to recall the substance of the topic and its circumstances as completely as possible. Probes were used when information was not disclosed in immediate responses and they were included primarily in interviews held later in the time period of the study; earlier ones were more open-ended since the main categories of the data were not established at that time. No distinctions in question content were made between selected and non-selected schools.[2] Although the interview structure was standardized, individual questions were varied depending upon the subject (principal, teacher, or volunteer) and, to some extent, the interests of the interviewee and interviewer. An outcome of that strategy was that not all questions were answered by all respondents.[3] This questioning arrangement may be called "partially structured" because it is more flexible than semi-structured interviewing that requires a strict order of questioning and does not permit queries to be modified by the questioner.[4]

Interviews usually took one hour. Interpretations of the impacts of factors or the certainty of effects were checked with the respondent during the session. Some subjects requested information about school voluntarism from their interviewer. Often, the investigator indicated an intention to send the interviewee a copy of the report of that portion of the study conducted in the district. In all cases, interviewers compiled their notes from the sessions and returned them to their respondents for a validation of facts and interpretations. When there was a discrepancy between the memory of the questioner and the altered notes, the change was taken as accurate.[5] Interviewers reported their experiences to be enjoyable and that they received full cooperation except in two instances in which interviews were terminated early by respondents. As principle investigator for the study, I conducted eleven interviews myself in order to learn first hand how people reacted to the questions. The conversations appeared to be highly meaningful to my respondents. Each encounter was challenging, intriguing, enjoyable, and tiring for me. In many cases, investigators observed that interviews exceeded the planned time because of respondents' enthusiasm to share their experiences and reflections. They seemed flattered to be asked.[6] Subjects' willingness to be interviewed may have been enhanced because they participated voluntarily. In the cases of interviews with teachers and volunteers, their principal's clearance of the interview also likely increased their level of cooperation.

A total of 185 principals, vice-principals, teachers, and volunteers were interviewed. Research team members asked contact persons in school districts for

TABLE A.1   Role and Sex of Interviewees in the Sample

	Principals	*Vice-Principals*	*Teachers*	*Volunteers*	*Total*	*Percentage*
Male	47	6	2	13	68	37
Female	11	5	31	70	117	63
Total	58	11	33	83	185	100
Percentage	31	6	18	45	100	

names of personnel who were highly informed about school volunteers. The persons identified were often principals and they were frequently interviewed. Most of the remaining interviewees were chosen by principals because they were familiar with volunteer work—they were teachers or volunteers.[7] Some interviewees were chosen because their (unselected) schools were not known for their volunteer programs. Persons were distributed across role and sex as shown in Table A.1.

Most administrators were male (77%) while most teachers and volunteers were female (87%). Persons who worked for pay in schools comprised 55% of the sample; 45% were volunteers.[8]

The Sample of Schools

A total of 72 public elementary schools formed the sample for the primary data. Fifty-four (75%) of them were selected on the basis of the reputation of their volunteer programs. They were chosen by the investigators (who typically worked in their respective districts) in conjunction with school district personnel, usually central office administrators and principals. A school qualified for inclusion when it was known to have considerable numbers of volunteers or when its volunteer program had produced special events or initiatives that gained attention.[9] No other school characteristics were used to include them in the sample. Eighteen were "typical" elementary schools that were not considered notable by the investigators and district contact persons in that regard. They were chosen on the basis of their proximity to the schools with many volunteers and are referred to as "nonselected" throughout this book. The data gathered from them were used to contrast with findings from selected schools. Once the sample of schools was identified, interviewee selection followed.

Investigators classified the schools, once they had been included in the primary data, in a number of ways. One was by location, defined as urban (in a large or medium-sized city of 50,000 or more people), suburban (outside a large or medium-sized city) or rural (in towns or relatively isolated areas). Another categorization was by relative wealth of the neighbourhoods that constituted the schools' catchments. Principals were asked to label their schools according to their socioeconomic status. Although no objective criteria were used, principals were assumed to have a sense of the background of the children with whom they worked on a daily basis. Their classifications were: schools in which most parents held professional or managerial positions (higher income), schools in which parents held mainly white collar positions or a balanced mix of all backgrounds (middle income), and schools in which most parents worked in blue collar occu-

TABLE A.2   Sample Schools Distributed by Location and Socioeconomic Status

	Urban	Suburban	Rural	Total	Percentage
Higher income	6	6	1	13	18
Middle income	4	20	12	36	50
Lower income	9	6	8	23	32
Total	19	32	21	72	100
Percentage	26	44	29	99*	

*Shows error due to rounding.

TABLE A.3   Sample School Enrollments and School Socioeconomic Status

	Small (40–200)	Medium (201–500)	Large (501–1100)	Total	Percentage
Higher income	1	10	2	13	18
Middle income	11	21	4	36	50
Lower income	10	10	3	23	32
Total	22	41	9	72	100
Percentage	31	57	13	101*	

*Shows error due to rounding.

pations (lower income). Table A.2 shows the school breakdown on these two dimensions.

Most schools were suburban and most were rated as middle income (28% of the sample schools fell in both categories). While lower income schools were evenly distributed across the three locations, higher income schools were located almost solely in urban and suburban areas. No substantial differences were observed between selected and unselected schools with regard to location or socioeconomic status. Seventeen of the total of 23 lower income schools were selected schools.[10]

The schools in the sample also varied considerably in size. The relationship between size and socioeconomic status is shown in Table A.3. Divisions of enrollments into small, medium, and large were largely arbitrary except that they reflected some natural "clumping" in the data.

Most schools fell in the medium sized category and the modal schools were both medium-sized and middle income, being 29% of the sample. Only one small school was located in a higher income neighbourhood. Although 19 of the schools were situated within urban areas,[11] only 9 were over 500 students in size. This outcome may reflect a tendency to build smaller schools to serve smaller neighbourhoods or a lack of urban density surrounding the schools studied. No particular pattern appeared to exist between enrollments and socio-economic status as measured. Selected and unselected schools showed little difference in average size.

Another basis for understanding the context of the schools in the primary sample is to see how they are distributed across their respective 17 districts, 11 of

TABLE A.4   Numbers of Schools Across District Wealth Categories

	Residential Assessed Value per Pupil	*Number of Sample Schools*	*Percentage*
High	$182,000–338,000	22	31
Medium	82,000–162,000	29	40
Low	43,000–75,000	21	29
Total		72	100

SOURCE: Ministry of Education, Province of British Columbia, 1992–1993, in Canadian dollars.

TABLE A.5   Numbers of Schools Across District Enrollment Categories

	Number of Students in District	*Number of Sample Schools*	*Percentage*
Small	800–3,000	4	6
Medium	4,000–10,000	27	38
Large	11,000–23,000	332	44
Extra Large	52,614	9	13
Total		72	101*

*Shows error due to rounding.

SOURCE: Ministry of Education, Province of British Columbia, 1992.

which are located in Greater Vancouver.[12] Schools were scattered across districts with highly varying residential assessed value per pupil,[13] as shown in Table A.4.

The divisions in the residential assessed value per pupil show natural breaks in the data. Most of the schools in the low category were located in rural areas, while most of the schools in the medium and high categories were in suburban or urban areas. If the residential assessed value per pupil averaged across districts is an accurate measure of the material resources surrounding schools, then these data reveal that the richest environments possess eight times the wealth of the poorest ones.[14]

A final indicator of school context is the elementary and secondary student enrollment of the districts in which schools in the primary data were located. District enrollments give some sense of schools' organizational and social environments. Table A.5 displays the breakdown.

All small districts were rural ones. The single, "extra large" urban district is Vancouver. Clearly, the typical school in this sample was embedded in a district that enrolled between 4,000 and 23,000 students. Divisions in the number of students reflect natural discontinuities in the data.

The Larger Setting

The 72 public schools comprising the primary sample were affected by circumstances beyond their respective neighbourhoods. While the greater environment most likely influenced different schools differently, two particular demands made upon schools in British Columbia prior to and during the period of the study may have caused similar effects that are relevant to the study of voluntarism. These were increases in the number of children for whom English was a second language, and the number of children with special needs.

The English as a Second Language (ESL) additions were a direct effect of Canadian immigration policies. During 1992, 20.7 percent of immigration was from the United States, Great Britain, and Europe while the remainder came mostly from countries in which English was not the primary language.[15] While 35 percent of persons in British Columbia had British origins, the second largest minority group was Chinese.[16] A total of 20.6 percent of persons resident in the province had a native language that is not English.[17] As a consequence of these federal immigration policies, total ESL student enrollment grew from 20,249 in 1988–89 to 48,990 in 1992–93, an increase of 142 percent in four years.[18]

Schools in British Columbia were also affected by the special education policies of the provincial government. Children with handicaps continued to be integrated into regular classrooms. Students who were moderately handicapped increased by 45 percent (from 33,080 to 47,875) while those who were severely handicapped increased by 40 percent (from 3,953 to 5,551) during the period 1988–89 to 1992–93.[19] Although additional dollars for both ESL and special needs children were provided by the province, there was recurrent controversy about the sufficiency of the resources given to classroom teachers. One reason that ESL and special education programs were contentious was that relatively few nonpublic schools in the province offered them.

In addition to these two issues, competition for students was a recurring concern on the part of the public school system prior to and during the study. One reason is that nonpublic schools receive public aid in British Columbia and in other provinces of Canada.[20] Table A.6 shows nonpublic school enrollments and grants and their trends over time.

During the period 1980–81 to 1992–93, the number of private schools expanded from 115 to 313, an increase of 172%. The span of twelve years shows considerable enrollment and funding growth for private schools in the province. Trends were less pronounced for the public schools, as shown in Table A.7.

During the twelve-year period cited in these figures, the public school teaching force expanded by 13.5. Elementary class sizes increased from 22.8 to 23.1 (+1%) and the pupil teacher ratio (including all certificated personnel) decreased from 17.3 to 16.6 (–4%) across the twelve years.[21]

A simple comparison of private and public enrollments shows that nonpublic schools served only 8.1 percent of the total school-aged children in the province during 1992–93. Clearly, most children attended public schools. Private schools received only 2.9 percent of the total funds for elementary and secondary education, a percentage far below their enrollment share. This was because their level of public funding was established at an average of 43.4 percent of that provided to public schools. For private schools, differences between the public funds received and their total yearly expenditures were made up from tuition and other private sources, including voluntarism.

Finally, another concern to public education in British Columbia during this study was the general capacity of its citizens to support their schools with monies

TABLE A.6 Nonpublic School Enrollments and Grants

	1980–81	*1992–93*	*Change*
Enrollment	20,925	43,965	+100%
Total Grants	$13 M	$99 M	+663%
Average per pupil grant	$684	$2,754	+303%

NOTE: The amount per pupil was increased during the period.

SOURCE: Ministry of Education, Province of British Columbia.

TABLE A.7 Public School Enrollments and Grants

	1981	*1992–93*	*Change*
Enrollment*	492,054	540,390	+9.8%
Total Grants	$1,602M	$3,367M	+110%
Cost per pupil*	$3,257	$6,345	+95%

*Reflects mainstreaming policy.

SOURCE: Ministry of Education, Province of British Columbia.

from taxation. The income of the average family in the province was $30,272 in 1980 and $54,894 in 1991, a rise of 81 percent as compared to the increase in the cost of living which was 70 percent for approximately the same period.[22] Although income growth exceeded inflation, a full 48 percent of the family's income was paid in taxes of various kinds during 1993.[23] Unemployment continued to stay at about ten percent of the labour force during this time. These figures show some of the reasons why the provincial government remained unenthusiastic about increasing the levels of support for public education. As a consequence of the demands of ESL and mainstreaming, along with competition from private schools and government unwillingness to increase expenditures greatly, public schools were given incentives to seek resources beyond those provided from public funds.[24]

Thus, an analysis of the larger context of the public schools in the primary sample reveals the heavy demands on them for ESL and mainstreaming services, the limited level of competition from nonpublic schools, and the province's reticence to provide them more dollars via taxation. These challenges will sound familiar to readers around the globe, particularly in the United States. But besides their financial and educational contexts, are Canadians in British Columbia sufficiently similar to Americans so that the experiences encountered in the schools there may be generalized? Fortunately, Seymour Martin Lipset has provided some answers to these questions in his extensive study that compared the two countries often seen as "children of a common mother."[25] Tracing the loyalist and rebel roots of the two societies, he paints a picture of Canadians as more elitist, law-abiding, statist, and collectively-oriented while Americans are seen as more individualist, achievement-oriented, egalitarian, and materialistic. His results show that Canadians rely more on government service while Americans remain suspicious of them. If that conclusion is correct, expressions of benevolence as gifts freely given should occur less frequently in Canada than in the United

States. Lipset found that Canadian governments spend more per capita than the U.S. and Canadian citizens give less per person for nonreligious causes.[26] That difference suggests that there should be less voluntarism directed toward public schools in Canada. If so, the "test of benevolence" based on Canadian data in this volume is a conservative one. Voluntarism for public education should be even more evident in America than the primary data show.

Yet, another interpretation of Lipset's work may be made. His central thesis is that many of these differences between the United States and Canada are actually small:

> the two resemble each other more than either resembles any other nation. Both are products of North American settler societies. They have many structures and classically liberal views in common, and they vary in comparable ways from postfeudal, mercantilist Britain and Europe. Their differences, as we have seen from many public opinion polls, are often in the range of 5 to 10 percent. (Lipset, 1990, p. 212)

An assertion of basic similarity is also made by some Canadian critics of Lipset's work. They even take issue with his overall levels of participatory differences.[27] If their position is accepted (that variation in giving between the two nations remains at 10% or less), then this volume's context of Canadian schools can be said to resemble American circumstances with respect to benevolence.

Conduct of the Study

The data collection and interpretation were structured with a principal investigator and a set of student researchers. The researchers, all of whom were at advanced stages of completing requirements for a master's degree in educational administration,[28] worked as teachers, vice principals, or principals. Entry into the master's program had required endorsement from their respective districts as having administrative potential; they were identified as promising "insiders." The student researchers were 10 men and 8 women who ranged in age from 30 to 45. Prior to gathering their data, they were asked to submit a proposal containing a literature review on some aspect of voluntarism in schools and a research plan with their samples and questions (including the common ones). Proposals were vetted by the principal investigator who provided guidelines for conducting partially-structured interviews. Once their proposals were revised, approved, and clearance was granted from the university and school districts, the researchers collected their data. Since most of the students were part-time, meetings and social events were held during the year to maintain contact and direction. On completion of their interviews, the student researchers analyzed and synthesized their data and then submitted their drafts for review. When the papers were completed to the satisfaction of the principal investigator, they were given to a second professor for further revisions. These checks served to overcome any obvious errors and to secure the integrity of the individual works. After final corrections, the graduating papers were accepted. Frequent communication between the principle investigator and the students and among students themselves enhanced the reliability of the data by ensuring some standardization of interview technique, which included the collection of verbatim responses, low-inference descriptors, and interview simulations.[29]

I am pleased to pause here and acknowledge the eighteen men and women whose work contributed directly to the primary data set. They constituted a group with unbridled curiosity, determination to excel, and persistence under professional circumstances that were sometimes difficult. They ventured into new terrains, braved challenging interviewing conditions, showed great appetite for new ideas and facts, and shared the trials of revisions with each other. Each made a significant contribution to the project. They were: Oscar Bisnar who explored the delicate area of cultural differences, Glynn Crew who persisted in doing more than he was asked, Dennis Dempster whose enthusiasm was hard to contain, Allan Douglas who gained important insights despite adverse conditions in his school, Harry Edwards whose work covered close-knit farming communities, Victor Kusaka who explored his two schools in depth, Pam Milburn who energetically pursued principals of small schools in rural areas, Susan Mirhady whose urban interviewees gave some very special insights, Diane Nelson who was captivated by the idea of mentorship, Debbie Osipov whose strong determination to gather ample evidence paid off well, Sandy Pearce whose school contrasts were delightful, Glen Rose who searched widely for the best possible cases, Jim Rowse whose demonstrations of voluntarism in action provided important input at a critical time in the study, Patricia Stapleton who pursued her interviewees enthusiastically, Doug Thompson who helped blaze the trail in the project's early days, Rosalie Tully who tackled the hard socio-economic questions head-on, Bill Vliegenthart who covered his district's wide terrain in depth, and Evelyn Wood who so ably linked her evidence to resource dependency theory. My resounding thanks go to all these people.

There are three other groups of students that I would like to add to the Martian honour roll where "Martian" is derived from the acronym of the project called "Marketing and the Attraction of Resources for Schools." The first conducted pocket studies and thus contributed indirectly to the background of this investigation of voluntarism. Unlike their fellows, they undertook to write their papers and collected data on topics that were outside the institutional or geographic boundaries of the primary sample. As they were subject to the same rigours as the other studies, their works advanced my thinking about voluntarism both conceptually and specifically via the provision of comparative data. The pocket studies group included Wyatt Boulton who explored giving behaviour on the part of public high school teachers, Paul Brazeau who looked at voluntarism in French immersion schools in Ontario, and Peter O'Loughlin who studied benevolence in Roman Catholic elementary and secondary schools. The breadth of perspective offered by their studies was most helpful. A second group of students was also instrumental in providing related ideas and evidence. They explored ideas and experience relating to school enterprise (in contrast to benevolence). While their number is too large to acknowledge them individually here, I thank them for their involvement in the overall MARS Project and their contributions to the exploration of how and why the pursuit of private resources is undertaken in public education. The third group of students were those in my course on school-community relations in the fall of 1993 who courageously agreed to criticize their professor's work by each assessing a chapter of this volume. Their analyses provided the some hard tests of the first draft and their efforts suitably were rewarded in a fair exchange, albeit an immediate one.

Returning to the specific research methods associated with the primary data, each of the student inquiries that contributed directly to the data set was conducted in accordance with the following general methodology. Specific answers of individual respondents were checked for factual confirmation with those of the 8–12 others within the immediate study. Responses were then aggregated across the interviews. Concordant and discordant answers were noted, patterns of data were observed and emergent topics were recorded. Metaphoric or factual quotations were highlighted. The results were synthesized to 15–20 pages and some initial conclusions were generated. A research paper of between 50 to 100 pages was written by each interviewer.

After the reports were submitted, the results were disaggregated and recompiled by the themes that had either been evident from the literature or that had emerged from the interviews independently. The abridged results were entered into files by themes into an outlining computer program.[30] A parallel set of files was built containing notes from the relevant literature on voluntarism, spanning the strictly conceptual to the highly empirical.

The ongoing analysis and synthesis of both the literature and the particular data can be described properly as an interactive exploration of voluntarism in public schools. Initially, the principal investigator reviewed the literature and wrote a research proposal. When funded, the project produced data that were generated in light of the literature but in a highly exploratory way. After a report assembling the knowledge to that date was written to the funding agency, the principal investigator and students searched the literature again in greater depth and the student team gathered further data. This time, more profound explanations for giving behaviour were encountered and the data became narrower in scope, for instance, fewer schools were included in more depth. A synthesizing article was written in order to assess the overall direction of the project.[31] Once again, the literature was investigated to determine the limits of what it had to offer and the remaining data were collected with more intense investigations into particular themes.[32] This book is the product of the "final" analysis and synthesis of the inquiry into benevolence in schools. Its development may be interpreted as a manifestation of David Krathwohl's research chain of reasoning that includes the components of data, questions, explanations, and research design.[33]

Spirit of the Research Method

The use of the partially-structured interviewing technique was accompanied by attempts to secure the internal and external validity of the study. The inquiry's internal validity, considered to be the level of agreement of interpretations and concepts between participants and researcher,[34] was strengthened in one rather significant way by the commonality in backgrounds between the student researchers and their respondents. All researchers were public schools teachers or administrators who had worked with school volunteers at some point in their professional lives. They had spent much of their time in the kinds of schools in which the interviews were conducted. All respondents had strong contacts with the public schools, either as persons who had built careers in them in the cases of principals and teachers, or as persons who had donated considerable amounts of time to them in them as volunteers. There was much common ground to build mutual understandings on all aspects of voluntarism.[35] Once the facts and interpretations were established tentatively, the investigators provided an integration of them that was also influenced by their immersion in the institution. The eighteen graduate students offered challenges to the tentative perspectives provided and forged some of their own explorations into the understanding of giving to schools. Additionally, it is quite likely that the researchers would not have been able to access the information that they did unless they had been received as credible colleagues.

What of the study's external validity, the ability to generalize from its results?[36, 37] Potential generalization was deliberately crafted in three particular ways: the first was the use of purposive sampling.[38] This technique selected not just schools but particular persons within them in order to gain depth of knowledge about benevolence. Consequently, generalizations are not to be made to the typical public elementary school, but to the prospect of what the typical school could be. The second way in which external validity was strengthened was the addition of the data from many other studies (some of them quantitative in orientation) to overcome the delimitations of the primary data set based exclusively on interviews. Many other investigations have been undertaken on both volunteers in general and on volunteers in schools—they made significant contributions to the secondary data available. The third way was to use a conceptual framework that encompasses many social perspectives brought to bear on the issue of voluntarism. Thus, the substantive explanations generated from the data were brought together with formal explanations from the literature, as suggested by Anselm Strauss and Juliet Corbin.[39]

Most of the data gathered in this study may be labeled "perceptual," that is, it emanates from respondents' interpretations of their social worlds. A weakness of such data is that the perceptions can simply be wrong, despite the agreement that interviewees have. However, a strength of this kind of data is that tests of perceived cause and effect may be applied. For instance, respondents were asked directly if they believed that specific factors influenced certain outcomes. When those connections were supported on the basis of several interviewees' experiences, they added information which could not be gleaned from any other data source. When the same connections were supported by many persons, the credibility of those links between potential causes and effects was strengthened. These techniques captured the special strengths of interviews.[40] Unfortunately, the same mechanisms are associated with some of the problems of interviewing, such as the predisposition on the part of some interviewees to either try to make a positive impression on the interviewer or to simply agree with the interviewer's remarks without thought.[41] While there is little doubt that some respondents, particularly principals, probably reacted in this manner, the reflective comments that the interviewers wrote in their reports concerning such potential biases suggested that such behaviour was encountered infrequently. Overall, the students saw almost all the interviews as being incidents of mutual exploration in which both positive and negative aspects of voluntarism were discussed frankly.

This inquiry could have been undertaken with a questionnaire. That form of data collection would have given a representative sample upon which generalizations could be made with the relative security of statistical inference to a population. The result would have been a "state of the art" assessment of voluntarism in public schools. Yet, it may have produced data of uncertain validity without any special meaning for educators, since questionnaires do not allow for the person-to-person interactions that permit meanings to be clarified and new ideas to be explored. Alternately, the inquiry could have been pursued using a single case study and resulted in rich description with an intense understanding of a voluntary school.[42] No other method could produce the relatively complete story of how, for instance, a voluntary school came to be. This approach, however, would have yielded a solitary account from which generalizations would have been precarious. Rather than pursue either of these two extremes of inquiry, the decision was made to undertake partially-structured interviews across a variety of schools that existed under a range of circumstances. This method resulted in some stability in numbers but not a great deal of depth of information into any given school. It produced some brief case statements but did not allow complete standardization of responses. The approach was therefore a compromise that maintained some strengths and inherited some weaknesses of the questionnaire and case study methods.[43, 44]

This general research strategy was also a compromise between two paradigms called conventional and constructivist as described by Egon Guba and Yvonna Lincoln.[45] They assert that researchers must choose between rigour or relevance, precision or richness, elegance or applicability, objectivity or subjectivity, and verification or discovery.[46] Very unhappy alternatives! A simple characterization of the present study is that it was more realist than relativist (an objective reality is assumed but the realities of others are invoked), more dualist than monist (researchers' and respondents' values were present though the researcher's values play some role), and more interventionist than hermeneutic (there is some supremacy of generality over context). In other words, this study assumed: there is one real world; causes influence our lives; people make choices freely; perceptual methods provide insights. Guba and Lincoln label this compromise "natural evaluation of the first kind," since it is a departure from the canons of quantitative research without fully embracing the tenets of qualitative research.[47] The method was certainly more modern than post-modern and intentionally so.[48]

Another way to characterize the spirit of this inquiry's research method in which conceptual work and empirical digging are undertaken alternately is "realism" as described by Norman Blaikie. Realist studies assume that social reality is socially constructed but exists independently of the observer. Researchers working within the realist tradition build models that aim to account for social phenomena by discovering their structures and mechanisms that through observing regularities from the outset of the inquiry. Their method of reason is neither strictly deductive or inductive but retroductive.[49] Realist studies require a combination of reason and imagination. Most importantly, social actors' constructions of reality comprise only one element in a realist social science.[50]

Regardless of the method chosen in social research, there is simply no certainty that the results are "right." As Peshkin says, "No research paradigm has a monopoly on quality. None can deliver promising outcomes with certainty. None have the grounds for saying 'this is it' about their designs, procedures, and anticipated outcomes" (p. 28). The work is hard and the choices are difficult. Why would anyone undertake this kind of inquiry? There are two simple responses. Coleman articulates one. He suggests that the purpose of social research is

> a search for knowledge for the reconstruction of society. As horizons become wider and possible directions of social progress multiply, knowledge about self and society, and their relation, gains a new importance and immediacy. (Coleman, 1990, p. 651)

This characterization of research gives it some noble aspirations and I find them persuasive. As with benevolence itself, inquiry connects the researcher with the social world. But there is also a more personal reason, as described by Everhart:

> People choose careers, spouses, places to live, and for scientists, their research questions and the manner of pursuing them in part as a way of coming to grips with who they are, where they have been, and where they wish to go. For social scientists, then, (and this includes those who focus upon issues of educational administration and policy), the study of others is, to a great extent, studying themselves. They are not involved just in objectively assessing the actions and meanings of others but also in a therapeutic relationship with themselves in a total autobiography. (Everhart, 1988 p. 723)

As shown by this study, social research in general (and inquiry into voluntarism in particular) is a meaningful enterprise, both in the social world and in the realm of the natural person.

Notes

1. The design and sampling of this study draws considerably from the guidelines on qualitative research provided by Schumacher and McMillan and was also influenced by the directions taken from Krathwohl.

2. See the next section for the difference between the two kinds of school in the sample.

3. Investigators were asked to "go for the gold." When they discovered an intriguing practice or explanation, they were instructed to seek elaboration of it. Although this tactic reduced comparability across respondents, it allowed some highly relevant data to be uncovered.

4. Krathwohl defines a continuum of interview structures which varies from unstructured to totally structured (p. 369).

5. Interviewees were given the opportunity to "take back their words" even when they were considered highly valuable to the inquiry.

6. This was especially true of the volunteers who were respondents.

7. A few were vice-principals who were classified as principals or administrators in this study since they offered a school-wide perspective on voluntarism.

8. The total number of principals and vice-principals (69) does not equal the total number of schools (72) reported in the next section because three small schools had head teachers.

9. See Bogdan and Biklen on purposeful sampling (p. 67).

10. The proportion of urban higher income schools in the sample is reflective of the relative wealth that is located within the borders of Vancouver, as may be found in most Canadian cities.

11. See Table A2.

12. The school sample of 72 constituted 14 percent of the total of 526 elementary schools in the 17 districts. Note that the selected schools were chosen solely on the criterion of the visibility of their volunteer programs while unselected schools were included because of their proximity to selected schools.

13. Residential assessed value per pupil is the total assessed value of all residential property in the district divided by the total district enrollment. It is a measure of district wealth and therefore an indicator of the ability of a district to finance educational services.

14. Note that these district environments are not equivalent to school neighbourhoods.

15. For instance, 47.5 percent were from Asia and Pacific countries. Interestingly the policy has effective a complete change since 1970, in which the net migration percentages were 63 percent from the United States and Europe and 22 percent from the Asia/Pacific region. See Statistics Canada.

16. See Statistics Canada.

17. The population of British Columbia grew from 2,883,367 in 1986 (the year of the world's fair, EXPO '86) to 3,282,061 in 1991, an increase of 13.8 percent. See Statistics Canada.

18. See Ministry of Education, Province of British Columbia.

19. See Ministry of Education, Province of British Columbia.

20. The terms "private" and "nonpublic" are used interchangeably here.

21. See Ministry of Education, Province of British Columbia.

22. Canadian cost of living figures were computed from 1981 to 1992. Statistics Canada.

23. See The Fraser Institute.

24. Provincial revenues fell during the period 1980–86. See Rekart for more background on the financial state of the province (pp. 32–56).

25. See Lipset.

26. See Lipset (p. 142).

27. See Curtis, Lambert, Brown, and Kay.

28. This program was normally taken as their sixth year of university education.

29. For a definition of reliability in qualitative analyses, see Schumacher and McMillan (pp. 385–391).

30. Originally called an idea processor, this program's main strength is its ability to categorize and order words by using an outline format.

31. See Brown (1993).

32. The content of the questions changed somewhat from comparatively global ones to others that were more thematic. See Krathwohl (p. 370) on this process.

33. See Krathwohl (pp. 58–68).

34. See Schumacher and McMillan (p. 391).

35. For the importance of matching characteristics between interviewer and interviewee, see Krathwohl (pp. 372–373).

36. This question has already been answered in part by the data on the respondents, schools, districts, and province and also by the brief comparison between Canada and the United States. See the other sections in this appendix.

37. For an account of external validity, see Schumacher and McMillan (pp. 394–397).

38. See Krathwohl for a description of purposive sampling (pp. 324–327).

39. See Strauss and Corbin (p. 23).

40. See Krathwohl (pp. 369–370) for an exposition of the virtues of the interview method, particularly when interviews are partially- or semi-structured.

41. Krathwohl (p. 392) reviews tendencies that can distort the kinds of information gathered.

42. A case study could have been carried out in accordance with the guidelines proposed in Strauss.

43. Krathwohl makes some useful recommendations as to choice of method (p. 352). For him, a qualitative approach is most appropriate when discovery is more important than validation, the subject matter is comparatively new, and well-grounded explanations are wanted. See Krathwohl (pp. 353–354) for hallmarks of qualitative methods and their special characteristics in contrast to quantitative methods.

44. The partially-structured interview technique also permitted the discovery of underlying processes which were not evident in the literature on voluntarism in education. While prior writings gave general directions, they did not specify fully the ways in which benevolence was encountered by those who work in schools. The literature was used in ways described by Strauss.

45. See Guba and Lincoln (pp. 79–102).

46. See Guba and Lincoln (p. 112).

47. Guba and Lincoln (p. 163).

48. For a thorough account of the impact of post-modernism on inquiry in the social sciences, see Rosneau.

49. Blaikie's example of retroductive reasoning is an inversion of the standard syllogism: all beans from this bag are white; these beans are white; therefore they are from this bag. It is not as rigourous as deductive reasoning but it is an accepted form of logic.

50. See Blaikie (pp. 58–62, 98, 162–163, 168, 202–205, and 209).

References

Alexander, Karl L., Entwisle, Doris R., and Thompson, Maxine S. (1987). School performance, status relations, and the structure of sentiment: Bringing the teacher back in. *American Sociological Review.* 52 (October) 665–82.

Allan, Graham. (1989). *Friendship: Developing a sociological perspective.* Boulder, CO: Westview.

Argyris, Chris and Schon, Donald A. (1978). *Organizational learning: a theory of action perspective.* Reading, MA: Addison-Wesley.

Batey, Carol S. (1996). *Parents are lifesavers: A handbook for parental involvement in schools.* Thousand Oaks, CA: Corwin Press.

Bausch, P. A. and Goldring, E. G. (1995). Parent involvement and school responsiveness: facilitating the home-school connection in schools of choice. *Educational Evaluation and Policy Analysis,* 17(1), 1–22.

Beare, Hedley. and Boyd, William. L. (1993). Introduction. In Hedley Beare and William. L. Boyd, (eds.) *Restructuring schools: An international perspective on the movement to transform the control and performance of schools.* London: Falmer Press, 2–11.

Becker, Gary S. (1991). *A treatise on the family.* (Enlarged ed.). Cambridge, MA: Harvard University Press.

Becker, Henry J., and Epstein, Joyce L. (1982). Parent involvement: A survey of teacher practices. *The Elementary School Journal.* 83 (2) 85–102.

Becker, Henry J., Kathryn Nakagawa, and Ronald G. Corwin. (1997). Parent involvement contracts in California's charter schools: Strategy for educational improvement or method of exclusion? *Teachers College Record.* 98 (3), Spring, 511–536.

Bell, Daniel A. (1993). *Communitarianism and its critics.* Oxford: Clarendon Press.

Bellah, Robert N., Masden, Richard, Sullivan, William M., Swidler, Ann, and Tipton, Steven M. (1991). *The good society.* New York: Alfred A. Knopf.

Benson, Charles. S. (1982). Household production of human capital: time uses of parents and children as inputs. In Walter W. McMahon and Terry G. Geske (eds.), *Financing education: overcoming inefficiency and inequity.* Urbana, Ill.: University of Illinois Press.

Bidwell, Charles E. (1965). The school as a formal organization. In James G. March (ed.), *Handbook of organizations.* Chicago: Rand McNally and Co., 972–1022.

Blaikie, Norman. (1993). *Approaches to social inquiry.* Cambridge UK: Polity Press.

Bogdan, R. C. and Biklen, S.K. (1992). *Qualitative research for education: An introduction to theory and methods.* (2nd ed.) Boston: Allyn and Bacon.

Boudon, Raymond. (1993). Beyond the alternative between the Homo Sociologicus and the Homo Oeconomicus: toward a theory of cold beliefs. In Aage B. Sorensen and Seymour Spilerman (eds.) *Social theory and social policy.* Westport, CT: Praeger, 43–57.

Boulding, Kenneth E. (1981). *A preface to grants economics: the economy of love and fear.* New York: Praeger.

Boulding, Kenneth E. (1989). *The three faces of power.* Newbury, CA: Sage Publications.

Boyd, William L. (1992). The power of paradigms: reconceptualizing educational policy and management. *Educational Administration Quarterly.* 28 (4) November, 504–528.

Boyd, William L. and Cibulka, James G. (eds.) (1989). *Private schools and public policy: international perspectives.* London: Falmer Press.

Boyd, William L. and Walberg, Herbert J. (eds.) (1990). *Choice in education: potential and problems.* Berkeley, CA: McCutchan.

Bradley, John P., Daniels, Leo F., and Jones, Thomas C. (Eds.) (1969). *The international dictionary of thoughts.* Chicago: J. G. Ferguson Publishing Co.

Bremner, Robert H. (1960). *American philanthropy.* Chicago: University of Chicago Press.

British Columbia Ministry of Education. (1992/93). *Public and Independent Schools Book.* Victoria, B. C.

Brown, Daniel J. (1990). *Decentralizationa and school-based management.* London: Falmer Press.

Brown, Daniel J. (1991). *Decentralization: the administrator's guide to school district change.* Newbury Park, CA: Corwin Press.

Brown, Daniel J. (1992). Review of Foundations of social theory by James S. Coleman, *Educational Administration Quarterly.* 28 (4), 563–556.

Brown, Daniel J. (1993). Benevolence in Canadian Public Schools. In Stephen L. Jacobson and Robert Berne (eds). *Reforming education: the emerging systematic approach.* Newbury Park, CA: Corwin Press, 191–208.

Brown, Daniel J. (1995). What is school enterprise? *Education Canada.* 35, (Spring) 33–39.

Brown, Daniel J. and Bouman, Claudette. (1995). Policies for School Fees. Unpublished manuscript, Vancouver, BC: University of British Columbia.

Brudner, Jefferey L. (1990). *Fostering volunteer programs in the public sector.* San Francisco: Jossey-Bass.

Bryk, Anthony S. (1988). Musings on the moral life of schools. *American Journal of Education.* 96 (2), 256–90

Bryk, Anthony S., Lee, Valerie E. and Smith, Julia B. (1990). High school organization and its effects on teachers and students: an interpretive summary of the research. In William H. Clune and John E. Witte (eds.) *Choice and control in American education,* Vol I. London: Falmer Press, 135–226.

Bryk, Anthony, S. and Driscoll, Mary E. (1988). *The school as community: theoretical foundation, contextual influences, and consequences for students and teachers.* Madison, WI: National Center for Effective Secondary Schools. University of Wisconsin.

Bryk, Anthony, S., Lee, Valerie E. and Holland, Peter B. (1993). *Catholic schools and the common good.* Cambridge, MA: Harvard University Press.

Butts, R. Freeman and Cremin, Lawrence A. (1953). *A history of education in American culture.* New York: Henry Holt and Company.

Cabot, E. L. (1914). *Volunteer help to the schools.* Boston, MA: Houghton Mifflin.

Caldwell, Brian and Spinks Jim M. (1988) *The self-managing school,.* Taylor and Francis, London

Caldwell, Brian J. and Spinks, Jim M. (1992). *Leading the self-managing school.* London: Falmer Press.

Callahan, Raymond E. (1962). *Education and the cult of efficiency.* Chicago: University of Chicago Press.

Carney, Juanita. (1983). A study of succeful elementary school volunteer parent participation programs. Unpublished doctoral dissertation, School of Education, University of Southern California, Los Angeles.

Chavkin, Nancy F. and Williams, David L. Jr. (1987). Enhancing parent involvement. *Education and Urban Society.* 19 (2) February, 164–84.

Chavkin, Nancy F. and Williams, Jr., David L. (1993). Minority parents and the elementary school: attitudes and practices. In Nancy F. Chavkin (ed.) *Families and schools in a pluralistic society.* Albany, NY: State University of New York Press, 73–83.

Cherlin, Andrew J. and Furstenberg, Frank F. Jr. (1986). *The new American grandparent.* Cambridge, MA: Harvard University Press.

Chubb, John E. and Moe, Terry. M. (1990). *Politics, markets, and America's schools.* Washington, DC: The Brooking's Institution.

Cibulka, James. G. (1994). Economic and financial dimensions of schooling: taxonomy and overview. University Council for Educational Administration Documentation. New York: McGraw-Hill, 40pp.

Clark, Reginald. (1983). *Family life and school achievement: why poor black children succeed or fail.* Chicago: University of Chicago Press.

Clune, William H. and Witte, John F. (eds). *Choice and control in American education, volumes 1 and 2.* London: Falmer Press.

Cole, Bob. (1988). Teaching in a time machine: the 'make-do' mentality of small-town schools. *Phi Delta Kappan.* 70 (2) 139–144.

Coleman, James S. (1988). Social capital in the creation of human capital. In Christopher Winship and Sherwin Rosen, (eds.) Organizations and institutions: sociological and economic approaches to the analysis of social structure. *American Journal of Sociology.* 94 Supplement, S95-S120.

Coleman, James S. (1990). *Foundations of social theory.* Cambridge, MA: Belknap Press of Harvard University Press.

Coleman, James S. and Hoffer, Thomas. (1987). *Public and private high schools: the impact of communities.* New York: Basic Books Inc.

Coleman, James S. and Schiller, Kathryn S. (1992). A comparison of public and private schools: the impact of community values. In Pearl R. Kane (ed.) (1992). *Independent schools, independent thinkers.* San Francisco: Jossey-Bass, 222–233.

Collins, Randall. (1988). *Theoretical sociology.* San Diego: Harcourt Brace Jovanovich.

Comer, James P. (1980). *School power: implications of an intervention project.* New York: The Free Press.

Comer, James P. and Haynes, Norris M. (1991). Parent involvement in schools: an ecological approach. *Elementary School Journal.* 91 (3), 271–277.

Conway, James A. and Stephen L. (1990). An epilogue: Where is educational leadership going? In S. L. Jacobson and J. A. Conway (Eds.), *Educational leadership in an age of reform.* New York: Longman. 181–195.

Conyers, John. (1996). Building bridges between generations. *Educational Leadership.* 53 (7) 14–16.

Cookson, Peter W. (1994). *School choice: the struggle for the soul of American education.* New Haven, CT: Yale University Press.

Cooley, Charles H. (1955). Primary groups. In Paul Hare et al. (eds.) *Small Groups.* New York: Alfred Knopf.

Coons, John E. and Sugarman, Steven D. (1978). *Education by choice: the case for family control.* Berkeley, CA: University of California Press.

Cooper, Bruce S. (1988). The changing universe of U.S. private schools. In James Thomas and Henry M. Levin (eds.). *Comparing public & private schools, volume 1: institutions and organizations.* London: Falmer Press, 18–45.

Cooper, Bruce S. (1993). Educational choice: competing models and meanings. In Stephen L. Jacobson and Robert Berne (eds). *Reforming education: the emerging systemic approach.* Newbury Park: Corwin, 107–130.

Corwin, Ronald G. (1987). *The organization-society nexus: a critical review of models and metaphors.* Westport, CT: Greenwood Press.

Craft, Maurice, Raynor, John, and Cohen, Louis (eds.) (1980). *Linking home and school: A new review.* London: Harper and Row.

Crenson, Matthew A. (1987). The private stake in public goods: overcoming the illogic of collective action. *Policy Sciences.* 20 (3), 259–76.

Crowson, Robert L. (1992). Schools and their communities; School-community relations and a changing profession. In *School-community relations under reform.* Berkeley: McCutchan, 23–61.

Cuban, Larry. (1990). Reforming again, again, and again. *Educational Researcher,* 19 (1), 3–13.

Cubberley, Ellwood, P. (1934). *Public education in the United States. A study and interpretation of American educational history.* (rev ed.) Boston: Houghtin Mifflin Co.

Curtis, James E., Lambert, Ronald D., Brown, Steven D., and Kay, Barry, J. (1989). Affiliation with voluntary associations: Canadian American comparisons. *Canadian Journal of Sociology.* 14 (2): 143–61.

Cyster, Richard and Clift, Phil. (1980). Parental involvement in primary schools: The NFER survey. In Maurice Craft, John Raynor, and Louis Cohen (eds.) *Linking home and school: A new review.* London: Harper and Row, 152–164.

Daniels, Arlene K. (1988). *Invisible careers: Women civic leaders from the volunteer world.* Chicago: University of Chicago Press.

Davies, Don. (1991). Testing a strategy for reform: the League of Schools reaching out. Presented at the annual meeting of the American Educational Research Association, Chicago, 26pp.

Davis, Jean N. (1988). Predictors of elementary teachers' attitudes toward parent volunteers in an large urban school district in Northern California. Unpublished doctoral dissertation, Curriculum and Instruction Program, University of San Francisco.

Decker, Larry E. (1994). Home-school-community relations: Trainer's manual and study guide. 150pp. ERIC ED 371822.

Delgado-Gaitan, Concha. (1991). Involving parents in the schools: a process of empowerment. *American Journal of Education*, 100 (November) 20–46.

Devins, Neal E. (ed.) (1989). *Public values, private schools*. London: Falmer Press.

Douglas, James. (1987). Political theories of nonprofit organization. In Powell, Walter W. (ed.) *The nonprofit sector: a research handbook*. New Haven: Yale University Press, 43–54.

Downs, Anthony. (1967). *Inside bureaucracy*. Little, Brown.

Drickamer, Lee C. and Vessey, Stephen H. (1986). *Animal behavior: concepts, processes, and methods*. Boston, MA: Prindle, Weber, and Schmidt.

Duchesne, Doreen. (1989). *Giving freely: volunteers in Canada*. Ottawa ON: Statistics Canada.

Eccles Jacquelynne. S. and Harold, Rena. D. (1993). Parent-school involvement during the early adolescent years. *Teachers College Record*. 94, 568–587.

Education Commission of the States and Center for School Change. (1995). Charter schools . . . What are they up to? Denver, CO: ECS. 40pp.

Edwards, Tryon. (1899). *A dictionary of thoughts*. Detroit: F. B. Dickerson, Co.

Eisenstadt, Abraham S. (1988). *Reconsidering Tocqueville's democracy in America*. New Brunswick: Rutgers University Press.

Elam, Stanley M., Lowell C. Rose, and Alec M. Gallup. (1996). The 28th annual Phi Delta Kappa/Gallup Poll of the public's attitudeses toward the public schools. *Phi Delta Kappan*. 78 (1) 10–17.

Elam, Stanley M., Rose, Lowell C., and Gallup, Alec M. (1992). The 24th annual Gallup/Phi Delta Kappa poll of the public's attitudes toward the public schools. *Phi Delta Kappan*. 74 (1) 41–53.

Ellis, Susan J. and Noyes, Katherine H. (1990). *By the people: a history of Americans as volunteers*. (rev. ed.) San Francisco: Jossey-Bass.

Elmore, Richard F. (1990). Options for Choice in Public Education. In William L. Boyd and Herbert J. Walberg (eds.) *Choice in education: potential and problems*. Berkeley, CA: McCutchan, 21–42.

Emerson, Ralph W. (1936, 1868). *The complete works of Ralph Waldo Emerson*, Volume I. XVII—Gifts 220–223.

Emlen, Stephen T. (1991). Evolution of cooperative breeding in birds and mammals. In John. R. Krebs and Nicholas. B. Davies (eds.). *Behavioural ecology*, (3rd ed.) Oxford: Blackwell Scientific Publications, 301–335.

Epstein, Joyce L. (1987). Parent involvement: what research says to administrators. *Education and Urban Society*. 19 (2) 119–136.

Epstein, Joyce L. (1990). School and family connections: theory, research, and implications for integrating sociologies of education and family. In D. G. Unger and M. B. Sussman (eds.), *Families in community settings: interdisciplinary perspectives*. New York: Haworth Press. 99–126.

Epstein, Joyce L. and Dauber, Susan L. (1991). School programs and teacher practices of parent involvement in inner-city elementary and middle schools. *The Elementary School Journal*. 91 (3), 289–305.

Epstein, Joyce L. and Susan L. Dauber. (1995). Effects on students of an interdisciplinary program linking social studies, art, and family volunteers in the middle grades. *Journal of Early Adolescence*. 15 (1) 114–144.

Epstein. J. L., and Lee, S. (1995). National patterns of school and family connections in the middle grades. In Ryan, B.A., G. R. Adams, T. P. Gulotta, R. P. Weissberg, and R. L Hampton (Eds.), *The family-school connection: theory, research and practice.* London: Sage publications, 108–154.

Erickson, Donald A. (1986). Choice and private schools: dynamics of supply and demand. In Daniel Levy (ed.) *Private education: studies in choice and public policy.* New York: Oxford University Press, 103–4.

Etzioni, Amatai. (1993). *The spirit of community: the reinvention of American society.* New York: Simon and Schuster.

Etzioni, Amitai. (1988). *The moral dimension: toward a new economics.* New York: Free Press.

Etzioni, Amitai. (1996). *The new golden rule: community and morality in a democratic society.* New York: Basic Books.

Everhart, Robert B. (1988). Fieldwork methodology in educational administration. *Handbook of Research on Educational Administration,* Norman J. Boyan, (ed.) New York: Longman. 703–728.

Fischer, Claud S. (1982). *To dwell among friends.* Chicago: University of Chicago Press.

Fischer, Lucy R. and Kay B. Schaffer. (1993). *Older volunteers: a guide to research and practice.* Newbury Park, CA: Sage.

Fowler, Frances; Boyd, William L.; and Plank, David N. (1993). International school reform: political considerations. In Stephen L. Jacobson, Stephen L. and Robert Berne (eds.), *Reforming education: the emerging systemic approach.* 153–168.

Frank, Jeffrey and Stephen Mihorean. (1996). Who gives to charity? *Canadian Social Trends.* (Winter) 8–13.

Friedman, Debra, and Hechter, Michael. (1990). The comparative advantages of rational choice theory. In G. Ritzer (ed.) *Frontiers of social theory: the new syntheses.* New York: Columbia University Press: 214–229.

Frymier, Jack. (1987). Bureaucracy and the neutering of teachers. *Phi Delta Kappan,* 69 (1) September, 9–14.

Fullan, Michael. G. (1991). *The new meaning of educational change.* New York: Teachers' College Press.

Furman, Gail C. and Merz, Carol. (1994). Schools, community and reform: applying a sociological framework. Presented at the annual meeting of the American Educational Research Association, New Orleans.

Galaskiewicz, Joseph. (1985). *Social organization of an urban grants economy.* Orlando, FL: Academic Press.

Getzels, J. Jacob. (1979). Communities of education. In Hope J. Leichter (ed.) *Families and ccmmunities as educators.* New York: Teachers' College Press, 95–118.

Glazer, Nathan. (1988). *The limits of social policy.* Cambridge, Mass.: Harvard University Press.

Goldberg, Michael. (1989). *Volunteers in the Burnaby School System.* Vancouver, BC: Social Planning and Research Council of British Columbia. 35pp.

Goodlad, John I. (1984). *A place called school.* New York: McGraw-Hill.

Guba, Egon, and Lincoln, Yvonna. (1989). *Fourth generation evaluation.* Newbury Park, CA: Sage.

Guthrie, James W. (1990). The evolution of educational management. In I. B. Mitchell and Luverne. L. Cunningham (eds.) *Educational leadership and the changing contexts of families, communities and schools.* Eighty-ninth yearbook of the National Society for the Study of Education. Part II. Chicago: University of Chicago Press, 210–231.

Hallinger, Philip and Murphy, Joseph E. (1986). The social context of effective schools. *American Journal of Education.* May, 328–355.

Hancock, Mary F. (1977). Factors related to umplementation of programs of parent volunteer classroom involvement in selected elementary schools of Florida. Unpublished doctoral dissertation, Educational Management Systems, Florida State University.

Hannaway, Jane. (1993). Decentralization in two school districts: Challenging the standard paradigm. In Jane Hannaway and Martin Carnoy, (eds.) *Decentralization and school improvement.* San Francisco: Jossey-Bass, 135–162.

Haughness, Hariette E. (1978). Administrative practices employed by principals in selected school volunteer programs. Unpublished doctoral dissertation, School of Education, University of Southern California, Los Angeles.

Hawley, W. D. (1988). Missing pieces of the educational reform agenda: Or, why the first and second waves may miss the boat. *Educational Administration Quarterly.* 24, 416–437.

Hechter, Michael. (1987). *Principles of group solidarity.* Berkeley, CA: University of California Press.

Hedges, H. G. (1972). *Using volunteers in schools.* Toronto, ON: Ontario Institute for Studies in Education.

Henderson, Anne T. (1988). Parents are a school's best friends. *Phi Delta Kappan.* 70, October 148–153.

Hess, Alfred. Jr. (1991). *School restructuring: Chicago style.* Newbury Park, CA: Corwin.

Hewitt, John P. (1989). *Dilemmas of the American self.* Philadelphia: Temple University Press.

Hill, Corrine P. (1980). A comparative study of formal volunteer programs in educational settings. Unpublished doctoral dissertation, Department of Educational Administration, University of Utah, Salt Lake City. 158pp.

Ho, Esther S. (1997). Parental involvement and student performance: the contributions of economic, cultural, and social capital. Unpublished Dissertation, Department of Educational Studies, University of British Columbia, Vancouver, B.C. 168pp.

Hodgkinson, Harold. (1991). Educational reform versus reality. In American Association of School Administrators/National School Board Association (Eds.), *Beyond the schools: How schools and communities must collaborate to solve problems facing America's youth.* Washington, DC: AASA/NSBA.

Hodgkinson, Virginia A. and Weitzman, Murray S. (1990). Volunteering and giving among American teenagers 14 to 17 years of age. Washington, DC: Independent Sector. ERIC ED 330 923

Hölldobler, Bert, and Wilson, Edward O. (1990). *The ants.* Cambridge MA: The Belknap Press of Harvard University Press.

Holmes, Stephen. (1990). The secret history of self-interest. In Jane J. Mansbridge (ed.) *Beyond self-interest.* Chicago: University of Chicago Press, 267–286.

Holy Bible. King James Version. London: Collins.

Hoover-Dempsey, Kathleen V. and Howard M. Sandley. (1997). Why do parents become involved in their children's education? *Review of Education Research.* 67 (1) 3–42.

Hostetler, John A. and Huntington, Gertrude E. (1992). *Amish children: Education in the family, school, and community.* (2nd ed.) Fort Worth, TX: Harcourt, Brace, Jovanovich.

Hoy, Wayne K. and Cecil D. Miskel. (1996). *Educational administration: theory, research, and practice.* (5th ed.) New York: McGraw-Hill.

Ilsley, Paul. (1990). *Enhancing the volunteer experience.* San Francisco, CA: Jossey-Bass.

Independent Sector. (1986). American volunteer 1985. Washington, DC: Independent Sector.

Jackson, Babara. (1991). Schools reaching out: perspectives from one school—PS 111—The Adoph Ochs School, a New York City Public School. Presented at the annual meeting of the American Educational Research Association, Chicago.

James, Thomas, and Levin, Henry M. (eds.) (1988). *Comparing public and private schools: institutions and organizations.* London: Falmer Press.

Jencks, Christopher. (1987). Who gives to what? In Walter W. Powell (ed.) *The nonprofit sector: a research handbook.* New Haven, CT: Yale University Press, 321–339.

Jennings, John F. (1996). Travels without Charley. *Phi Delta Kappan.* 78 (1 September) 10–17.

Johanson, Donald C. and O'Farrell, Kevin. (1990). *Journey from the dawn: Life with the world's first family.* New York: Villard Books.

Johns, Roe L. and Morphet, Edgar L. (1975). *The economics and financing of education, a systems approach.* Englewood Cliffs, New Jersey: Prentice-Hall, Inc.

Johnson, Susan. (1990). *Teachers at work.* New York: Basic Books.

Jordan, W. K. (1959). *Philanthropy in England 1480–1660.* London: Allen and Unwin.

Kane, Pearl R. (ed.) (1992). *Independent schools, independent thinkers.* San Francisco: Jossey-Bass.

Katz, Michael B. (1987). *Alternative models for American education. Chapter in reconstructing American education.* Cambridge, MA: Harvard University Press.

Kerbow, David and Bernhardt, Anette. (1993). Parent intervention in the school: the context of minority involvement. In James S. Coleman and Barbara Schneider (eds.) *Parents, their children, and schools.* Boulder CO: Westview Press, pp. 115–146.

Kirst, Michael, McLaughlin, Milbrey, and Massell, Donald. (1989). *Rethinking children's policy: Implications for educational administration.* Stanford, CA: Stanford University, College of Education, Center for Educational Research.

Knight, Brian. (1993a). *Financial management for schools.* Oxford: Heinemann.

Knight, Brian. (1993b). Delegated financial management and effectiveness. In Clive A.J. Dimmock, *School-based management and school effectiveness.* London: Routledge, 114–141.

Knoke, David, and Wright-Isak, Christine. (1982). Individual motives and organizational incentive systems. *Research in the sociology of organizations, Volume 1,* 209–254.

Kohn, Alfie. (1990). *The brighter side of human nature.* New York: Basic Books.

Kraft, Richard J. (1996). Service learning: an introduction to its theory, practice, and effects. *Education and Urban Society.* 28 (2), 131–159.

Kramer, Ralph M. (1987). Voluntary agencies and the personal social services. In Walter W. Powell (ed.). *The nonprofit sector: a research handbook.* New Haven: Yale University Press, 240–257.

Krathwohl, David R. (1993). *Methods of educational and social science research.* White Plains, NY: Longman.

Kraznow, Jean H. (1990). *Improving family-school relationships: teacher research from the Schools Reaching Out Project.* Boston, MA: Institute for Responsive Education. 160pp.

Krumm, Volker, et al. (1990). *Parent involvement or teacher involvement? Results of a comparative study in Austria, Taiwan, and the United States.* Institut für Erziehungswissenschaften, Universität Salzburg.

Lagemann, Ellen C. (1992). Philanthropy, education, and the politics of knowledge. *Teachers College Record.* 93 (3) 361–369.

Lareau, Annette. (1989). *Home advantage: Social class and parental intervention in elementary education.* London: The Falmer Press.

Lawton, Stephen B. (1995). *Bustin' bureaucracy to reclaim our schools.* Montreal: Institute of Research on Public Policy.

Levitt, B. and March, J. (1988). Organizational learning. *Annual Review of Sociology.* 14, 319–340

Lightfoot, Sarah. (1978). *Worlds apart: relationships between families and schools.* New York: Basic Books.

Lipset, Seymour Martin. (1990). *Continental divide: The values and institutions of the United States and Canada.* New York: Routledge.

Little Lake City Elementary School District, (1984). Painting the outside of the entire school, Santa Fe Springs, CA, EDRS ED 240 734.

Litwak, Eugene and Szelenyi, Ivan. (1969). Primary group structures and their functions: kin, neighbors, and friends. *American Sociological Review* (34) 465–81.

Litwak, Eugene, and Meyre, Henry J. (1974). *School, family and neighborhood: the theory and practice of school-community relations.* New York: Columbia University Press.

Lortie, Daniel C. (1975). *Schoolteacher: a sociological study.* Chicago: University of Chicago Press.

Lutz, Frank W. and Merz, Carol. (1992). *The politics of school/community relations.* New York: Teachers College Press.

MacIntyre, Alisdair. (1981). *After virtue. A study in moral theory.* London: Duckworth.

Malen, Betty and Ogawa Roger T. (1988). Professional-patron influence on site-based governance councils: a confounding case study *Educational Evaluation and Policy Analysis.* 10 (4), 251–270.

Mansbridge, Jane J. (1990). On the relation of altruism and self-interest. In Jane J. Mansbridge (ed.) *Beyond self-interest.* Chicago: University of Chicago Press, 133–143.

McLaughlin, Milbrey W. (1988). Business and the public schools. In Monk, David H. and Underwood, Julie, (eds.) *Microlevel school finance: Issues and implications for policy.* Cambridge, MA: Ballinger, 63–80.

McLaughlin, Milbrey W. and Schields, Patrick M. (1987). *Phi Delta Kappan.* 69 (2) October 156–160.

McPherson, J. Miller, and Smith-Lovin, Lynn. (1986). Sex segregation in voluntary associations. *American Sociological Review.* 51 (February) 61–79.

Michael, Bernard. (ed.) (1990). *Volunteers in public schools.* Committee on the Use of Volunteers in Schools; Commission on Behavioral and Social Sciences and Education, National Research Council. Washington, D.C.: National Academy Press.

Ministry of Education, Province of British Columbia. (1993/94 and 1992/93). *Comparative and analytic data.* Victoria, British Columbia.

Mintzberg, Henry. (1979). *The structuring of organizations: a synthesis of the research.* Englewood Cliffs, NJ: Prentice-Hall.

Moles, Oliver C. (1993). Colleaboration between schools and disadvantaged parents: obstacles and openings. In Nancy F. Chavkin (ed.) *Families and schools in a pluralistic society.* Albany, NY: State University of New York Press, pp. 21–49.

Monk, David H. and Haller, Emil J. (1986). Organizational alternatives for small rural schools. Final report to the Legislature of the State of New York. Department of Education, New York State College of Agriculture and Life Sciences, Cornell University.

Morgan, Gareth. (1986). *Images of organization.* Beverly Hills, CA: Sage Publications.

Mort, Paul R. and Reusser, Walter C. (1941). *Public school finance: its background structure, and operation.* New York: McGraw-Hill.

Muller, Chandra and Kerbow, David. (1993). Parent involvement in the home, school, and community. In James S. Coleman and Barbara Schneider (eds.) *Parents, their children, and schools.* Boulder CO: Westview Press, pp. 13–42.

Munch, Richard. (1992). Rational choice theory: a critical assessment of its explanatory power. In James S. Coleman and Thomas J. Fararo (eds.) *Rational choice theory: advocacy and critique.* Newbury Park, CA: Sage, 137–160.

Murphy, Joseph. (1991). *Restructuring schools: Capturing and assessing the phenomena.* New York: Teachers College Press.

Murphy, Joseph. (1992). School effectiveness and school restructuring: Contributions to educational improvement. *School Effectiveness and School Improvement.* 3 (2), 90–109.

Murphy, Joseph. (1993). Restructuring: in search of a movement. In Joseph Murphy and Philip Hallinger (eds.). *Restructuring schooling: learning from ongoing efforts.* Newbury Park, CA: Corwin Press, 1–31.

Murphy, Joseph. (1994). Transformational change and the evolving role of the principal: early empirical evidence. In Joseph Murphy and Karen S. Louis (eds.) *Reshaping the principalship: insights from transformational reform efforts.* Thousand Oaks, CA: Corwin Press, 20–53.

Murphy, Joseph, and Hallinger, Philip (eds.). (1993). *Restructuring schooling: learning from ongoing efforts.* Newbury Park, CA: Corwin Press.

Nanaimo Free Press (1989). Vol. 116, No. 154, p. 3, October 16.

Nathan, Joe. (1996). Possibilities, problems, and progress: Early lessons from the charter movement. *Phi Delta Kappan.* 78 (1) 18–23.

National Center for Educational Statistics. (1989). Education Partnerships in Public Elementary and Secondary Schools. Washington, D.C.: U.S. Department of Education, Office of Educational Research and Improvement. CS-89-060.

National Center for Educational Statistics. (1990–91, 1987–88). Schools and staffing in the United states: a statistical profile. Washington, DC: U.S. Department of Education, Office of Educational Research and Improvement.

New shorter Oxford English dictionary. (1993). Oxford: Clarendon Press.

Nisbet, Robert. (1962). *Community and power.* New York: Oxford University Press.

Noddings, Nel. (1988). An ethic of caring and its implications for instructional arrangements. *American Journal of Education.* 96, February, 215–230.

Olmsted, Patricia P. (1983). Parent involvement: perspectives from the Follow Through experience. In Ron Haskins and Diane Adams (eds.) *Parent education and public policy.* Norwood, NJ: Ablex Publishing Co. 112–140.

Olson, Jr., Mancur. (1965). *The logic of collective action: Public goods and the theory of groups.* Cambridge, MA: Harvard University Press.

Onishi, Esther and Erica Peto. (1996). Training students as technology assistants. *Technology Collection.* 3 (3), May, 19 and 31.

Ortner, Maria L. (1994). An alternative approach to increase parent involvement among culturally diverse families. Ed. D. Practicum, Nova University, 55pp.

Owen, David. (1964). *English philanthropy.* Cambridge, Mass.: Harvard University Press.

Pawlas, George E. (1995). *School-community relations.* Princeton Junction, NJ: Eye on Education.

Peshkin, Alan. (1978). *Growing up American: Schooling and the survival of community.* Chicago: University of Chicago Press.

Peshkin, Alan. (1993). The goodness of qualitative research. *Educational Researcher.* 22 (2) March, 23–29.

Pfeffer, Jeffrey. (1982). *Organizations and organization theory.* London: Pittman.

Phillips, Charles E. (1957). *The development of education in Canada.* Toronto: W. J. Gage.

Powell, Walter W. and Dimaggio, Paul J. (1991). *The new institutionalism in organizational analysis.* Chicago: University of Chicago Press.

Raywid, Mary Anne. (1995). The Struggles and Joys of Trailblazing: a Tale of Two Charter Schools. *Phi Delta Kappan.* 76 (7), March, 555–560.

Rekart, Josephine. (1993). *Public funds, private provision: the role of the voluntary sector.* Vancouver, B.C.: University of British Columbia Press.

Reynolds, Mary I. (1975). A rationale and recommendations for using retired citizens as volunteers in public schools. Unpublished doctoral dissertation, Department of Educational Administration and Services, Northern Illinois University, Dekalb, Illinois.

Rioux, J. William and Nancy Berla. (1993). *Innovations in parent and family involvement.* Princeton Junction, NJ: Eye on Education.

Ritzer, George. (1992). *Contemporary sociological theory.* (3rd ed.) New York: McGraw-Hill.

Roberts, Val. (1989). Parental involvement in middle schools: a case study. *Research in Education.* 41, May, 27–37.

Robinson, Floyd, et al. (1971). Volunteer helpers in elementary schools. Toronto: Ontario Institute for Studies in Education.

Rosneau, Pauline M. (1992). *Post-modernism and the social sciences: insights, inroads, and intrusions.* Princeton, NJ: Princeton University Press.

Salamon, Lester M. (1987). *Partners in public service: the scope and theory of government-nonprofit relations.* 99–117.

Salloum, K. (1985). Private funding for elementary and secondary public education in British Columbia for 1983–84. Unpublished Masters Thesis, Faculty of Education, Burnaby, BC: Simon Fraser University.

Saxe, Richard W. (1984). *School-community relations in transition.* Berkeley, CA: McCutchan.

Schmuck, Richard A. and Schmuck, Patricia A. (1992). *Small districts, big problems.* Newbury Park, CA: Corwin Press.

Schumacher, Sally and McMillan, James H. (1993). *Research in education: a conceptual introduction.* (3rd ed.) New York: Harper Collins.

Schwartz, Barry. (1986). *The battle for human nature: science, morality and modern life.* New York: W. W. Norton.

Sciulli, David. (1992). Weaknesses in rational choice theory's contribution to comparative research. In James S. Coleman and Thomas J. Fararo (eds.) *Rational choice theory: advocacy and critique.* Newbury Park, CA: Sage, 161–180.

Scott, W. Richard. (1981). *Organizations: Rational, natural, and open systems.* Englewood Cliffs, NJ: Prentice-Hall.

Sergiovanni, Thomas J. (1994). *Building community in schools.* San Francisco: Jossey-Bass.

Smrekar, Claire. (1992). Building community: the influence of school organization on patterns of parent participation. Presented at the annual meeting of the American Educational Research Association, San Francisco.

Sorokin, Pitirim A. (1950). *Altruistic love: a study of American 'good neighbors' and Christian saints.* Boston: The Beacon Press.

Sorokin, Pitirim A. (1954). *The ways and power of love.* Boston: The Beacon Press.

Southgate, Henry. (n.d.). *Many thoughts of many minds. First Series.* (31st ed.). London: Charles Griffin and Co.

Statistics Canada. (1991). *Census of Canada.* Ottawa, ON: Queen's Printer.

Strauss, Anselm L. (1987). *Qualitative analysis for social scientists.* New York: Cambridge University Press.

Strauss, Anselm, and Corbin, Juliet. (1990). *Basics of qualitative research.* Newbury Park, CA: Sage.

Strayer, George D. and Haig, Robert M. (1923). *The financing of education in the state of New York.* Report of the Educational Finance Ineuqiry Commission, Vol. 1. New York: Macmillan.

Streit, John F. (1975). The effect of an instructional volunteer program on an elementary school. Unpublished doctoral dissertation, Department of Secondary Administration and Supervision, Detroit: Wayne State University.

Sundeen, Richard A. (1988). Explaining participation in coproduction: a study of volunteers. *Social Science Quarterly.* 69 (3), 547–68.

Swanson, Austin D. (1993). A framework for allocating authority in a system of schools. In Hedley Beare and William L. Boyd, (eds.) *Restructuring schools: an international perspective on the movement to transform the control and performance of schools.* London: Falmer Press, 218–234.

Swanson, Austin D. and King, Richard A. (1997). *School finance: its economics and politics.* (2nd ed.) New York: Longman.

Swap, Susan M. 1993. *Developing home-school partnerships.* New York: Teachers College Press.

Swedberg, Richard. (1990). *Economics and sociology.* Princeton, NJ: Princeton University Press.

Taylor, Charles. (1989). *Sources of the self: The making of the modern identity.* Cambridge, MA: Harvard University Press.

Tierce, Jerry W. (1982). The role of the secondary school volunteer as perceived by school volunteer coordinators. Unpublished doctoral dissertation, Graduate College, Texas A&M University.

Titmuss, Richard M. (1970). *The gift relationship: From human blood to social policy.* New York: Random House.

Tocqueville, Alexis. (1835). *Democracy in America.* George Lawrence (trans.), J. P. Mayer and Max Lerner (eds.) New York: Harper and Row, 1966.

Tonnies, Ferdinand (1940). *Fundamental concepts of sociology.* Charles Loomis (trans.) New York: American Book Company.

Van Til, Jon, and Associates. (1990). *Critical issues in American philanthropy.* San Francisco: Jossey Bass.

Verba, Sidney, Norman H. Nie, and John R. Petrocik. (1976). *The changing American voter.* Cambridge, Mass: Harvard University Press.

Wagstaff, Lonnie, and Gallagher, K. (1990). Schools, Families and Communities: Idealized images and new realities. In I. B. Mitchell and L. L. Cunningham (eds.) *Educational leadership and the changing contexts of families, communities and schools.* Eighty-ninth yearbook of the National Society for the Study of Education. Chicago: University of Chicago Press. 90–117.

Waller, Willard. (1932). *The sociology of teaching.* New York: Wiley.

Weisbrod, Burton A. (1988). *The nonprofit economy.* Cambridge, Mass.: Harvard University Press.

Willower, Donald J. (1989). Waller on schools as organizations: an appreciation and criticism. In Donald J. Willower and William L. Boyd (eds.) *Willard Waller on education and schools: a critical appraisal.* Berkeley, CA: McCutchan, 9–38.

Wilson, Bruce L. and Corcoran, Thomas B. (1988). *Successful secondary schools: Visions of excellence in American public education.* London: Falmer Press.

Wilson, Edward O. (1978). *On human nature.* Cambridge, MA: Harvard University Press.

Wilson, James Q. (1993). *The moral sense.* New York: Free Press.

Wise, Arthur E. (1979). *Legislated learning: the bureaucratization of the American classroom.* Berkeley: University of California Press.

Wohlstetter, Priscilla and Buffet, Thomas. (1992). Promoting school-based management: Are dollars decentralized too? In Allen Odden (ed.), *Rethinking school finance: An agenda for the 1990's.* San Francisco: Jossey-Bass, 128–165.

Wuthnow, Robert. (1991). *Acts of compassion.* Princeton, NJ: Princeton University Press.

Yao, Esther L. (1993). Strategies for working effectively with Asian immigrant parents. In Nancy F. Chavkin (ed.) *Families and schools in a pluralistic society.* Albany, NY: State University of New York Press, 149–156.

Young, John, and Levin, Benjamin. (1998). *Understanding Canadian schools.* (2nd ed.) Toronto: Harcourt Brace and Company.

Index